Reach for It

A Handbook of Health, Exercise and Dance Activities for Older Adults

Second Edition

David E. Corbin, Ph.D. and Josie Metal-Corbin, M.Ed.

with Selected Chapters by

Frank Fong

Rita Frickel

Vicki Roitman

and

Judy Vann

Cover Design and Original Drawings by

Frances Thurber

Photography by

David E. Corbin

eddie bowers publishing company

Dubuque, Iowa 52001

To the memory

of Belle Corbin, Charles Metal

and Charles Wolford

eddie bowers publishing company
2600 Jackson Street
Dubuque, Iowa 52001

ISBN 0–945483–00–7

Printed in the United States of America.

9 8 7 6 5 4 3 2 1

Table of Contents

Foreword to the Second Edition
by Jane F. Potter, M.D.

Most individuals reach the peak of their abilities sometime between 25 and 30 years of age. While some decline can be expected after that, there is a great individual variability and with training activity and interest, many older individuals substantially out-perform others a fraction of their age. Among the most modifiable effects of "aging" are decrements in the musculoskeletal system. Taken for granted by the young, physical abilities are critical to successful independent living in old age.

The authors of this text have for some time been proponents and educators in this important aspect of successful aging. In this text, they share their wisdom and experience and cross several disciplines to synthesize programs of activity and exercise for the able and the not-so-able. In so doing, the authors have created a valuable resource for older persons, those who work with the aged and those assisting cross-generational groups.

This expanded Second Edition provides background information on additional aspects of physical functioning including changes in the body with age, nutrition, and sexuality, as well as common disorders that improve with programs of regular exercise.

Finally, I must note that the foreword to the first edition of this text was written by Representative Claude Pepper who ably demonstrated that physical and mental activity preserves function and makes important contributions possible throughout late life.

Dr. Jane F. Potter is Chief of the Section of Geriatrics and Gerontology, University Geriatric Center, University of Nebraska Medical Center, Omaha, NE.

Foreword to the First Edition
by Rep. Claude Pepper

It is with great pleasure that I accept the invitation to write the foreword to this unusual handbook, the authors' contribution to the welfare of the elderly. Gerontology has grown into a discipline of its own, its importance derived originally from the fact that a great deal of physiological and medical relevance attaches to it. To this end, greater attention will be given to the role of exercise and dance as a means to improve the quality of life of senior citizens. The House Select Committee on Aging's Subcommittee on Health and Long-Term Care, which I chair, has found that exercise not only maintains fitness, but stimulates the mind, and helps to prevent premature dependence on others. Inactivity can lead to immobility, the precursor to institutionalization.

I believe that *Reach for It: A Handbook of Exercise and Dance Activities for Older Adults* is an appropriate response to the problems associated with inactivity. I submit this handbook to your attention in the hope that in some measure it may contribute toward enhancing the lives of all who read it, physically, mentally and emotionally.

Apropos is the statement by Victor Hugo: "Greater than the tread of mighty armies is the idea whose time has come." The time has come for this handbook. Read it, and be alive as long as you live.

The Late Rep. Claude Pepper was deemed by *Time* magazine to be the "Spokesman for the Elderly" in America. As chairman of the House Select Committee on Aging, he championed many bills that benefited older Americans. He was the recipient of the Medal of Freedom, the nation's highest civilian award and upon his death at age 88 Congress ruled that he should lie in state in the Capitol Rotunda. He was the 27th American to be so honored.

Preface

The spirit of this book can best be captured in the saying, "If you don't use it, you lose it." Staying active is important throughout a person's life. It is never too late to change a sedentary lifestyle or to learn new things.

The title of this book, *Reach for It,* is meant to convey the movement inherent in some of the exercise and dance activities as well as to convey the more figurative interpretation that suggests that each individual reach for goals and reach out in new directions, regardless of age.

The material in this book is directed toward older adults and those who lead older adults in health, exercise and dance programs. It is based upon our many years of experience in conducting health, exercise and dance classes and workshops with older adults and leaders of older adults in many different parts of the United States and Great Britain.

The ideas and concepts presented include not only our own observations and research but also that of others in the fields of physical education, exercise physiology, dance education, dance therapy, health education, gerontology, recreation and sports medicine. The older adults with whom we have worked have, of course, contributed the most to the ideas included in this book.

In writing this book for and about "older adults," we have not meant to imply that all older people are alike or have the same needs. Older adults are in fact, more heterogeneous than most age groups and their individual differences in physical ability levels and health knowledge are great. Indeed, an older person's fitness level or health status is more likely to be related to his or her past and current lifestyles than it is to his or her chronological age. Nevertheless, as with other age groups, older adults, in general, do have specialized needs that are unique. It is to these needs that we have addressed our book.

Although this book was written primarily for older adults, we do not believe that older adults should exercise and dance exclusively with people their own age. In fact, we strongly advocate an intergenerational approach to all aspects of life, where people can reach out to others and share their life experiences. We believe that integrating different generations is an excellent way to break down age stereotypes. In intergenerational settings, there are opportunities for the generations to teach each other and to learn from one another. We have addressed our beliefs about intergenerational education in a chapter entitled "Uniting the Generations" in the third edition of *Introduction to Educational Gerontology* edited by D. Barry Lumsden.

For the most part, the exercises and dance activities in this book were selected because they can be performed in small spaces on a limited budget using free, inexpensive or no equipment. Some are designed for individuals and others are for small or large groups. The major portion of this book is devoted to descriptions, suggestions and procedures for exercises and dance activities and they may be read in any sequence. However, we suggest that before beginning any of these activities, Chapters 1–5 be read first. These chapters present an introduction to the demographics of aging, a summary of theories about the aging process, a rationale or basic philosophy about exercise and aging, and important guidelines and precautions that should be followed throughout the rest of the book. Chapter 4 contains warm-up activities that you may wish to perform before embarking on the exercise or dance sessions. Chapters 13, 14, and 16 present methods for incorporating relaxation techniques into everyday living through use of stress management skills, t'ai chi ch'uan and yoga. It is our firm belief that not only exercise but also relaxation should be an integral part of everyone's life.

In this second edition of the book we have added many new exercises and dances and we have included six entirely new chapters. Chapter 1 Demographics of an Aging Society and Chapter 2 — The Aging Body will help the reader have a stronger foundation for working with older adults. Chapter 11 — Water Exercises offers an exercise alternative for people who have access to a swimming pool. Chapter 17 — Nutrition for the Older Adult, Chapter 18 — Drugs and the Older Adult, and Chapter 19 — Sexuality and Aging will all help you to envision a more holistic approach to health.

There are references and resources at the end of many chapters in this book. Chapter 20 expands on these references and resources more comprehensively by listing books, records, tapes, films, videotapes, organizations and associations dealing with health, exercise, dance and gerontology.

Although we have experienced success with the ideas presented in this book, we offer them merely as a foundation for you to use when designing and fulfilling the needs of your own exercise or dance programs.

D. E. C.
J. M-C.

Acknowledgments

We are indebted to many people for their assistance and encouragement in the writing of both the first and second editions of this book. We were fortunate to have had the opportunity of gaining our initial experience with exercise and dance programs for older adults at Vintage, Inc., in Pittsburgh, PA and at the downtown Omaha Center for Seniors at Paxton Manor in Omaha, NE. We are also appreciative of the contributions of the exercise and dance program participants at Underwood Tower in Omaha where we have led exercise and dance classes for almost six years and for the support of Cecilia Holzhey and the residents of Oak Grove Manor.

Much of the background in this book was provided by numerous teachers. Each opened a uniquely different and important window to our understanding of health, exercise, dance and aging. Some, we have only encountered for short periods of time, nevertheless their influence has remained with us. Some teachers who have been very influential in the development of activities for this book were Erna Caplow Lindner, Leah Harpaz, and Edith Clarke. In addition, the Beth Johnson Foundation, North Staffordshire Health Authority, North Staffordshire Polytechnic, and the University of Keele, all in England, provided many enriching and inspiring experiences for us.

Frank Fong, Rita Frickel, Vicki Roitman and Judy Vann have each authored a chapter in this second edition and we are grateful for their contributions. We are fortunate that Frances Thurber has created more of her sensitive drawings for the second edition of *Reach for It*.

We are indebted to the following people who so graciously agreed to pose for the photos in this book:

Ed Aide, June Aide, Irene Benbennek, Ada Brotherton, Bruce Clark, Rita Corell, Eva Derry, Kerry Ecklebe, Jodi Fretz, Addie Greening, Erna Hanselmann, Dorothy M. Hill, Tom Hostetter, Charlie Hutchison, Bertha Kolnick, Nick Kostelac, Elizabeth Layton, Glenn Layton, May Luenenberg, Emma Meininger, Beverly Mendoza, Charles Metal, Josephine E. Metal, Ruth Middleton, Howard Milder, Blanche Morrison, Alta Moser, Marjorie Price, Ruth Quigley, Robert Rodriguez, Elva Sheard, the Silver Streak Dancers, and Marie Waite. We are also grateful to the many students (too numerous to mention individually) from the School of Health, Physical Education and Recreation and the Gerontology Department at the University of Nebraska at Omaha who assisted us with health, exercise and dance programs. Working with them has reaffirmed our belief that different generations can and should do things together. We would also like to acknowledge our daughter Quinn Corbin, who has been a regular and enthusiastic participant in our Underwood Tower Program.

Chapter 1

The Demographics of an Aging Society

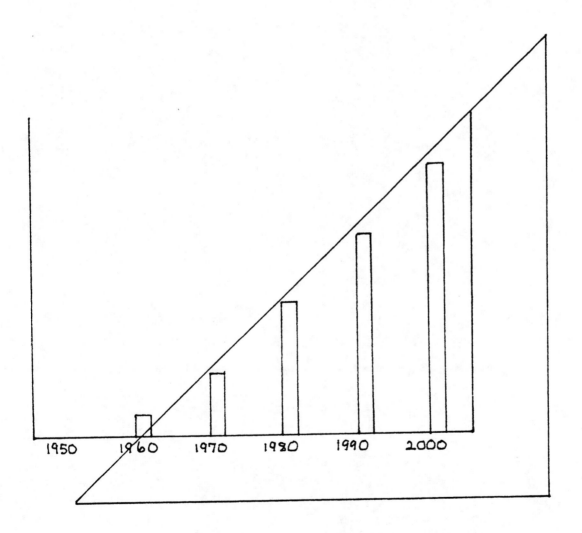

Chapter 1
The Demographics of an Aging Society

The Graying of America

We have all heard about the "graying of America" but what does this mean? Before anyone can adapt to meet the needs of an older population it is necessary to know more about them. Who is the new generation of older Americans? Where and how do older people live? What are the trends? The Administration on Aging and the American Association of Retired Persons compiled "A Profile of Older Americans" flyer in 1987 and much of the following information comes from that flyer.

The population of Americans 65 years or older numbered 29.2 million in 1986. They represented 12.1% of the population. This represents an increase of 14% since 1980, compared to an increase of 5% for the under-65 population.

Since 1900, the percentage of older Americans has tripled. The older population itself is getting older. In 1986 the 65-74 age group was eight times larger than in 1900, but the 75-84 group was 12 times larger and the 85+ group was 22 times larger. In 1986 a 65 year old could expect to live an additional 16.9 years (18.6 for women and 14.8 for males). About 5,900 Americans per day reach the age of 65. The older population is continuing to grow and the greatest spurt is expected between the years 2010 and 2030 when the "baby boom" generation reaches age 65. By the year 2000 the over 65 generation will represent about 13% of the population and by 2030 this percentage is expected to reach 21%!

Marital Status

Most older men are married (77%) and most older women aren't (40%). Widows outnumber widowers 5 to 1. Only about 4% of older Americans are divorced. The main reasons for the disparity between widows and widowers is that women outlive men, in general, and today's older women were more likely to have married men older than they.

Income

Older Americans are among the richest and the poorest in our society. Older women, blacks, and hispanics are more likely to be living below the poverty level than older white men. The median (50% above-50% below) net worth of older households ($60,300) was well above the U.S. average of $32,700 in 1984. Net worth was below $5,000 for 16% of older people's households but was above $250,000 for 7%. Older people are more likely to be asset rich and cash poor than younger people. About 11% (3 million) older Americans are still in the work force.   More than half of these people work only part-time.

Education

The educational level of older people is steadily increasing.   Betweeen 1970 and 1986, the median level of education increased from 8.7 years to 11.8 years and the percentage who completed high school rose from 28% to 49%. About 1 in 10 had four or more years in college.   The median number of years in school varies considerably by ethnicity: 12.1 for whites, 8.3 years for blacks, and 7.2 years for hispanics.

Health Status

The great majority of older Americans rate their health as either good or excellent. Only 30% assessed their health as fair or poor compared to 7% for people under age 65.   Older blacks were much more likely to rate their health as fair or poor (45%) than whites (29%). Older people averaged 32 days per year in which activities were restricted due to illness or injury.   Most older people have at least one chronic condition and many have several conditions. The most frequently occurring conditions for older adults in 1986 were: arthritis (48%), hypertension (39%), hearing impairment (29%),   heart disease (30%),   orthopedic impairments and sinusitis (17% each), cataracts (14%), diabetes and visual impairments (10% each), and tinnitus (ringing in the ears) (9%), (see Table 2 in Chapter 2).   The 12.1% older population accounted for 31% of the hospital stays and 42% of all days of care in hospitals in 1986.   The average length of a hospital stay was 8.5 days for older people and 5.4 days for younger people.   Older people averaged more visits to doctors in 1986 (9 visits) versus five visits for younger people.

In 1984 the 65+ group represented 12.1% of the population but was projected to account for 31% of total personal health care expenditures.   These expenditures were expected to total $120 billion and to average $4,202 per year for each older person, more than 3 times the $1,300 spent on each younger person. About $1000 or one-fourth of the average expenditure was expected to come from direct ("out-of-pocket") payments by older persons.   Hospital expenses were projected to account for the largest share (45%) of health expenditures for older persons in 1984, followed by physicians and nursing home care (21%). About two-thirds of these health expenditures were projected to be covered by government programs like Medicare and Medicaid compared to only one-third for people under age 65.

Living Arrangements

About two-thirds of older non-institutionalized people lived in a family setting in 1986.   At any given time only about 5% of older adults are institutionalized, however by age 85, 22% live in institutions.   About 40% of the noninstitutionalized women and 15% of the noninstitutionalized men lived alone in 1986.   A

1984 study found that 4 out of 5 older persons had living children and of these two-thirds lived within 30 minutes of a child. Sixty-two percent had at least weekly visits with their children and three-fourths talked on the phone at least weekly with their children.

Geographic Distribution

In 1986, 49% of people 65+ lived in eight states: California, New York, Florida, Pennsylvania, Texas, Illinois, Ohio, and Michigan. Ten states have populations with more than 13.6% of the pupulation over the age of 65. They are:

Florida	17.7%
Pennsylvania	14.6%
Rhode Island	14.6%
Iowa	14.5%
Arkansas	14.5%
South Dakota	13.9%
Missouri	13.7%
West Virginia	13.6%
Nebraska	13.6%
Massachusetts	13.6%

In eleven states the 65+ population increased by 20% or more between 1980 and 1986. They are:

Alaska	55%
Nevada	51%
Hawaii	36%
Arizona	33%
New Mexico	25%
South Carolina	24%
Florida	23%
Delaware	22%
Utah	22%
North Carolina	21%
Washington	21%

Note that only Florida appears on both lists. It has the highest percentage of older people and it is seventh in terms of growth of its older population.

Older people are less likely to move than other age groups. In 1985 only 16% of people 65+ had moved since 1980. By comparison, 45% of people under 65 had moved in those same five years. In 1985, only about 3% moved out of their home state. Most of them moved to Southern or Southwestern states.

Political Power

According to the Census Bureau, people older than 65 were more likely to vote in the 1988 election than any other age group. Sixty-seven and eight tenths percent of people age 65+ reported that they voted. This compares with 67.7% of the 45-64

year olds, 54% of the 25-44 year olds, and 36.2% of the 18-24
year olds.   Older people are increasingly interested in federal,
state, and local health care issues.   Organizations such as the
American Assocation of Retired Persons (over 27 million strong),
the Older Women's League, and the Gray Panthers are continuing to
grow and exert more and more political clout than any groups of
older people have ever previously done.   This older population
has a considerable amount of skill and more leisure time in which
to mobilize.   They are a force to be reckoned with.

<u>Summary</u>

There are more older people in increasing percentages in the
United States than ever before. The great majority of this older
generation is educated and healthy.   Although they consume more
health care dollars and are more likely to have chronic health
conditions, they remain largely independent.   Older people are
politically active and astute.   They are, as a group, among the
richest and the poorest Americans.   The older population is
continuing to grow and as it does the needs for services for
older adults will also increase.   The special needs of older
people regarding special needs for health education, physical
education, recreation and dance need to expand and adapt to the
meet the demands of a changing society.

Reference

Fowles, D.G.   (1987). <u>A profile of older Americans--1987</u>.
Washington, DC: Association of Retired Persons, 1987.

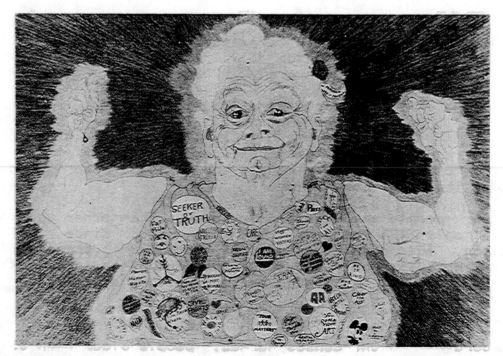

In this Elizabeth Layton drawing "Her Strength Is In Her Principles"
   the buttons illustrate some of her many beliefs.

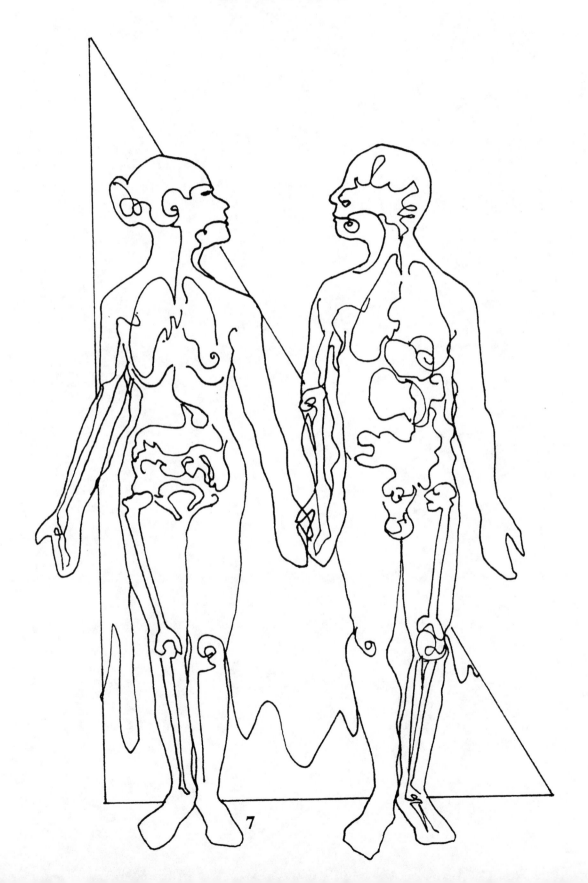

Chapter 2
The Aging Body

Aging is <u>not</u> a disease. It is a natural process that is just beginning to be understood. Some important questions about aging were addressed by the National Institute on Aging (part of the U.S. Department of Health and Human Services) in their "Answers About Aging" series pamphlets: "New Pieces to an Old Puzzle" and "The Aging Man" and "The Aging Woman." Some of this information is excerpted, adapted, summarized, or amplified in this chapter.

How and why do we age? Why is individual aging so varied? Which of the many diverse theories of aging are valid? How can answering the previous questions help to improve the quality, if not the quantity of life? What is the difference between normal aging and diseased aging? What are the common changes that occur in aging human beings? These are questions about aging that most of us would like to have the answers to. Some of these questions have answers and some have only theories. Let's start with the theories.

Despite the intense interest in longevity by so many cultures throughout the ages, scientists do not yet agree on precisely why or how humans age. Investigations into the nature of aging have been under way for many years, especially in the last decade. Much of the recent emphasis on understanding aging comes from our increasing awareness of the growth of the older population. Understanding the underlying mechanisms of aging is crucial to development of a system that considers the special health needs and medical conditions of America's older population.

It appears that human aging cannot be explained by one theory. Table 2.1 summarizes the most popular theories of aging. It is probable that several theories may be needed to explain all aging phenomena. The theories in Table 2.1 can be divided into two general types: error theories and programming theories. Error theories are based on the premise that the rate of aging in a given organism is directly related to the organism's rate of living and that random events like environmental assaults, cause damage to the body's cells. This damage accumulates over time, resulting in cellular, molecular, and organ malfunction or errors. This can be likened to a dirty copying machine that gets dirtier and dirtier through the years until the copies are ultimately illegible. The error theories include causes of aging that are extrinsic or outside the working of the body.

Table 2.1

THEORIES OF AGING

"Error Theories"	Proponent
Wear and Tear Theory*	Pearl (1924)
Rate of Living Theory*	Pearl (1928)
Metabolic Theory*	
Cross-Linking Theory**	Bjorkstein (1968)
Collagen Theory**	Vertzar (1957)
Free Radical Theory	Harman (1955)
Error Catastrophe Theory	Orgel (1963)
Somatic Mutation Theory	Sziliard (1959)

"Programming Theories"	Proponent
Programmed Senescence Theory	Hayflick (1961)
Immunological Theory	Walford (1969)
Endocrine Theory	Korenchevsky (1947)

* may represent the same theory
**may represent the same theory

Adapted from National Institute on Aging, "Answers About Aging: New Pieces to an Old Puzzle."

Programming theories are based on the assumption that aging is an event that is programmed into the cell itself and is intrinsic or inside the body. These theories maintain that aging is the natural and expected result of a purposeful sequence of events written into the genes. To continue the copying machine analogy to explain the programming theory, imagine that you made a copy and then made a copy of the copy and then a copy of that copy and on and on until eventually the copy would be illegible. In the human body (and for that matter, in any living being) there are only so many doublings that it can endure before it dies. This is thought to be internally programmed.

Error Theories

One of the oldest theories of aging is the wear and tear theory, which states that humans have vital parts which "run down" with time, leading to aging and death. This is based on the principle that nothing can last forever and sooner or later different parts begin to break down. Some parts can regenerate themselves but eventually the mechanisms by which parts or cells regenerate themselves also break down. This ultimately leads to chronic health conditions and eventually to death.

The rate of living theory, or metabolic theory, postulates that the faster an organism lives, the quicker it dies. This would explain the long lives of tortoises and the short lives of mice. One of the most dramatic methods of lengthening the lives of laboratory animals is to greatly decrease their caloric intake. In some experiments the animals lived up to 30% longer. Indeed, caloric restriction appears to be the only intervention repeatedly shown to alter the rate of aging in animals. The explanation of this phenomenon is that reducing food intake may lower the animal's metabolic rate and thus slow the aging process, perhaps by reducing the rate of DNA or cellular damage. It is known that calorie restriction can change certain hormonal responses, the composition of blood fats, and declines in the immune system. To date, however, there is little evidence that calorie restriction can alter lifespan in humans because there are no systematic longterm studies on humans who are on low calorie diets.

The cross-linking theory speculates that aging results from an accumulation of so-called cross-links in proteins. Cross-linking occurs when certain small molecules with at least two chemically active sites attach to two protein molecules; or when active groups on separate protein molecules interact with each other. One particularly abundant protein, collagen (the material which supports our cells and tissues), is found in tendons, cartilage, and bones. With aging, more and more cross-links form between collagen molecules. This makes the collagen less pliable or more rigid. This process (collagen theory) can explain many age-related changes, such as the reduced ability of the skin to stretch and flex, but is is unlikely that this is the major contributor to aging.

The free-radical theory of aging is essentially an example of the cross-linking theory. It points to damage resulting from chemical reactions between stable molecules and highly unstable chemical fragments called free-radicals. These free-radicals that are produced during normal metabolism can readily react with and often damage other molecules. Over time, an age-related accumulation of free-radical damage may ultimately interfere with the vital functioning of key cell structures. Recent media attention given to the free radical theory (even though it was first proposed over 30 years ago) have suggested that certain vitamins such as C and E and certain drugs and supplements such as centrophenoxine and superoxide dismutase (SOD) can help to stop or retard the damage done by an overaccumulation of free-radicals in the human body. The studies are not sophisticated enough at this time to determine if any positive results are the result of inhibiting free-radicals or decreased caloric restriction and weight loss as increasing survival in laboratory animals. The free-radical theory of aging has had an important effect on the scientific and lay communities in terms of longevity. It introduced the idea that we may be able to intervene in the aging process, not just to prolong life, but to alter the way in which we age. This notion may have provided a vital impetus for further and more complex studies of aging mechanisms.   In addition, it may have alerted more people to consider lifestyle and diet as important variables in the quality and quantity of their lives.

The   error catastrophe theory proposes that when damage to the protein-making machinery of the body occurs, faulty proteins will be synthesized and will gradually accumulate.   Because certain proteins are involved in making more proteins, this would result in even more erroneous proteins.   This continuing process of accumulating faulty proteins leads to "catastrophes," such as damaged cells, tissues, and organs.   Recent experiments have revealed that the error catastrophe theory does not appear to be valid, although many experts suggest that currently available methods of detecting the degree of damage that would be needed to alter cellular functions are not precise enough to support or refute this theory at this time.   A first step in resolving this question would be to identify functions or processes that clearly decline with age and then detemine whether any protein components involved in these processes show unusually high levels of damaged molecules.

The somatic mutation theory proposes that mutations occur more often with age, causing cellular deterioration and malfunction. Some investigators have not found this theory to be true and others have found that chromosome abnormalities do increase with age.   More sophisticated tools that are now being developed may be able to settle these contradictions.

The Programming Theories

The programmed senescence theory is one of the oldest.   It states that aging and death are built-in, programmed events. This theory does not specify mechanisms by which this happens, rather it views aging as a result of the sequential switching on and off of certain genes.   This theory postulates that there are biological "clocks" that are genetically controlled.   These clocks bring on menarche and menopause and the shrinkage of the thymus gland, which plays an important role in the aging of the immune system.   It was discovered in the 1960s that cells in culture in the laboratory had limited abilities to divide.   The normal number of divisions was found to be between 40 and 60. After that, the cells no longer divide.   Although this was an important discovery, it does appear to be an oversimplification to say that people age and die because their cells stop dividing, but it does provide interesting new directions to finding what systems might control the ability of cells to divide.

Some   scientists believe that there is a "death hormone" (endocrine theory) that is secreted at some point in the aging body and that this contributes ultimately to death.   This hormone, however, has never been isolated.   DHEA (dehydroepiandrosterone), however, is a hormone that may play a role in the aging process.   In studies on laboratory animals, DHEA has delayed certain chronic conditions and immune dysfunctions.   These DHEA treated animals also did not gain as much weight and, as was explained earlier, weight reduction and caloric restriction are the best predictors of longevity. So this could be the mechanism by which DHEA may work. To date, there are no studies that prove the value or safety of DHEA use in humans.

The immunological theory asserts that at least some aspects of aging are attributed to a programmed decline in the immune system. By reducing the body's ability to fight infection, fend off cancer, and even repair DNA damage, a decline in the immune system may be the single most important event in the aging process.

Regardless of which theory or theories of aging are valid, there is promise that by either controlling environmental hazards or by altering life-long habits there is the potential for being able to live better and longer lives. There is little doubt that smoking cessation, judicious exercise programs, balanced nutrition, and other proven healthy behavior, such as wearing seatbelts in automobiles, can contribute to these ends.

Changes in the Aging Body

The National Institute on Aging (NIA) is dedicated to the goal of understanding how the body ages, and to separate normal human aging from disease. The previous part of this chapter summarized many of the theories of aging that the NIA believes to be among the most important. The rest of this chapter will summarize some of the normal changes that occur with aging. It will attempt to separate the gerontological from the geriatric. Too often people confuse aging processes with disease processes. According to Morgan (1987) gerontology has "been hijacked by geriatrics." Morgan added that "aging is increasingly being presented as a disease requiring medical treatment. Medical conceptualizations tend rapidly to gain ascendancy, eclipsing alternative views of the same phenomena. Yet there is so much more to aging than can possibly be seen from a medical viewpoint."

Another problem is the self-fulfilling prophesy of believing that aging and disease are synonymous. Upon visiting a doctor for a knee problem, the 90+ year old George Burns observed that he got little constructive help. The doctor indicated that Burns should expect problems at his age. Burns replied: "but my other knee is the same age!" Maladies need to be treated, aging "per se" doesn't.

Indeed, age is not a very reliable predictor of health or activity levels. One of the best predictors of good health in later years is the number and extent of healthy lifestyles that were established in earlier life. But what are the reasonable expectations of an aging human being? What are the differences between what often does happen and what could or should happen? Let's examine what the NIA feels are the normal aspects of aging.

Skin and Hair

Two of the most obvious changes that occur with aging are the graying of the hair and the wrinkling of the skin. One study showed that women in their thirties and forties dread wrinkles more than they fear any other part of being old. The expectation of "looking old" seems to be worse than the reality. That same study found that by the time a woman reaches 65 her fears have become more sensible, and her wrinkles don't even bother her! The amount and extent of wrinkling are determined by genes and exposure to the sun. By far the most important determinant of wrinkling is the sun (or other "tanning" equipment). When exposed to the sun it is wise to wear high-protection sunscreens. Sunscreens also help to prevent skin cancer, a type of cancer that is almost entirely preventable by staying out of the sun. Most the damage to the skin in terms of wrinkling and skin cancer occurs before age 20, but it is wise to protect the skin from ultraviolet rays regardless of age. Damage that has already occurred cannot be reversed, but further damage can be minimized. Glasses with ultraviolet protection may also help to prevent cataracts. Getting prescription glasses or sunglasses fitted properly will also help to keep the damaging ultraviolet rays from reaching the eyes from the top or sides of the glasses. Sun exposure between 10 a.m. and 2 p.m. is the most damaging because ultraviolet rays are most intense at this time.

Men tend to wrinkle about 10 years later than women, because their skin tends to be thicker and oilier than women's. Also, dermatologists believe that the scraping of the razor across the skin's top layer hastens rejuvenation of the lower layers. Women who daily use gentle abrasive cleansers on their faces can mimic this process.

Recently a prescription cream called Retin-A has proved to be a popular means to reduce wrinkling. Notice that this cream is prescribed by doctors. Beware of over-the-counter creams with similar looking or sounding names. They do not have the same effects as Retin-A. It is also worth considering that the attractiveness or unattractiveness of wrinkles are in the eyes of the beholder. It makes no sense for a society that encourages a so-called "healthful" tan in youth as a sign of attractiveness, to then do an about face in later years and consider the results of that tanning to be unattractive. Functionally, of course, neither tanning or wrinkling serve a purpose. Regardless of what people might think, ultraviolet rays are harmful to the body, but wrinkles, per se, are not.

Graying of the hair is caused by a slowed production of pigment in the hair follicles. The timing of this process is determined by genetics. Although wrinkling, graying, and baldness are considered to be signs of aging, none of them are signs of aging in any other body system. A so-called "youthful look" has prompted some people to jokingly refer to the "graying of America" as the "tinting of America." Again, many people in older generations have let younger generations set the standards for what beauty should be. Why youthful standards are sought after in looks is not well understood. We ordinarily don't let youth determine most standards in politics, finance, law enforcement, or justice, so why so much influence in looks? Often the youthful standards for looks are either unattainable, unrealistic, silly, or even unhealthy (i.e., tanning) regardless of the age of the person trying to achieve them. Perhaps it is time to nurture new, more accommodating standards about what is attractive.

If the skin becomes dry and itchy then it is a good idea to take cool baths, use moisturizers, and avoid overuse of antiperspirants, soaps, perfumes, long hot baths, and overexposure to dry air.

The Eyes

Most older people wear glasses. Presbyopia (literally "elderly vision") results in the inability of the lens to focus on near objects. The muscles that hold the lens in place, and that flex it or flatten it to change its focus, gradually lose their tone, which also contributes to presbyopia. This can be corrected by magnifying glasses or bifocals (for those already wearing glasses for distance vision). Bifocals are available in contact lenses, too. As a person ages he or she is more sensitive to glare, less likely to produce tears, and less able to adapt to sudden changes in lighting. By age 80 a woman needs three times more light than she did at age 20 to achieve the same visual clarity. More than half of all visual impairments occur in people over age 65. In addition, a great many eye diseases are associated with aging. The most common are age-related macular degeneration (AMD), cataracts, and glacoma. Laser therapy is successful in preventing or delaying AMD, cataracts are treated by surgery (and as mentioned in the previous section, avoiding ultraviolet exposure to the eyes can help prevent or delay cataracts), and glaucoma is not curable but it can be treated with drugs or laser surgery. People over age 40 should have periodic eye examinations that check for these diseases.

Hearing

Hearing loss is a more common problem in older men than older women. There are basically two types of hearing loss. Conduction deafness is a blockage of the ear canal caused by excessive ear wax, abnormal structures in the outer ear, or infection. Most of these cases are treated by flushing the ear, by medicines, or by surgery. Central or sensorineural deafness results from damage to the nerve centers within the brain. This can include damage to the cells in the organ of Corti (the organ of hearing) which can result from exposure to loud noises, disease, and certain drugs. Vascular diseases in particular can cause hearing loss by cutting off the blood supply to the ear. Tinnitus is an annoying ringing or buzzing in the ear whose exact cause is unknown. Some cases are caused by excessive use of aspirin, certain antibiotics, or diuretics (water pills), all of which are more commonly used by older adults. Tinnitus may also be caused by tumors. Heredity may play a part in as much as 50 percent of age-related hearing loss and loud noise may be more to blame than aging in many cases of hearing loss. Hearing aids can help many different types of hearing losses. It is essential that hearing aids be well fitted and well maintained.

The Musculoskeletal System

Both men and women lose muscle mass as they age, and their bodies develop higher proportions of fat. An average 20-year-old woman's body is 16.5% muscle and 26.5% fat. A 20-year-old man's body is 18% fat. As people age their percent body fat increases to a lifetime high of 42% for women in their fifties, which then begins a gradual decline to about 36% in women in their sixties and seventies. What isn't completely understood is how much of these variations in body fat are due to aging and how much are due to sedentary lifestyles. Master athletes, for example, do not demonstrate such high percents of body fat with age. In general, however, an aged muscle looks different from a young muscle, revealing cell loss, atrophy of cells, accumulation of fat and collagen, and loss of contractility. These changes don't necessarily mean a loss of function, though; what they primarily mean is that an older person is more likely to experience strains, pulls, and cramping after exercising. All of this just means that it is essential for older people to warm-up before exercising and cool down after exercising. A well-conditioned person of 65 can be in far better physical shape than a desk-bound person of 25.

There is currently considerable debate about what "ideal" weights and percent body fats ought to be among older adults. Being extremely thin or extremely fat does place older adults at a higher risk of premature death. But some researchers have indicated that current height-weight tables should be adjusted upward for older adults. In other words, older adults can weigh more than younger people without increasing their mortality rate (Andres, et al., 1985).

Women are more likely to develop osteoporosis and arthritis as they age. Men, however, are not immune to these maladies. Because bone mass reaches its peak at about age 35, good nutritional and exercise practices prior to that are essential. Despite all of the hoopla in current advertising, the benefits of calcium supplementation after menopause is unclear. Estrogen replacement therapy (ERT) in women is known to decrease a woman's risk of osteoporosis, but it is controversial since the estrogen must be continued indefinitely, perhaps for 20 or more years. This may produce untoward side effects of yet unknown severity.

It is thought that alcohol consumption, carbonated beverages, red meat, coffee ingestion, and cigarette smoking can all contribute to osteoporosis. Weight bearing exercises like walking, cycling, and jogging may help prevent osteoporosis.

The Cardiovascular System

Studies that have monitored the rate of aging over a period of years indicate that the heart of a healthy 80-year-old performs about as well as that of a man in his twenties. In the absence of disease, the heart functions smoothly and even adapts to the normal changes of age. Changes that do occur in the heart with age are thought to help maintain normal function. Such changes include thickening of the left ventricle of the heart, which sends the blood with oxygen to the body. The aging heart also compensates for a slower heart rate during exercise by increasing the amount of blood pumped per heartbeat.

Heart disease, specifically coronary artery disease, is the number one cause of death in men over age 40, and accounts for 50 percent of all deaths among older people. When blood flow cannot reach the heart muscle due to a clogged coronary artery, then damage to the heart muscle ensues, resulting in an often fatal myocardial infarction or heart attack. While some risk factors for heart disease are uncontrollable (genetic makeup and age), others like smoking, high blood pressure, stress management skills, and high blood cholesterol can be modified to reduce the risk of heart disease. How these factors can be changed are dealt with in later chapters in this book.

Cerebrovascular disease or strokes are other main types of blood vessel diseases. Strokes are the third leading cause of death among older adults. A stroke occurs when blood is cut off to a region in the brain because of blocked blood vessels or a rupture with bleeding (hemorrhage) into surrounding tissues. The loss of blood may result in permanent damage to the brain cells, and related mental or physical disability or death. Risk factors for stroke are the same as those mentioned above for coronary heart disease. In addition, people who drink excessive amounts of alcohol, people who are overfat, and people who have diabetes are at greater risk of developing a stroke.

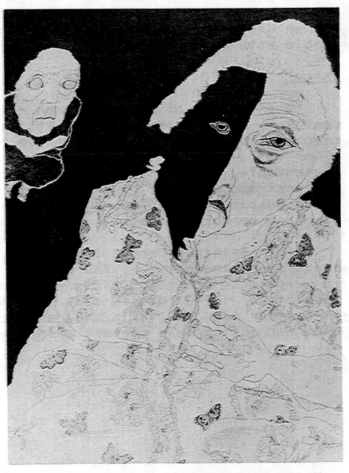

"Stroke" by Elizabeth Layton

Women develop cardiovascular disease, on the average, about 10 to 20 years later than men do. This remains true even when you control such risk factors as smoking, blood cholesterol levels, and family histories of heart disease. Between the ages of 45 and 54, women die of cardiovascular disease at the rate of 84 per 100,000 per year. By the time they reach age 65, that rate jumps to a whopping 1,958 per 100,000 per year. This latter figure is almost as high as the rate for men of that age. Women, however, tend to develop milder forms of cardiovascular disease. A man's first and only symptom might result in sudden death from a massive heart attack. A woman's symptoms are more likely to involve angina, a condition of chest pain on exertion that indicates that the heart muscle is not getting enough oxygen. Perhaps estrogen helps to protect women from cardiovascular disease, because the amount of estrogen is related to the level of high density lipoproteins (HDL's) which help to decrease blood cholesterol. Many experts feel that post-menopausal estrogen replacement therapy may help reduce the risk of heart disease.

Although women are less susceptible to coronary heart disease than men, their risk of hypertension is greater. Hypertension, or high blood pressure, becomes more common with advanced age (see Table 2.2). Hypertension has been called "the silent killer" because it generally has no symptoms. Nevertheless, it can cause serious damage to the eyes, kidneys, and blood vessels. Hypertension can often be controlled by proper diet, exercise, relaxation techniques, or medication, but people with hypertension should be under a doctor's care.

Cancer

The rates of cancer increase with age. One out of eight deaths in women over 65 can be attributed to cancer, particularly cancer of the large intestine, the breast, and the lungs. Among older men, lung cancer is by far the most common and the most preventable. Colon and rectal cancer are the next most common killers among men. The American Cancer Society recommends a sigmoidoscopic exam (commonly known as a "procto") every 3 to 5 years to detect colorectal cancer.

The American Cancer Society estimates that one-half of all cancers are preventable. The biggest single contributor to cancer is cigarette smoking. This will be dealt with in more depth in Chapter 18. The role of diet in cancer prevention is addressed in Chapter 17. The "Skin and Hair" section in this chapter dealt with methods to help prevent skin cancer.

Table 2.2

Selected Reported Conditions per 1,000 Persons, by Sex and Age:
United States 1985

Number of Chronic Conditions per 1,000 Persons

Type of Chronic Condition	Female 65 Years and Over	Male 65 Years and Over
Arthritis	550.5	361.5
Hypertension	458.4	351.4
Hearing Impairment	245.9	364.2
Heart Disease	288.1	328.0
Cataracts	205.7	104.3
Deformity or Orthopedic Impairment	193.6	138.1
Visual Impairment	91.5	103.6
Frequent Constipation	75.4	31.7
Cerebrovascular Disease	50.3	76.7
Glaucoma	41.1	33.5
Disorders of Bone or Cartilage	29.4	7.4
Gastritis or Duodenitis	27.2	12.5
Ulcer	27.1	43.9
Emphysema	21.9	80.1

Source: National Center for Health Statistics,
Vital and Health Statistics, Series 10, No. 160

Breast cancer is the type of cancer that kills the most women although in some states breast cancer has been surpassed by lung cancer due to increased smoking practices among females over the past few decades. It is recommended that women practice monthly breast self-exams (call for a free pamphlet from your local affiliate of the American Cancer Society) and past age 50 all women should have an annual mammogram, which can detect breast cancer at its earliest, most treatable stage.

Among men, prostate cancer is the second most common after lung cancer. Fortunately, prostate cancer is usually slow in progression so it is often very successfully treated. Men over the age of 50 should have an annual rectal exam to check the prostate for abnormalities.

The American Cancer Society recommends that all people be alert to the seven warning signs of cancer. It should be kept in mind that usually these symptoms are false alarms and not cancer, but as the saying goes: "It is better to be safe than sorry." Notice that the first letters of the seven warning signals spell out C-A-U-T-I-O-N. This mnemonic device might be used to help remember these seven symptoms.

1) Change in bowel or bladder habits (which might indicate bowel or prostate cancer).

2) A sore that does not heal (possibly mouth or skin cancer).

3) Unusual bleeding or discharge (perhaps indicating uterine or bowel cancer).

4) Thickening or lump in breast or elsewhere (a sign of breast or testicular cancer).

5) Indigestion or difficulty in swallowing (stomach or esophagus cancer).

6) Obvious change in warts or moles (skin cancer).

7) Nagging cough or hoarseness (lung or larynx cancer).

Sleep

For an activity that we spend so much of our life doing, it is amazing that we know so little about the purpose and need for sleep. Everyone sleeps but the individual differences are extremely varied. Although in our society we acknowledge developmental changes in most aspects of our lives, we tend to think in terms of a "healthful" or oftentimes "magical" eight hours of sleep per night (except in the childhood years). The fact is that our sleep cycles change with age but too many people seem to try to force old sleep patterns on a changing body.

Sleep research clearly shows that compared to young adults, older people have more broken sleep which is more vulnerable to disturbance by noise, less deep sleep, and fewer hours spent asleep. In addition, the stages of sleep are generally altered, i.e., less time is spent in rapid eye movement (REM) or dream sleep among older people than among younger people.

Most of the above information flies in the face of what people normally think of when they think of older people and sleep. The stereotype is of people who sleep more, nap often, and since they are more likely to be hard of hearing, they are less bothered by noise. As with many other aspects of aging, it is difficult to separate what actually happens with what should happen or to separate the "normalcy" from the other attendant diseases that older people are more likely to have. For example, do older people nap more because they have more of an opportunity or more of a need? Would younger people nap more if given the same opportunity? In some cultures it is the the norm to take a mid-day "siesta."

Although older people tend to sleep less than younger people, they are more likely to spend more time in bed. Their "sleep efficiency index" (i.e., total sleep time divided by the total time spent in bed) is decreased. This, combined with the age old dictum: "Most people need about 7 or 8 hours of sleep per night," seems to preoccupy the minds of countless older people. If they aren't getting this much sleep they may turn to sleeping pills that in the longterm may cause more harm than good. As Kevin Morgan (1987), author of the book <u>Sleep</u> <u>and</u> <u>Ageing</u> said: "At the professional level, it is also clear that a medical tradition has developed which seems to assume that insomnia in old age is often due to some form of benzodiazepine [sleeping pill] deficiency." According to Dr. Morgan, most younger people <u>might</u> need 7 or 8 hours of sleep per night, "most elderly people certainly <u>do</u> <u>not</u>." Morgan went on to say:

> . . . expectations of sleep are more likely to be influenced by inherited or "common" knowledge rather than by direct observation. It is interesting to note, therefore, that much conventional wisdom about sleep, as contained in popular maxims, seems to assume a quite unrealistic (and misleading) life-long stability in sleeping patterns. For example, such pearls as "early to bed, early to rise . . ." etc., or "an hour before midnight is worth more than one hour after midnight" are of little value to elderly people who would be better advised to go to bed as late as possible so that their sleep stretches at least till dawn (p. 141).

If insomnia results from illness, disease, or bereavement, then the best course of action would be to treat the cause not the symptom. As with many of the other problems mentioned in this chapter many of the problems with sleep can be controlled by the individual. Sleep-wake cycles can be strengthened by maintaining regular personal habits and routines. "Regular times of going to bed and getting up, regular preparations for bedtime, and regularly scheduled daytime naps can all help to re-establish and maintain regular sleep-rhythms." (Morgan, 1987). In addition, certain stress management techniques and exercise several hours prior to bedtime may be beneficial.

Mental Functioning

The phrase "use it or lose it" applies to both the physical and mental capabilities of older men and women. In general, older people remain intelligent and creative. The myth that older people will automatically lose their mental capabilities still persists. Words like "senile" are used pejoratively to mean "out of touch." The word senile originally came from a Latin word and meant old. The problem of expectations of automatic mental dysfunction in old age, as mentioned in other parts of this chapter, is the difficulty of distinguishing those characteristics that are attributed to aging from those attributed to disease. It is true that older people are more likely to suffer from diseases like Alzheimer's disease but it is also true that the great majority of older adults do not get Alzheimer's disease or any of the other types of dementias. Mental confusion can also be caused by poor nutrition, depression, hypothyroidism, and adverse reactions to drugs (see Chapter 18). Small strokes can block blood flow to the brain, resulting in the death of brain tissue and subsequent disability. As mentioned previously, the risk of strokes can be diminished by controlling blood pressure and cholesterol, eating properly, and exercising to improve circulation.

For those victims and families of the various disease forms of dementias, there are support groups and associations to help all of those affected to cope with the problem. One example is the Alzheimer's Association.

Another condition called "pseudo-dementia" is the mental changes caused by an underlying depression. Oftentimes these people are "written off" to the ravages of aging by families and even by physicians. But depression in later life can be treated by psychotherapy and medications. The controversial electroshock therapy is helpful to some sufferers of depression. An estimated three-quarters of older depressed people can be cured.

Suicide increases dramatically with age in men, from 23 per 100,000 men aged 35 to 44 to more than 50 per 100,000 for men over the age of 85. But as women age they to not seem to experience the same depths of despair. Suicide rates for women decline after the age of 54, when it peaks at 10 per 100,000.

Dimensions of Successful Aging

Besides the preventative factors mentioned in the previous parts of this chapter, another important aspect of aging is to have a positive attitude. Many older people have the same negative stereotypes about aging that young people do. They too often see aging as all bad and no good. Their expectations become self-fulfilling prophecies. Words and phrases like "over-the-hill", "one foot in the grave," "senile", or "geezer" set up the older person for a life of despair. It is important for people of all ages to realize that many older people do not necessarily want to be young again. Older people who view life positively, see both the advantages and disadvantages of aging. They often see that the former outweighs the latter. Fortunately, most older people rate their health as either good or excellent. Studies have shown that positive attitudes can also be self-fulfilling, i.e., those who see themselves as healthy act as healthy people should. They are more likely to maintain good health behaviors and to live longer (Mossey & Shapiro, 1982; Corbin, 1981).

Fries and Crapo (1981) expounded on a "new syllogism" which is based on the premise that: 1) the human life span is fixed; 2) the age at first infirmity will increase (i.e., infirmity will occur later in life); therefore, 3) the duration of infirmity will decrease. What this means is that life expectancy will not greatly increase, but people will live healthier years before their deaths. The physical and mental declines with age will be further and further delayed so that people will be able to live full and productive lives almost right up to the time of death, like the "one hoss shay" in Oliver Wendall Holmes' poem, "The Deacon's Masterpiece" (see the boxed item). This is what leading a healthy life can offer us all; not immortality, but fulfillment. Not more years in our life, but more life in our years. Gerontologist Ken Dychtwald (1989) commented on a conversation that he had with Monsignor Charles Fahey. Fahey suggested that although aging bodies may decline with age, that the spirit has the capability of soaring to new heights as we age. He intimated that "the growth and evolution of the inner life may be the unique and special opportunity that the aging of America will bring" (Dychtwald & Flower, 1989).

References

Andres, R., Elahi, D., Tobin, M.D., Muller, B.A., & Brant, L. (1985). Impact of age on weight goals. Annals of Internal Medicine, 103 (6), part 2, 1030-1033.

Corbin, D.E., (1981). Psychological and physical aspects of self-perceived health status among older adults. Dissertation: University of Pittsburgh. Dissertation Abstracts, No. 8210620, Universal Abstract Service, 300 Zeebe Rd., Ann Arbor, MI 48106.

Dychtwald, K. & Flower, J. (January/February 1989). The third age. New Age Journal, 50-59.

Fries, J.F. & Crapo, L.M. (1981). Vitality and aging, San Francisco: W.H. Freeman.

Morgan, K. (1987). Sleep and ageing, London: Croom Helm.

Mossey, J.M. & Shapiro, E. (1982). Self-rated health: A predictor of mortality among the elderly. American Journal of Public Health, 72, 800-808.

National Institute on Aging, (n.d.). Answers about: The aging woman/the aging man, U.S. Department of Health and Human Services.

National Institute on Aging, (n.d.). Answers about aging: New pieces to an old puzzle, U.S. Department of Health and Human Services.

Thomas, L. (1979). The medusa and the snail. New York: The Viking Press.

The Deacon's Masterpiece

The brightest and most optimistic of my presentiments about the future of human health always seem to arouse a curious mixture of resentment and dismay among some very intelligent listeners. It is as though I'd said something bad about the future. Actually, all I claim, partly on faith and partly from spotty but unmistakable bits of evidence out of the past century of biomedical science, is that mankind will someday be a disease-free species.

Except for gaining a precise insight into the nature of human consciousness (which may elude us for a very long time, perhaps forever), I cannot imagine any other limits to the profundity of our understanding of living things. It may happen within the next few centuries, maybe longer, but when it does it will bring along, inevitably, the most detailed sorts of explanations for human disease mechanisms. It is an article of faith with me that we will then know how to intervene directly, to turn them around or prevent them.

Something like this has already happened for most of the major infections. Even though we are still in a primitive, earliest stage in the emergence of biology, as compared, say, to physics, we have accomplished enough basic science to permit the development of specific antimicrobial antiserums and an impressive list of safe, rational viral vaccines. Within fifty years after the recognition of bacteria as pathogens we had classified them and learned enough of their metabolic intricacies so that the field was ready for antibiotics. In the years since the late 1940s the first great revolution in technology in all the long history of medicine has occurred, and infectious diseases that used to devastate whole families have now been almost forgotten.

Events moved rapidly in the field of infection, and this may have represented abnormally good luck. For some of the others -- heart disease, cancer, stroke, the senile psychoses, diabetes, schizophrenia, emphysema, hypertension, arthritis, tropical parasitism, and the like -- we may be in for a longer, more difficult pull, but maybe not. With the pace of research having increased so rapidly in the last two decades, and the remarkable new young brains enlisted for the work of biology, we could be in for surprises at almost any time. Anyway, sooner or later, they will all become nonmysteries, accountable and controllable.

These prospects seem to me exciting and heartening, and it is hard to face the mute, sidelong glances of disapproval that remarks along these lines usually generate. You'd think I'd announced an ultimate calamity.

The trouble comes from the automatic questions, "Then what?" It is the general belief that we need our diseases -- that they are natural parts of the human condition. It goes against nature to tamper and manipulate them out of existence, as I propose. "Then what?" What on earth will we die of? Are we to go on forever, disease-free, with nothing to occupy our minds but the passage of time? What are the biologists doing to us? How can you finish life honorably, and die honestly, without a disease?

This last is a very hard question, almost too hard to face, and therefore just the sort of question you should look around for a poem to answer, and there is one. It is "The Deacon's Masterpiece, or, the Wonderful 'One-Hoss Shay,'" by Oliver Wendell Holmes. On the surface, this piece of rather dreadful nineteenth-century doggerel seems to concern the disintegration of a well-made carriage, but inside the verse, giving it the staying power to hold on to our minds for over a full century, is myth about human death.

Moreover, it is a myth for the modern mind. It used to be the common wisdom that the living body was a vulnerable, essentially ramshackle affair, always at risk of giving way at one point or another, too complicated to stay in one piece. These days, with what is being learned about cellular biology, especially in the form and function of subcellular structures and their macromolecular components, and the absolutely flawless arrangements for drawing on solar energy for the needs of all kinds of cells, the most impressive aspect of life is its sheer, tough power. With this near view, it becomes a kind of horrifying surprise to realize that things can go wrong -- that a disorder of one part can bring down the whole amazing system. Looked at this way, disease seems a violation of nature, an appalling mistake. There must be a better way to go.

Thus, a detailed anatomy of Holmes's carriage can be read as a metaphor for a live organism -- or, for that matter, a cell:

> Now in building of chaises, I tell you what,
> There is always <u>somewhere</u> a weakest spot--

In hub, tire, felloe, in spring or thill,
In panel, or crossbar, or floor, or sill,
In screw, bolt, thoroughbrace--lurking still . . .
And that's the reason, beyond a doubt,
That a chaise <u>breaks</u> <u>down</u>, but doesn't <u>wear</u> <u>out</u>.

This was the nineteenth-century view of disease, and the source of our trouble today. It assumes that there is always, somewhere, a weakest part, as though foreordained. Without fundamental, localized flaws in the system, it might simply age away. As it is, it is doomed to break down prematurely, unless you can figure out how to find and fix the flawed item. Dr. Holmes, in the sicence of his day, saw little likelihood of this, but he did see, in his imagination, the possibility of sustained perfection. The Deacon is his central, Olympian Creator, symbolizing Nature, incapable of fumbling. What he designs is the perfect organism.

. . . so built that it <u>couldn't</u> break daown . . .
. . . "the weakes' place mus' stan' the strain;
'N' the way t' fix it, uz I maintain,
Is only jest
T' make that place uz strong uz the rest."

Then, the successive acts of creation, collectively miraculous, scriptural in tone:

. . . the strongest oak,
That couldn't be split nor bent nor broke . . .
He sent for lancewood to make the thills;
The crossbars were ash, from the straightest trees,
The panels of white-wood, that cuts like cheese,
But lasts like iron for things like these. . .

Step and prop-iron, bolt and screw,
Spring, tire, axle, and linchpin too,
Steel of the finest, bright and blue;
Thoroughbrace bison-skin, thick and wide;
Boot, top, dasher, from tough old hide . . .
That was the way he "put her through."
"There!" said the Deacon, "naow she'll dew!"

And dew she did. The chaise lived, in fact, for a full, unblemished hundred years of undiseased life, each perfect part supported by all the rest. It was born from the Deacon's hands in 1755, the year of the great Lisbon earthquake, and it died on the earthquake centenary, to the hour, in 1855.

The death was the greatest marvel of all. Up to the last minute, the final turn of the splendid wheels, the thing worked perfectly. There was aging, of course, and Holmes concedes this in his myth, but it was respectable, decent, proper sort of aging:

A general flavor of mild decay,

A general flavor of mild decay,
But nothing local, as one may say.
There couldn't be -- for the Deacon's art
Had made it so like in every part
That there wasn't a chance for one to start.

And then, the hour of death:

. . . the wheels were just as strong as the thills,
And the floor was just as strong as the sills,
And the panels just as strong as the floor . . .
And the back crossbar as strong as the fore . . .
And yet, <u>as a whole</u>, it is past a doubt
In another hour it will be <u>worn out</u>!

What a way to go!

First of November, 'Fifty-five!
This mourning the parson takes a drive.
Now, small boys, get out of the way!
Here comes the wonderful one-hoss shay,
Drawn by a rat-tailed, ewe-necked bay.
"Huddup!" said the parson. Off went they.

And the death scene itself.   No tears, no complaints, no
listening closely for last words. No grief. Just, in the way of
the world, total fulfillment. Listen:

All at once the horse stood still,
Close by the meet'n'-house on the hill.
First a shiver, and then a thrill,
Then something decidedly like a spill--
And the parson was sitting upon a rock,
At half past nine by the meet'n'-house clock--

And, finally, the view of the remains:

What do you think the parson found,
When he got up and stared around?
The poor old chaise in a heap of mound,
As if it had been to the mill and ground! . . .
. . . . it went to pieces all at once--
All at once, and nothing first--
Just as bubbles do when they burst.

My favorite line in all this is one packed with the most
abundant meaning, promising aging as an orderly, drying-up
process, terminated by the most natural of events: "As if it had
been to the mill and ground!"

This is, in high metaphor, what happens when a healthy old
creature, old man or old mayfly, dies. There is no outside evil
force, nor any central flaw. The dying is built into the system
so that it can occur at once, at the end of a preclocked,
genetically determined allotment of living.   Centralization

ceases, the forces that used to hold cells together are
disrupted, the cells lose recognition of each other, chemical
signaling between cells comes to an end, vessels become plugged
by thrombi and disrupt their walls, bacteria are allowed free
access to tissues normally forbidden, organelles inside cells
begin to break apart; nothing holds together; it is the bursting
of billions of bubbles, all at once.

What a way to go!

Chapter 3

How Exercise and Dance Can Improve the Health of Older Adults

29

Chapter 3

How Exercise and Dance Can Improve
the Health of Older Adults

We have all heard about the fitness boom in the United States. But is the fitness boom going bust, or was the fitness boom just an illusion in the first place? Certainly, there are still countless magazines, books, videotapes, and television shows touting the advantages of different types of exercise and dance programs. But are people actually doing anything about fitness other than reading about it?

It is difficult to obtain accurate information about how many Americans are physically active because different studies define physical activity in different ways. But it is safe to say that far too many Americans get little or no exercise. Some studies suggest that older adults, as an age group, have been more likely to take up exercise in recent years than other age groups, but they may also have a longer way to go. Sallis, et al. (1985) indicated that 92% of older women and 75% of older men reported no vigorous activities at all. Fifteen percent of the women and 17% of the men reported that they engaged in no moderate activity. In Britain, Dallosso et al. (n.d.) found that "customary engagement in many activities was found to be low" among two groups of older adults (aged 65-74 and aged 75 and over). Low levels of activity may cause older adults to drift dangerously near to the threshold of their capacity to maintain an independent lifestyle. If this is true then there is a need for more information about exercise for older adults. If there are contradictions surrounding the benefits and hazards of exercise among young people (and there are), the contradictions are even more pronounced with respect to the benefits and hazards of exercise among older adults, mainly because researchers have only recently devoted more time to studying the effects of exercise on older people.

The inactivity of older adults is often the result of overprotection by well-meaning family members, friends, or even physicians. Many older adults, even peole who have been active all their lives, are encouraged to limit their activity drastically as they get older. They are told, "Take it easy," or "Don't do too much -- you'll hurt yourself." As a consequence, some older adults become overcautious and afraid to exert themselves. They then suffer a further loss in function stemming from their sedentary lifestyle (Corbin, C. & Lindsey, 1984).

In an effort to clear up some of these contradictions, this chapter will summarize what is now known about the effects of exercise on the mental and physical health of older adults. (Chapter 5 will discuss exercise guidelines and precautions for older adults). Whether the fitness boom is a mirage or a reality for most people, is open to debate, but there will always be a need for more information about the benefits of exercise and dance for older adults who do wish to remain active, even if they remain in the minority.

It is no major revelation to say that various physical diseases and disorders can, and often do, affect both the mental and physical health of people of all ages. The consequences, however, are likely to be more profound among older people than among younger people because diseases and disorders among older people are more likely to be chronic (of long duration) in nature. Indeed, 86% of older persons have one or more chronic disease or disorder (Butler & Lewis, 1982).

There is evidence that carefully planned exercise programs can help to prevent and/or diminish the severity of many common chronic health conditions that afflict most older people. In addition, exercise and dance can be fun and rewarding. As the Health Education Authority in Great Britain says: "It doesn't have to be hell to be healthy."

Following are some important examples of the benefits of exercise and dance:

<u>Cardiovascular disease</u>. Despite recent declines in cardiovascular disease rates, it remains the number one cause of death in the United States. Included among these cardiovascular diseases are hypertension, heart attacks and strokes, all of which are prevalent among older persons (see Table 2 in Chapter 2) all of which are associated with diet, smoking, stress and exercise. That aerobic or endurance exercise (continuous exercise done regularly for at least 20 minute durations three or more times per week) can positively affect the cardiovascular system and therefore decrease the risk or severity of these cardiovascular diseases is well known. However, most of that evidence has been gathered on young people. Even with young people it may not be necessary to exercise as vigorously as most books claim and with older people regular moderate exercise may be very beneficial. Paffenbarger, Hyde, Wing & Hsieh (1986) showed that death rates were one quarter to one third lower among Harvard alumni who expended 2000 or more calories per week than among the less active Harvard men in their longterm study. The more active alumni were estimated to have lived on average one and one quarter years longer than less active men (Paffenbarger, Hyde, Hsieh, & Wing (1986). This does not mean that older people who have been active all of their lives cannot or should not exercise aerobically, it simply means that exercise does not necessarily have to be "aerobic" to be of benefit to the cardiovascular system and other systems. Aerobic exercise can be

started late in life as long as it is worked up to gradually and as long as the participant has the capabilities and the motivation. But it is misleading for people to believe that exercise can only benefit people if it is twenty minutes of continuous exercise that is performed a minimum of three times per week. Kasch, Wallace, & Van Camp (1985) in an eighteen year longterm study, showed that there was very little decline in physical work capacity among thirteen men who regularly exercised throughout their lives. Maximal oxygen uptake remained almost constant when compared with the initial test eighteen years earlier. At twenty years into the study Kasch (1987) concluded that the men in his study "aged" 39% less than average due to their exercise intervention. There was a decline in the cardiac output over the twenty years, but it was much less than among those who didn't exercise.

What can exercise do to benefit the cardiovascular systems of older people? Exercise can:

1) Increase heart volume & heart weight.
2) Increase blood volume.
3) Increase maximal stroke volume and cardiac output.
4) Decrease arterial blood pressure.
5) Increase maximal oxygen consumption.
6) Decrease resting heart rate. (Wiswell, 1980).

All of the above benefits make for a stronger, more efficient heart and vascular system, thus resulting in decreased risk of cardiovascular disease or decreased severity of cardiovascular disease if it does occur. Even if exercise doesn't add years to life (and there is certainly no guarantee that it will), it certainly can add life to years. Exercise can increase the years of feeling good--"to be alive as long as you live " (Frankel & Richard, 1977). If you make exercise fun, rather than strictly a prescription for a disease, then your quality of life will certainly increase.

Arthritis. Arthritis affects approximately 32 million Americans. Ninety-seven percent of all people aged 60 and over have arthritis that is detectable by X-ray. (Arthritis Foundation, 1978). Arthritis can cause severe pain, disfigurement and incapacity. Because of this, some people cannot participate in normal daily activities, they may withdraw from society and public functions and they may have to take medications that may precipitate or cause physical and mental side effects. Certain types of arthritis can be reduced in severity or treated through flexibility exercises prescribed by a knowledgeable physician, physical therapist or physical educator. These exercises, that do not overstress the arthritic areas, can aid in the preservation of joint and muscle function. The Arthritis Foundation (1983) gives the following guidelines for choosing appropriate physical activities.

1) The exercise shouldn't cause pain.

2) There should be no stress to the involved joints.
3) Exercise sessions should be balanced with rest.
4) Body or limb positions that contribute to joint stress or deformity should be avoided.
5) Do less when the disease is more active or when the joints are more painful.
6) Respect individual limitations.

Good exercise or dance programs can increase mobility, decrease the need for medication and encourage people to emphasize the physical tasks they can do rather than dwelling on the activities they cannot do. Exercise and dance are not panaceas, and all people and all types of arthritis will not respond favorably to them, but for millions of Americans exercise and dance can open paths to more mobility, less pain and increased self-concept. If a chronic condition produces depression, then the amelioration of that condition can certainly serve to eliminate that depression. Exercise and dance are important means to that end.

Obesity. Being extremely overweight is a major health hazard in America. Obese individuals are more likely to suffer from chronic conditions like cardiovascular disease, osteoarthritis, and diabetes (Kart, Metress & Metress, 1988). Some types of surgery are more hazardous when performed on obese patients. In addition, the obese person often exhibits a low self-concept and is often subject to public scorn and ridicule. This is likely to produce poor mental health. One must not overlook the fact that poor mental health can lead to overeating which can lead to obesity, which can lead to even poorer mental health leading to more overeating, thus producing a vicious cycle.

Exercise is, of course, a major factor in weight control. Endurance type activities, like walking or dancing are excellent for weight control purposes. Of course, exercise along with a well-balanced, controlled diet is the best prescription for long-term weight control (see Chapter 17). Compulsive eaters should, in addition, be receiving psychological counseling aimed at the investigation of any psychological contributors or causes of obesity. Of course, some people are genetically predisposed to obesity but this does not negate the importance of exercise and good nutrition.

Diabetes. Approximately 2 million people over age 65 suffer from diabetes. Many of these people can control their diabetes by carefully regulating their diet and exercise habits and by avoiding obesity. The added benefit of being able to control a chronic condition without drugs or with minimal medical intervention is an extremely important aspect of health, particularly to those people who previously believed that they had no control or mastery over their own health. Exercise is an important way for people to begin to take charge of their own health. Diabetes control through exercise is an excellent example of how this can be done.

Osteoporosis. Osteoporosis is a disease that affects between 15 to 20 million older Americans--mostly women. It is a disease that is characterized by bone loss. As the bones become more fragile, the chances of falls, resulting in broken bones, increase. Because of the fear of falls and broken bones, many people with osteoporosis remain homebound, fearing to explore all but the most familiar territory. There is increasing evidence (although not clearly defined) that weight bearing exercise can diminish the onset and/or severity of osteoporosis (Smith, 1982). If a person with severe bone loss can increase bone mineral mass, then that person is more likely to become more independent and more self-assured as a result of becoming physically or structurally stronger.

Constipation. Many older people complain of constipation. "It is estimated that 40 to 60 percent of the elderly use laxatives regularly. Advertising techniques tend to heavily exploit the elderly population with strong emotional pitches that are often family or nostalgia oriented. More than 700 over-the-counter constipation remedies exist " (Kart, Metress & Metress, 1988). A large percentage of older people who use these laxatives regularly become dependent on them and consequently suffer a great deal of pain and discomfort as a result of chronic constipation. Exercise (particularly when combined with a well-planned diet) offers a natural and easy alternative to laxatives. Regular, rhythmic exercises speed up the transit time of food through the digestive tract, thereby relieving symptoms of or decreasing the chances of constipation without the cost or side effects of commercial laxatives.

Insomnia. Exercise is a natural sleep producer and tranquilizer (USHHS, 1981). According to deVries (1975) ". . . (an) exercise modality should not be over-looked when a tranquilizer effect is desired, since in single doses, . . . exercise has a significantly greater effect, without any undesirable side effects, than does Meprobamate, one of the most frequently prescribed tranquilizers."

Tranquilizer drugs can adversely effect the quality of sleep, including suppression of necessary dream sleep. Good quality and quantity of sleep are essential for optimal mental and physical functioning. Mild exercise a few hours prior to bedtime may help to alleviate insomnia without adversely affecting the quality of sleep (see the section on sleep in Chapter 2).

Stress related diseases. "In judging the adaptations of older persons, it is vital to remember that they commonly deal with more stresses (in actual number, frequency, and profundity) than any other age group " (Butler & Lewis, 1982). The stress related diseases that accompany the stressors of old age range from asthma to ulcers. Certain types of physical exercises like T'ai Chi Ch'uan (Chapter 13) and Yoga (Chapter 14) can relieve stress, and indeed they have served that purpose for thousands of years. Western culture has become more receptive to the value of these exercises and their ability to help people deal with stress.

Exercise is also a good stress reducer. Noncompetitive exercises and dance activities provide an outlet for the physical tensions and the stress hormones that key us up for a "fight or flight" response. Exercise can help to increase one's tolerance to future stress and can provide increased feelings of well-being, tranquility and even transcendence (Dusek-Girdano, 1979). Dance sessions for older adults can provide stress reducing activities that help to re-confirm self-awareness and expression of feelings (Samuels, 1974). (Chapter 16 addresses stress reduction in more detail).

Mental health. There is ample evidence that exercise and dance can improve the mental health of older people in very direct ways. The variety of stimulations that are evoked by dance movements often result in emotions that produce a sustained feeling of well-being. The good feeling that the older adult experiences during dance sessions is not only an immediate result of the physiological benefits of exercise but is often linked to carefree feelings that are rekindled and associated with movement sequences. Group dance activities, structured so that there is ample opportunity for tactile experiences such as touching and hugging, can help to break through the isolation and loneliness that sometimes accompanies old age (Samuels, 1974). Berryman-Miller (1988) concluded that a dance/movement program positively influenced the self-concepts of older adult participants.

In a more objective vein, researchers have reported positive changes in "surgence," "self-sufficiency," "emotional stability," "composure," "adventurousness," "confidence," "anxiety," and "depression" as a result of participation in exercise programs. Several notable physicians have attested to the beneficial psychological changes that accompany physical exercise, but they based most of their observations and research on young people who used jogging as a method of exercise.

In two studies researchers focused more specifically upon the anti-depressant effects of exercise on older adults. In these studies, it was demonstrated that exercise does have a significant effect on depression in those subjects that were already depressed (Bennett, Carmach & Gardner, 1982; Brown Ramirez & Taub, 1978). The effects of exercise on the mood of people who were not already depressed was less definitive.

Moore (1982) reviewed the meaning of the studies which showed increased endorphin levels in the plasma after exercise. Endorphins are often described as the body's own versions of opiates that could be responsible for mood elevation during and after exercise. Endorphins may also provide an explanation for the so-called "runner's high." Moore (1982) though intrigued by the bio-chemical explanations of mood changes during and after exercise, believes too little is known about the meaning of increased plasma levels of endorphins. It could be that these plasma levels do indeed affect the brain, but the evidence at this time is far from being conclusive. Research has also indicated that plasma endorphin levels increase less dramatically as a result of exercise in persons over age 40.

Whether it is endorphins or some other mechanism that influences mood during and after exercise, there is enough evidence to indicate that, at least for some older people, exercise can help relieve depression, and increase self-esteem.

<u>Summary</u>. Exercise is not a mental or physical health panacea, but the evidence is mounting that it is very important to the health of older adults. The physical and mental health of older adults can be directly and indirectly influenced by exercise and its relationship to cardiovascular disease, arthritis, obesity, diabetes, osteoporosis, constipation, insomnia, stress related diseases, and depression. Yet perhaps the most important aspect of all is that exercise and dance can be fun, fulfulling and can help people of all ages to "be alive as long as they live" (Frankel & Richard, 1977).

References

Arthritis Foundation. (1978). <u>Arthritis: the basic facts</u>. Atlanta, GA.

Arthritis Foundation. (1983). <u>Self-care for osteoarthritis and rheumatoid arthritis</u>. University of California, San Francisco.

Bennett, J., Carmach, M.A., & Gardner, V.J. (1982). The effect of a program of physical exercise on depression in older adults. <u>The Physical Educator</u>,<u>39</u> (1), 21-24.

Berryman-Miller, S. (1988). Dance/movement: Effects on elderly self-concept. <u>Journal of Physical Education, Recreation, and Dance</u>. May/June, <u>59</u> (5), 42-46.

Brown, R.S., Ramirez, D.E., & Taub, J.M. (1978). The prescription of exercise for depression. <u>The Physician and Sportsmedicine</u>,<u>6</u> (12), 35-45.

Butler, R.N., & Lewis, M.I. (1982). <u>Aging and mental health: Positive psychosocial and biomedical approaches</u> (3rd ed.). St. Louis: C.V. Mosby.

Corbin, C. B. & Lindsey, R. (1984). <u>The ultimate fitness book</u>. New York: Leisure Press.

Dallosso, H.M., Morgan, K., Bassey, E.J., Ebrahim, S.B.J., Fentem, P.H., & Arie, T.H.D. (n.d.). <u>Levels of customary physical activity among the old and the very old living at home</u>. Unpublished manuscript, University of Nottingham Medical School, Queen's Medical Center, The Activity and Ageing Research Group, Departments of Physiology and Pharmacology and the Health Care of the Elderly, Nottingham, England.

deVries, H.A. (1975). Physiology of exercise and aging. (Chapter 12) In D.S. Woodruff & J.E. Birren (Eds.), <u>Aging: Scientific perspectives and social issues</u>. New York: D. Van Nostrand.

Dusek-Girdano, D. (1979). Stress reduction through physical activity. (Chapter 15) In D. Girdano & G. Everly, <u>Controlling stress and tension</u>. Englewood Cliffs, NJ: Prentice-Hall.

Frankel, L.J., and Richard, B.B. (1977). <u>Be alive as long as you live</u>. Charleston, WV: Preventicare Publications.

Kart, C.S., Metress, E.K., & Metress, S.P. (1988). <u>Aging and health: Biologic and social perspectives</u>. Boston: Jones and Bartlett.

Katch, F.W. (1987, June). <u>Aging and exercise -- A long-term study</u>. Paper presented at the American Alliance for Health, Physical Education, Recreation and Dance, Council on Aging and Adult Development Workshop, St. Louis, MO.

Katch, F.W., Wallace, J.P., & Van Camp, S.P. (1985). Effects of 18 years of endurance exercise on the physical work capacity of older men. <u>Journal of Cardiopulmonary Rehabilitation</u>, <u>5</u>, 308-312.

Moore, M.(1982). Endorphins and exercise: A puzzling relationship. <u>The Physician and Sportsmedicine</u>, <u>10</u> (2), 111-114.

Paffenbarger, R.S., Hyde, R.T., Wing, A.L., & Hsieh, C. (1986). Physical activity, all-cause mortality, and longevity of college alumni. <u>The New England Journal of Medicine</u>, <u>314</u>, 605-613.

Paffenbarger, R.S., Hyde, R.T., Hsieh, C. & Wing, A.L. (1986). Physical activity, other life-style patterns, cardiovascular disease and longevity. <u>Acta Medica Scandinavaica</u>. (Suppl). <u>711</u>, 85-91.

Salles, J.F., Haskell, W.L., Wood, P.D., Fortmann, S.P., Rogers, T., Blair, S.N. & Paffenbarger, R.S. (1985). Physical activity assessment methodology in the five-city project. <u>American Journal of Epidemiology</u>, <u>121</u> (1), 91-106.

Samuels, A. (1974). Dance therapy for geriatric patients. In P.M. Plunk-Burdick (Ed.), <u>Dance therapist in dimension: depth and diversity</u>. Proceedings of the Eighth Annual Conference, Columbia, MD: American Dance Therapy Association.

Smith, E. (1982). Exercise for prevention of osteoporosis: a review. <u>The Physician and Sportsmedicine</u>, <u>10</u> (3), 72-83.

U.S. Department of Health and Human Services. (1981). <u>Exercise and your heart</u>. (Publ. No. 81-1677). Bethesda, MD: National Heart, Lung and Blood Institute.

Wiswell, R.A. (1980). Relaxation, exercise, and aging. (Chapter 39) In J. Birren and B. Sloane (Eds.), <u>Handbook</u> <u>of</u> <u>mental</u> <u>health</u> <u>and</u> <u>aging</u>. Englewood Cliffs, NJ: Prentice-Hall.

Chapter **4**

Exercises in Futility:
Reasons People Give for Not Exercising

Chapter 4
Exercises in Futility:
Reasons People Give for Not Exercising

Many people believe in the benefits of exercise for other people but when it comes to actually exercising themselves, they can find all sorts of reasons for not exercising. In this chapter we will try to respond to some of these myths and excuses.

There are, of course, legitimate reasons why certain types of exercises cannot be done by certain people (see Chapter 5). However, there are very few people who cannot find an exercise program that can benefit them and be suited to their specific needs. Following are some responses to common reasons given by older adults for not exercising:

I'm too old to exercise or dance. (Or the older you are, the less exercise you need). In Chapter 3 the mental and physical health advantages of exercise and dance for older adults were pointed out. In general, older people benefit from regular exercise and dance just as much or more than younger people. Age need not be a limitation to exercise or dance activities. What is important, no matter what your age is adapting your exercise or dance program to your own fitness level.

I don't have the time to exercise. Exercise does not have to take more than 20-40 minutes, three times a week. Besides, the change of pace from other daily routines can give you time to relax. This relaxation, combined with the increased physical fitness you gain, can help to make you more efficient in carrying on other daily tasks and chores.

'I CONSIDERED A ROCKING CHAIR — THEN I DECIDED TO PEDAL 100,000 MILES INSTEAD...'

All cartoons in this chapter are from All You Could Forget About Older People by Leo Missinne and Ed Fischer, used by permission of R and E Publishers, P.O. Box 2008, Saratoga, CA 95070.

BEING OF SOUND MIND AND A — SO-SO BODY...

The invested time is not wasted; its payoff in better health and a good sense of well-being are more than paid back in the long-term benefits. Group exercises and dance activities are also ways to socialize and meet new people, making the time invested even more worthwhile.

<u>Exercise makes me tired, sore and stiff</u>. This statement is true in reference to exercise that is only done sporadically, but if a person is exercising on a regular basis in gradual increments (which is as it should be done), then the statement is not true. Most people, as their bodies get in better shape, feel that exercising gives them more energy.

<u>The weather is too bad</u>. There is enough variety in exercises that they can be performed indoors, outdoors, in large spaces or in small spaces. The exercise and dance activities in this book offer you enough options so that the weather should be of no consequence. But even for those people who prefer to exercise in the outdoors, proper clothing and proper safety precautions make this possible most of the time.

<u>Exercise equipment, exercise clothing, and exercise spas and clubs are too expensive.</u> There is no doubt that some exercise equipment, spas and clubs and clothing are expensive, but there is also no doubt that a person can get fit with very little capital outlay. Indeed many of the exercises and dance activities in this book require little or no cost and can be done at home or in rooms requiring little or no special equipment.

<u>I'm not very skilled, I look stupid dancing, or You have to be an athlete to exercise.</u> Exercise for health and fitness purposes need not require a great amount of skill or athletic ability. Many people who disliked sports or found sports too difficult in their younger years have found that many health and fitness activities are easy to do and are enjoyable. In both exercise and dance, skill, grace, and coordination can be important for those who choose to make it important, but they are not necessary for acquiring or maintaining health and fitness. Many people think of dance only as a performing art for a selected few. Yet recreational dance, expressive dance, and improvisational activities can provide movement experiences that are worthwhile and fun for all levels of abilities.

The old adage "act your age" has done little more than stereotype and limit the behavior of older adults. Young people hold no patents on expressive movement (or any other type of movement for that matter).

Exercise is too boring. Some exercise is boring but some is exciting, fun, and fulfilling (and this can vary from person to person and from day to day). The important thing to do if your exercise program becomes intolerable is to find several types of exercise that are attractive to you and vary your program from time to time as you become weary of the old program. Boredom itself, however, need not be a bad word. Boredom is a necessary part of life and it becomes negative only if it is perceived that way. Many routine aspects of life, rather than being boring in a negative sense, become relaxing and rewarding experiences--like knitting, reading, sleeping, and, of course, exercising.

I'm too ill or handicapped to exercise. There are illnesses and handicaps that preclude certain types of exercise, but many people with various diseases and handicaps can and indeed should exercise. Too many people wrongly assume that they can't or shouldn't participate in physical activities despite the lack of medical contraindications. It is important that you ask your physician about your medical limitations so that you know what you can do and what you can't do in terms of physical activity. It is a good idea to consult with a physical educator, physical therapist, or physician who is knowledgeable about exercise and older adults. Too often even health professionals may submit to cultural stereotypes and they may advise older people to "take it easy" or "get plenty of bed rest" even though there may be no medical reason for not allowing exercise. These professionals are simply giving advice they think older people should hear or want to hear. If you suspect this, then you need to look for a health care professional who has studied exercise physiology or sports medicine along with gerontology. These people may be difficult to find, but they do exist. These are the health care professionals who are best able to prescribe exercise for older adults.

Summary.   There are many reasons people can think of for not taking part in exercise or dance activities. The inhibitions may be physical, environmental, temporal, psychological, social, medical, or financial.   Although there is some truth to all of these reasons for not exercising or dancing, they can all be overcome and/or modified so that the exercise or dance activity is both suitable and enjoyable.   If you truly believe in the benefits of both exercise and dance, then you need to act on these beliefs. As the old song said "accentuate the positive and eliminate the negative."

Reference

U.S. Department of Health and Human Services. (1981). Exercise and your heart.   (Publ. No. 81-1677).   Bethesda, MD: National Heart, Lung and Blood Institute.

Precautions, Guidelines, and Assessments

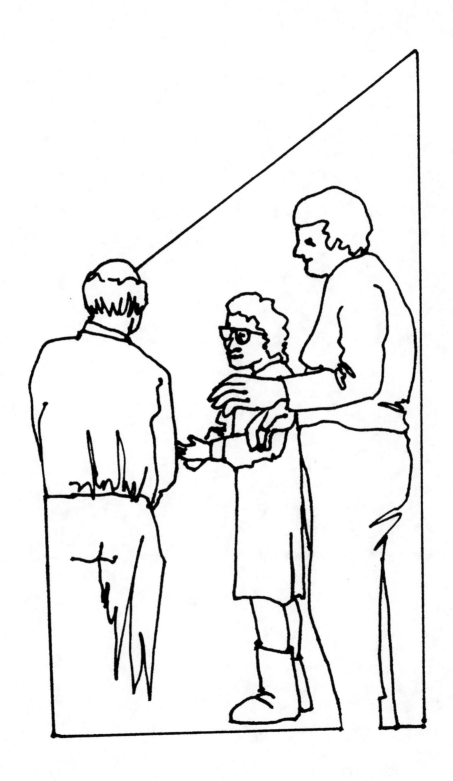

Chapter 5

Precautions, Guidelines, and Assessments

Most people do not experience any danger when they start a gradual, sensible exercise program, but there are some special caveats to consider before older people embark on a new exercise program. Older people should first do the self-assessment exercise in Box 1 on the next page before reading on.

If any of the items in Box 1 were checked it is best to talk to a doctor who is knowledgeable about exercise before you start. If you've checked none of the items, you can start on a gradual, sensible exercise program tailored to your needs. However, if you are unsure about the safety of any of the exercises you do, you should consult with a physical educator, physical therapist, or physician (see Box 3). Keep in mind that research on exercise has come a long way in the past several years. Some exercises that used to be standard aspects of many programs have been found to be harmful or ineffective. If you are not familiar with the current exercise research, then seek competent consultation before starting out on your own. Take this book to your physician and show him or her the exercises you would like to do. Discuss the pros and cons of each.

It is recommended that all older participants and exercise leaders become familiar with the "AAHPERD Guidelines for Exercise Progams for Older Persons (Age 50 and Older)" (see Box 2). In addition the "AAHPERD Council on Aging and Adult Development Medical/Exercise Assessment for Older Adults Form" should be completed before participation in an exercise program (see Box 3) if any of the items in Box 1 were checked.

The information in Boxes 2 and 3 are reprinted with the permission of the American Alliance for Health, Physical Education, Recreation, and Dance (AAHPERD), 1900 Association Dr., Reston, VA 22091.

Box 1

Mark those items that apply to you.

Your doctor said you have heart trouble, a heart murmur, or you have had a heart attack.

You frequently have pains or pressure--in the left or midchest area, left neck, shoulder, or arm-- during or right after you exercise.

You often feel faint or have spells of severe dizziness. You experience extreme breathlessness after mild exertion.

Your doctor said your blood pressure was too high and is not under control or you don't know whether or not your blood pressure is normal.

Your doctor said you have bone or joint problems such as arthritis.

You are over age 60 and not accustomed to vigorous exercise.

You have a family history of premature coronary artery disease.

You have a medical condition not mentioned here which might need special attention in an exercise program. (For example, insulin- dependent diabetes.)

Reprinted from Exercise and Your Heart, National Heart, Lung and Blood Institute.

Box 2

AAHPERD Guidelines for Exercise Programs
for Older Persons (Age 50 and Older)

There can be risk in sudden, unregulated and injudicious use of exercise. However, the risk can be minimized through proper preliminary screening and individualized prescribing of exercise programs. It is important for older persons entering an exercise program to have a medical evaluation by a physician knowledgeable about physical exercise and its implications.

For programs involving vigorous exercises (i.e., exercises that exceed the level of intensity encountered in normal daily activities such as walking and climbing stairs), the medical evaluation should ensure that the individual can participate in vigorous exercise without any undue risk to the cardiovascular and other bodily systems. Normally, a test that ascertains an individual's cardio-respiratory adjustment to the stress of exercise is an advisable part of the examination. Minimally, it would ascertain if the cardiovascular system, by such appropriate indicators as heart rate and blood pressure, can adequately adjust to vigorous exercise.

For exercise programs involving low intensity exercises (i.e., exercises that do not exceed the level of intensity encountered in normal daily activities), participants should have their personal physician's approval.

Regardless of whether or not a program of exercises is vigorous or of low intensity, the following guidelines to ensure the safety of the participants are offered:

(1) In that each person's response to the stress of exercise is specific to that individual, it is important that each person's response to exercise be monitored periodically for signs of undue stress (unduly high heart rate, nausea, dyspnea, pallor, pain). Participants should be taught to monitor their own heart rates and to recognize these indicators of stress. Unusual responses should be reported to the exercise leader immediately. Exercise leaders, also, should be vigilant of these warning signs.

(2) Every exercise program must have a well-defined emergency plan for exercise leaders to follow in the event of cardiac arrest or other accidents.

(3) Exercise programs must have adequate supervision. Exercise leaders should be trained in Cardio-Pulmonary Resuscitation (CPR) Techniques. At the very minimum, CPR-trained personnel should be present during every exercise session or in close proximity to the exercise program.

Courtesy of American Alliance for Health, Physical Education, Recreation and Dance. Developed by the Alliance Committee on Aging; Approved by Alliance Board of Governors, 10/4/81.

Box 3
AAHPERD--COUNCIL ON AGING AND ADULT DEVELOPMENT
Medical/Exercise Assessment for Older Adults
(Courtesy of CAAD of AAHPERD, Reston, VA)

Name_____ Phone_____/_____Date_____
Street_____ City_____State____Zip_____

PART I - TO BE FILLED OUT BY PARTICIPANT

A. ACTIVITY HISTORY
   1. How would you rate your physical activity level
      during the last year?
      _____ LITTLE - Sitting, typing, driving, talking - NO
                     exercise planned.
      _____ MILD - Standing, walking, bending, reaching
                     (less than once /week)
      _____ MODERATE - Standing, walking, bending, reaching
      _____ ACTIVE - Light physical work, climbing stairs,
                     exercise 2-3 days a week
      _____ VERY ACTIVE - Physical work or regular
                     exercise 4 or more days a week

   2. What exercise and recreational activities are you
      presently involved in? How often? _____
      _____

B. HEALTH HISTORY
   Weight _____ Height_____ Recent weight loss/gain_____
   Please list any recent illnesses:_____
   _____
   Please list any hospitalizations and reasons (during the
   last five years):_____

   PLEASE CHECK THE ITEMS BELOW WHICH APPLY TO YOU:
   _____ Anemia   _____ Heart Conditions
   _____ Arthritis/Bursitis   _____ Hernia
   _____ Asthma   _____ Indigestion
   _____ Blood Pressure_____   _____ Joint Pain on Walk-
   _____ Bowel/Bladder Problems   ing
   _____ Chest Pains   _____ Lung Disease
   _____ Chest discomfort while   _____ Shortness of Breath
          exercising   _____ Passing Out Spells
   _____ Diabetes   _____ Osteoporosis
   _____ Difficulty with Hearing   _____ Low Back Condition
   _____ Difficulty with Vision   _____ Other Orthopedic
   _____ Dizziness or Balance   Conditions (list)
          Problems   _____

   SMOKING: _____ Never smoked; _____ Smoke now (how much?)
   _____; _____ Smoked in the past.
   ALCOHOL CONSUMPTION: _____ None; _____ Occasional (less than
   5 drinks/week); _____ Often (how much and how often?)_____
   List any existing health concerns:_____
   List medications and/or dietary supplements you regularly
   take:_____

<u>**PART II - TO BE FILLED OUT BY PHYSICIAN**</u>
     Date of last examination _____
A.   PHYSICAL EXAMINATION   - Please check if it applies   to   the
patient or fill in the appropritate information.
     _____ Chest ausculation abnormal _____ Thyroid abnormal
     _____ Heart size abnormal   _____ Any joints abnormal
     _____ Peripheral pulses abnormal _____ Abnormal masses
     _____ Abnormal heart sounds   _____ Other _____

     PRESENT PRESCRIBED MEDICATION(S)_____

B.   CARDIOVASCULAR LABORATORY EXAMINATION (Within one year of the
     present date if recommended by physician) DATE: _____
     <u>Resting</u> ECG: Rate_____ Rhythm_____
        Axis_____ Interpretation _____
     <u>Stress</u> <u>Test</u>: Max H.R._____ Max B.P._____ Total Time_____
        Max VO2_____METS_____ Type of Test_____

     Recommendation   for exercise.   MODERATE is   defined   as
standing,   walking,   bending,   reaching and light exercise 3
days/wk. Please <u>check</u> one:
     _____ There is no contraindication to participation in a
            MODERATE exercise program.
     _____ Because of the above analysis, participation in a
            MODERATE exercise program may be advisable, but
            further examination or consultation is necessary,
            namely: STRESS TEST, ECG, OTHER _____.
     _____ Because of the above analysis, my patient may
            participate   only under direct supervision of a
            physician. (CARDIAC REHABILITATION PROGRAM).
     _____ Because of the above analysis, participation in a
            MODERATE exercise program is inadvisable.

C.   SUMMARY IMPRESSION OF PHYSICIAN
     1. Comments on any history of orthopedic and neuromuscular
        disorders that may affect participation in   an   exercise
        program - especially those checked._____
        _____
     2. Message for the Exercise Program Director:_____
        _____

     Physician:_____ Signature:_____
              (Please Type/Print)
     Address:_____ Phone:_____/_____
     _____

<u>**PART III - PATIENT'S RELEASE AND CONSENT**</u>

     _____ RELEASE: I hearby release the above information to
                        the Exercise Program Director.

     _____ CONSENT: I agree to see my private physician or
                        medical care professional and agree to
                        have an evaluation by him/her once a year,
                        if necessary.
SIGNED:_____ DATE:_____

Box 4 tells you the best way to pace yourself when doing exercises. It also lets you know how hard you should exercise in order to benefit the heart, lungs, and circulatory system.

Box 4

Determining Exercise Intensity

How do I
pace myself?

Build up slowly. If you've been inactive for a long while, remember it will take time to get into shape. But no matter where you begin, you will be able to build up your exercise time or pace as your body becomes more fit. Just remember that you will feel more fit after a few weeks than when you first started.

How hard
should I
exercise?

You can find out how hard to exercise by keeping track of your heart rate. Your maximum heart rate is the fastest your heart can beat. Exercise above 75 percent of the maximum heart rate may be too strenuous unless you are in excellent physical condition. Exercise below 60 percent gives your heart and lungs little conditioning.

Therefore, the best activity level for cardiovascular benefits is 60 to 75 percent of this maximum rate. This 60-75 percent range is called your target heart rate zone.

When you begin your exercise program, aim for the lower part of your target zone (60 percent) during the first few months. As you get into better shape, gradually build up to the higher part of your target zone (75 percent). After 6 months or more of regular exercise, you can exercise at up to 85 percent of your maximum heart rate--if you wish. However, you do not have to exercise that hard to stay in good condition.

Adapted from **Exercise and Your Heart**,
National Heart, Lung and Blood Institute.

Box 5 tells you how to determine your target heart rate zone or your heart rate while doing aerobic or cardiovascular exercise. Keep in mind that target heart rates for older adults are based mainly upon research done on younger subjects. It may not be appropriate to use the standards of youth to determine exercise levels for older adults. For example, does it make sense for a forty year old exercise leader to insist that an eighty-five year old man reach a certain heart rate for so many minutes per exercise period despite the fact that this participant is healthy and already living beyond the average life expectancy? Perhaps the best course of action is for the older participant to monitor symptoms such as those given at the end of this chapter and be less worried about a more or less arbitrary target. Indeed, insisting on reaching target heart rate zones for some segments of the older population may increase dropout rates and decrease adherence to exercise programs. It is better to exercise regularly at a lower intensity than to not exercise at a so-called higher intensity. Nevertheless, target heart zones can be useful for the more fit and they are also useful for teaching people to become more interested in self-care and self-monitoring when they are overdoing their exercises.

Ornstein and Sobel's (1989) final analysis after reviewing the literature on health and exercise is: "It doesn't take much exercise to make a difference." Their chapter on exercise and health is entitled "Why Kill Yourself to Save Your Life?" Their arguments for moderate exercise are particularly prudent for older adults who have not been very active in the past. Exercise is vital to the health of most people , but it need not be the standard fare of 15-60 minutes of continuous exercise 3-5 times per week to benefit the participant. It is important to keep exercise fun!

Paffenbarger, Hyde, Wing & Hsieh (1986) examined the physical activity levels of 16,936 Harvard alumni over a period of 12-16 year and they found that death rates declined as energy expenditure increased from less than 500 to 3500 calories per week. "By the age of 80, the amount of additional life attributable to adequate exercise, as compared with sedentariness, was one to more that two years." What all of this means is that exercise (even mild exercise) is beneficial to health. Being sedentary is a risk factor for dying at an earlier age.

Box 5

Target Heart Rate Zone

Your target heart rate zone is the range in which you want your heart rate to fall in order to produce an exercise effect on the heart.

To determine your target heart rate zone, look for the age category closest to your age and read the line across. For example, if you are 60, your target zone is 96-120 beats per minute. If you are 57, the closest age on the chart is 55; the target zone is 99-123 beats per minute.

Your maximum heart rate (the fastest your heart can beat) is usually 220 minus your age. However, the above figures are averages and should only be used as general guidelines.

It is important to note that some medications for high blood pressure lower the maximum heart rate and thus the target heart zone. If you are taking anti-hypertension medications, consult your physician to find out if your exercise program needs to be adjusted.

To see if you are within your target heart rate zone, take your pulse immediately after you stop exercising or dancing. (See Box 6).

Age	Target Zone (60-75%)	Average Maximum Heart Rate (100%)
55 years	99-123 beats/min.	165
60 years	96-120 beats/min.	160
65 years	93-116 beats/min.	155
70 years	90-113 beats/min.	150

Adapted from Exercise and Your Heart, National Heart, Lung and Blood Institute.

Box 6

The most convenient spot to take the pulse is on the inside of your wrist, (radial pulse) just below the base of the thumb. When you stop exercising, quickly place the tip of your index and middle finger over your radial pulse while timing for 6 seconds. Multiply by 10 by simply adding a zero to the pulse rate you counted. This gives you your heart rate per minute.

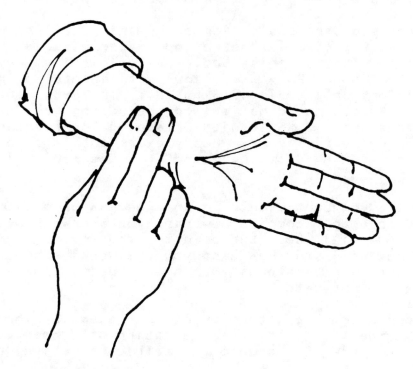

Taking the Radial Pulse

Taking the pulse is easy to do, particularly immediately after exercising when the pulse beat is most pronounced. With practice the counting and timing become even easier.

If you have just started an exercise program, it is a good idea to monitor your pulse before, during and after exercising. If your pulse is below your target heart rate zone, then exercise a little harder. If you are above your target heart rate zone, then slow down. If your heart rate falls within your target heart rate zone, you're doing fine.

Six seconds of time, to take your pulse, is not much of an inconvenience. If you have trouble seeing the second hand of a watch, then arrange to stop exercising near a large clock with an easy-to-read second hand or get a friend to time the six seconds for you.

Other Methods of Monitoring Exercise Intensity

A common test to determine whether or not you are exercising too hard is the TALK TEST. If you can keep up a conversation, sing a song, or whistle while performing the exercise, it is generally not too strenuous.

If you experience nausea, shortness of breath, labored breathing dizziness or prolonged weakness during or after exercise, you are overdoing it--slow down or stop.

Another popular scale for determining how hard you are working during exercise is the rating of perceived exertion (RPE) scale (Noble, 1982). This scale was originally developed by psychologist Gunnar Borg to allow participants to rate their physical effort on a scale of 6 to 20. In 1986, the American College of Sports Medicine revised the rating to an exertion scale ranging from 0 to 10 with 0 meaning "no exertion at all" and 10 meaning "very, very, heavy exertion." If you perceive that you are working "somewhat hard" (a desirable level), the rating on the scale is a 4.

The more you participate in an exercise program, the more you will be able to recognize how hard you are working. Through practice, you will be "tuned in to" your overall feeling of effort. You will know how hard you are working by the way you are breathing, the rate of your heart beat, how tired your muscles are feeling, etc.

By monitoring the intensity of your exercise through target heart rate, the talk test, or the rating of perceived exertion, you will be able to create a safe, effective program of activities.

For other special precautions see Boxes 7 and 8.

Box 7

On hot, humid days:

Exercise during cooler parts of the day such as early morning or early evening after the sun has gone down. Exercise less than normal for a week until you become adapted to the heat. Drink lots of fluids, particularly water. You do not need extra salt because you get enough salt in your diet. Also, a well-conditioned body learns to conserve salt so that most of the sweat is water. Watch out for signs of heat stroke--feeling dizzy, weak, light-headed, and/or excessively tired; sweating stops; or body temperature becomes dangerously high. Wear a minimum of light, loose-fitting clothing. Avoid rubberized or plastic suits, sweatshirts, and sweat pants. Such clothing will not actually help you lose weight any faster by making you sweat more. The weight you lose in fluids by sweating will be quickly replaced as soon as you begin drinking fluids again. This type of clothing can also cause dangerously high temperatures, possibly resulting in heat stroke.

On cold days:

Wear one layer less of clothing than you would wear if you were outside but not exercising. It's also better to wear several layers of clothing rather than one heavy layer. Use old mittens, gloves, or cotton socks to protect your hands. Wear a hat, since up to 40 percent of your body's heat is lost through your neck and head.

Reprinted from <u>Exercise</u> <u>and</u> <u>Your</u> <u>Heart</u>,
National Heart, Lung and Blood Institute.

Box 8

To avoid dizziness when performing rhythmic exercises, pause briefly before changing the direction of the exercise.

Breathe deeply and rhythmically during and between exercises. DO NOT HOLD YOUR BREATH WHEN EXERCISING!

Avoid strenuous exercise immediately after eating a large meal.

Wear loose fitting clothing to allow for freedom of movement.

When doing stretching exercises--hold the stretch--DO NOT BOUNCE!

Take 5 minutes, after strenuous exercises, to cool down. For example, the contraction and relaxation of the leg muscles, while doing a slow walking cool down, helps the heart return blood from the feet and legs. Thus, the heart rate returns to normal faster than if you sat down immediately after exercise.

It cannot be stressed enough that you should build up your level of activity gradually. Do not set your initial goals too high. Pay attention to body pains--they are good warning signals that you are overdoing.

Be aware of the following possible signs of heart problems.

1) Pain or pressure in the left or midchest area, left neck, shoulder, or arm during or just after exercising. (Vigorous exercise may cause a side stitch while exercising--a pain below your bottom ribs--which is not the result of a heart problem).

2) Sudden dizziness, cold sweat, pallor, or fainting.

Ignoring these signals and continuing to exercise may lead to serious heart problems. Should any of these signs occur, stop exercising and call your doctor.

Warm-up activities for exercise and dance are important for people of all ages and fitness levels. Chapter 6 gives examples of warm-up exercises.

Following the references in this chapter, the Council on Aging and Adult Development Functional Fitness Assessment for Adults over 60 Years is included. This is the first battery of assessments of fitness for older adults.

References

Exercise and Your Heart, Publ. No. 81-1677, U.S. Department of Health & Human Services, National Heart, Lung and Blood Institute, Bethesda, MD 20205.

Noble, B.J. (1982). Clinical applications of perceived exertion. Medicine and Science in Sport and Exercise. 14, 406-411.

Ornstein, R. and Sobel, D. (1989). Healthy pleasures. Reading, MA: Addison-Wesley.

Paffenbarger, S., Hyde, R.T., Wing, A.L. & Hsieh, C. (1986). Physical activity, all-cause mortality, and longevity of college alumni. The New England Journal of Medicine, 314 (10), 605-613.

Pep Up Your Life: A Fitness Book for Seniors. Marketing Services Department, The Travelers Insurance Companies, One Tower Square, Hartford, CT 06115.

Appendix to Chapter 5

FUNCTIONAL FITNESS ASSESSMENT
FOR
ADULTS OVER 60 YEARS
(A FIELD BASED ASSESSMENT)

The American Alliance
for Health, Physical Education, Recreation and Dance

Association for Research, Administration, Professional Councils
and Societies

Council for Aging and Adult Development

The AAHPERD Fitness Task Force includes:
Wayne Osness, Chairperson, University of Kansas
Marlene Adrian, University of Illinois
Bruce A. Clark, University of Missouri, St. Louis
Werner W.K. Hoeger, Boise State University
Diane Raab, University of Wisconsin
Robert Wiswell, University of Southern California

This article is adapted with permission from the Journal of Physical Education, Recreation & Dance, March 1989, 66-71. The Journal is a publication of the American Alliance for Health, Physical Education, Recreation and Dance, 1900 Association Drive, Reston, VA 22091

Rationale for the Test

This assessment program has been designed to use the latest scientific information available as it relates to the noninvasive assessment of the older adult and the physiological systems that support the physical function of the older adult. It is a functional assessment that can be conducted in a field based setting using large numbers of individuals. Each individual can then be compared to age and sex related norms to assess the present condition as well as to assess functional change over time.

When dealing with the older population, one must recognize the increased risks associated with physical activity, particularly during physical assessments when maximal efforts are desired. This battery of tests relates to a functional maximal performance which means the individual performs to the best of her or his capacity without discomfort or unusual risk. It is recognized that there is a psychological factor related to the intensity of one's performance which will affect the end result. However, the individual is expected to perform to the best of her or his ability within the confines of her or his present condition. For the older individual, this condition may be affected by several different kinds of anatomical, physiological, or pharmaceutical factors. Although these factors are very important, it is recognized that these same factors would be involved in the development of an exercise prescription designed to enhance physical functionality. The parameters tested and the test items used were selected because each relates to general fitness and the total battery of tests provide a comprehensive evaluation of the individual, considering the guidelines previously expressed in this document.

Body composition is measured by ponderal index which involves the relationship between height and weight. The use of anthropometric measurements was discarded because of the need for specific equipment and techniques. In addition, the formulas that use this information to project percent body fat have not been shown effective for older populations. The hydrostatic weighing technique is simply inappropriate for a field testing situation.

Flexibility is measured by the sit and reach test which actually measures the flexibility of the lower back and upper leg. The sit and reach test was selected because this test is a reasonable indicator of total body flexibility in the normal older adult. The procedure was developed to use a measuring stick to avoid the need for specific equipment that may not be available in a field setting.

Agility and dynamic balance is measured using a new test involving total body activity. It involves straight ahead movement, change of direction, and changing body position. The test closely relates to the functional movement of the older individual in daily life situations and also provides for a quantitative assessment of this ability. It is the most comprehensive of all test items used in the test battery.

The coordination test also relates to daily function and concentrates on the neuromuscular efficiency of the arms and hands. It is a practical test and one that also has good reproducibility as well as finite measurement potential.

Strength was considered an important component of the test battery. The measurement of strength also included an endurance factor using the number of repetitions through a range of motion. The measurement involves the upper body but also has shown good predictability of the total body strength of the older individual. This test was chosen because it was more quantifiable than some of the other field tests for dynamic strength that are dependent on body weight and moving the body through space.

The endurance test provides a functional assessment of walking ability in older adults. As an assessment of aerobic capacity, the validity is moderate but comparable with other walk/run tests based solely on time. The walk test may be administered in any open, well lighted area with an appropriate surface (even and non-slippery).

Each of the test items used is subject to motivation and psychological factors. These factors cannot be totally eliminated in a field test situation but care has been taken to provide the test administrator with appropriate directions to standardize the procedure in such a way that the effect of these factors would be minimized.

Test Items

The test items have complete protocols that must be used for the conduct of the test. The protocols should not be altered in any way so that norms can be used to evaluate the data on a given individual using norms established for a given age and sex. Each parameter and test item includes the equipment needed, the procedure, the scoring, trials and special considerations. The test administrator is asked to carefully review the special considerations for the appropriate safety of the participant and the validity of the data.

PARAMETER: BODY COMPOSITION

Test Item: Ponderal Index

Equipment: Body weight and height are determined using the procedures detailed in the sub parameters below. The measured weight in pounds is found on the right scale of Figure 2A and measured height is found on the left scale of Figure 2A. A straight line is determined using these two points and a straight edge connecting them. The intersection of the center scale provides the reading of the Ponderal Index. The higher the Ponderal Index, the greater the degree of leanness.

Scoring: Record Ponderal Index to the nearest .1 of one unit as the score.

Trials: Single trial.

Sub Parameter: Body Weight

Test Item: Weight

Equipment: Calibrated scale with increments of one pound or smaller.

Procedure: Set the scale on a firm, flat, horizontal surface. Check that the scale is accurate by using known loads prior to testing.
Ask the person to remove shoes and overgarments, such as coat, jacket, and sweater.
Ask the person to step onto the scale and stand without moving.
With subject standing on scale as directed, read the scales to the nearest pound. (Fig. 1A).

Scoring: Record weight in pounds as the score.

Trials: Single trial.

Special Considerations: None.

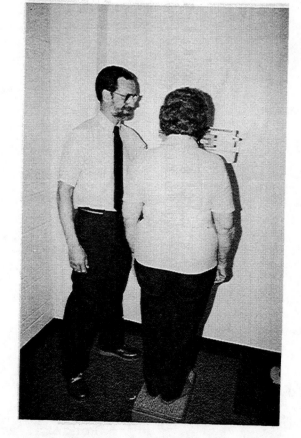

Fig. 1A

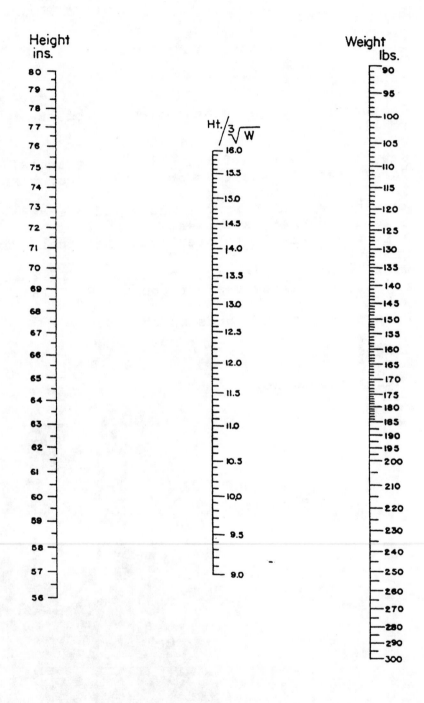

Fig. 2A
Ponderal Index

Sub Parameter: Standing Height Measurement

Test Item: Height

Equipment: Tape measure or other graduated scale of length, masking tape, and wall.

Procedure: Vertically attach a tape measure to a wall that has no molding strip or other protuberances. Ask the person to remove shoes, and to turn and place the heels together. Ask the person to stand erect with head upright and eyes looking straight ahead. With the person standing as directed, place a flat object, such as a 2" X 4" X 6" long wood block, ruler or clipboard, horizontally on the top of the crown of the head with one end against the wall. Read to the nearest half inch the intersection point of the flat object and the tape measure. If it is difficult to see, ask the subject to stoop slightly and step to one side.

Scoring: Record height in feet and inches to nearest half inch as the score. (Fig. 3A).

Trials: One trial.

Special Considerations: None.

Fig. 3A

PARAMETER: FLEXIBILITY

Test Item: Trunk/Leg Flexibility

Equipment: A yardstick, chalk, and masking tape.

Set Up: Draw a line approximately twenty inches long on the floor, or you may use masking tape for this line. Tape the yardstick to the floor perpendicular to the line, with the twenty-inch mark directly over the line. If masking tape is used for the line, the twenty-inch mark should be right at the edge of the tape.   Next, draw two marks on the line, each six inches away from the center of the yardstick (Fig. 4A).

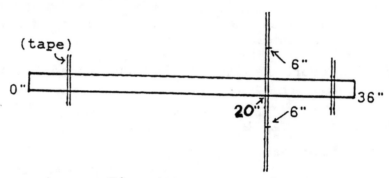

Fig. 4A

Procedure: The subject should remove the shoes for this test and sit on the floor with legs extended, feet twelve inches apart, toes pointing straight up, and heels right up against the line (at the twenty-inch mark, and each heel centered at the six-inch marks on the line).   The yardstick should be between the legs, with the zero point toward the subject.   The hands are placed one directly on top of the other. (Fig. 5A).

Fig. 5A

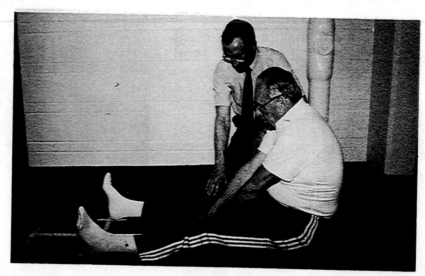

The subject may then slowly reach forward sliding the hands along the yardstick as far as possible, and must hold the final position for at least two seconds. The technician administering the test should place one hand on top of one knee (only) to insure that the subject's knees are not raised during the test. (Fig. 6A).

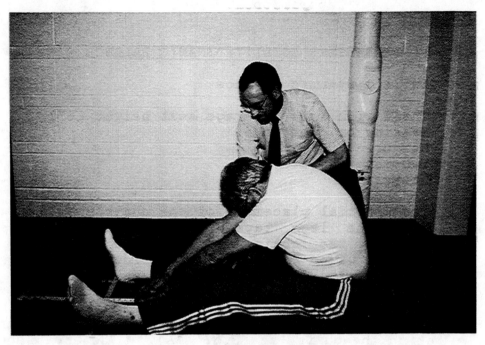

Fig. 6A

Scoring: Record the number of inches reached to the nearest one half inch for each trial (.0 or .5). The best trial is recorded as the score.

Trials: Two practice trials followed by two test trials are given. Only the score for the two test trials are recorded.

Approximate Range of Scores: Five to thirty inches.

Special considerations: Be sure that the subjects are properly warmed-up prior to this test. Speciic exercises related to this task should be conducted prior to the test. Help all subjects into the sitting position and subsequently when getting up from the floor. The forward reach should be a gradual movement along the top of the yardstick, the tip of the middle fingers must remain even during the entire reaching action, and the final position must remain even during the entire reaching action, and the final position must be held for at least two seconds.

must be held for at least two seconds. Be sure that the toes are straight up and that the legs are kept as straight as possible. If feet start turning outward or the knees start to come up during the reaching action, ask the subject to maintain the correct position.

PARAMETER: AGILITY/DYNAMIC BALANCE

Test Item: Agility/Dynamic Balance

Equipment: Chair with arms (average seat height 16")
Masking or duct tape
Measuring tape
Two cones
Stopwatch

Set Up: The initial placement of the chair should be marked with the legs taped to the floor, if possible, because the chair tends to move during the test. Measure from the spot on the floor (X) in front of the chair where the feet will be placed. The cones are set up with their farthest edge located six feet to the side and five feet behind the initial measuring spot (X). One cone is set up at either side behind the chair (see Fig. 7A). The area should be well lit, the floor even and nonslippery. Arrows should be placed on the floor in appropriate locations to remind the subjects of the proper pathway.

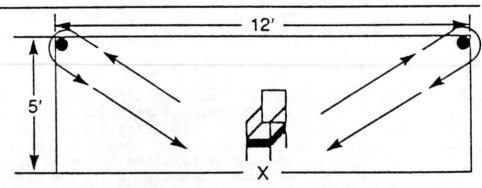

Fig. 7A

Procedure: The person begins fully seated in the chair with his or her heels on the ground. On the signal "Ready Go" the person gets up from the chair, moves to his or her right going to the inside and around the back of the cone (counterclockwise) (Fig. 8A), returns directly to the chair and sits down. Without hesitating the person gets up immediately (Fig. 9A), moves to his or her left again going to the inside and around the back of the cone (clockwise) (Fig. 10A) returns directly to the chair and sits down completing one circuit. The person gets up immediately and repeats a second circuit exactly as the first. One trial consists of two complete circuits (going around the cones four times (right, left, right, left).

Fig. 8A

Fig. 9A

Fig. 10A

During the test, after circling the cones, the person must sit down fully in the chair. This means having the person lift his or her feet 1/2 inch from the floor before getting up. Ther person must use his or her hands to help get in and out of the chair. The person should go as fast as he or she feels comfortable without loosing his or her balance or falling.

Explain the test procedure then walk the person through the course to make sure he or she circles the cones correctly and lifts his or her feet each time he or she sits down.

Give the following instructions to the subject: "Walk as fast as comfortable without feeling you will lose your balance or fall. One trial consists of circling the cones four times. The first time, go to your right, then to your left, right, and left. Go around the cone from the inside to the outside, come back and sit down after circling each cone. Sit down fully and lift your feet off the floor each time. Use your hands to help you get in and out of the chair without falling. If you feel dizzy, light-headed, or if you feel any pain, stop immediately and tell me."

Give directions, supervise practice and start each trial with "Ready Go." Start the stopwatch when the person begins to move, stop the watch when the person sits down the fourth time.

During the test give verbal directions (e.g., right, left, around, sit down, etc.) so the person does not have to stop or hesitate because he or she is confused. Make sure the person lifts his or her feet each time he or she sits down.

If the person moves the chair, the technician should readjust it to the original position during the trial.

Trials: A practice "walk through" should be administered until the person demonstrates that he or she understands the test. Two trials are administered with thirty seconds rest provided after each trial.

Score: Record the time for each trial to the nearest 0.1 seconds. The best trial is recorded as the score.

Approximate Range of Scores: Most people will score between 15 and 35 seconds.

PARAMETER: COORDINATION

Test Item: "Soda Pop" Coordination Test.

Equipment: Three unopened (full) cans of soda pop, a stopwatch, 3/4 " masking tape, a table, and a chair.

Set Up: Using the 3/4" masking tape, place a 30" strip of
             tape on the table, about five inches from the edge of
             the table.   Draw six marks exactly five inches away
             from each other along the line of tape, starting a 2
             1/2" away from either edge of the tape.   Now place
             six strips of tape, each three inches long, centered
             exactly on top of each of the six marks previously
             drawn.   For the purpose of this test, each little
             "Square" formed by the crossing of the long strip of
             tape and the three-inch strip of tape is assigned a
             number starting with 1 for the first square on the
             right to 6 for the first square on the left (Figs.
             11A and 15A).

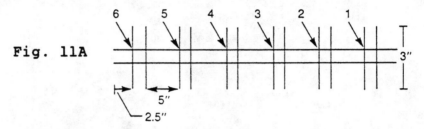

             Fig. 11A

Procedure: To administer the test, have the subject   sit
             comfortably in front of the table, the body centered
             with the diagram on the table. The preferred hand is
             used for this test. If the right hand is used, place
             the three cans of pop on the table in the following
             manner: can one is centered on square 1 (farthest to
             the right), can two on square 3, and can three on
             square 5.   To start the test, the right hand, with
             the thumb up, is placed on can one and the elbow
             joint should be at about 100-120 degrees. (Fig. 12A).
             When the tester gives the signal, the stopwatch is
             started and the subject proceeds to turn the cans of
             pop upside down, placing can one over square 2, (Fig.
             13A), followed by can two over square 4, and then can
             three over square 6; Immediately the subject returns
             all three cans, starting with can one, then can two,
             and can three - turning them right side up -- to
             their original placement. On this "return trip," the
             cans are grasped with the hand in a thumb down
             position (Fig. 14A).   This entire procedure is done
             twice, without stopping, and counted as one trial.
             In other words, two "trips" down and up are required
             to complete one trial. The watch is stopped when the
             last can of pop is returned to its original position,
             following the second trip back.   The preferred hand
             in this case, the right hand) is used throughout the
             entire task (a graphic illustration of this test is
             provided in Fig. 15A). The object of the test is to
             perform the task as fast as possible, making sure
             that the cans are always placed over the squares. If
             a can misses a square at any time during the test,
             the trial must be repeated from the start.   A miss
             indicates that a can did not completely cover the

entire square formed by the crossing of the two
strips of tape (Fig. 16A).

Fig. 12A

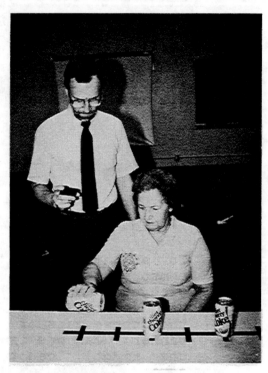

Fig. 13A

Fig. 14A

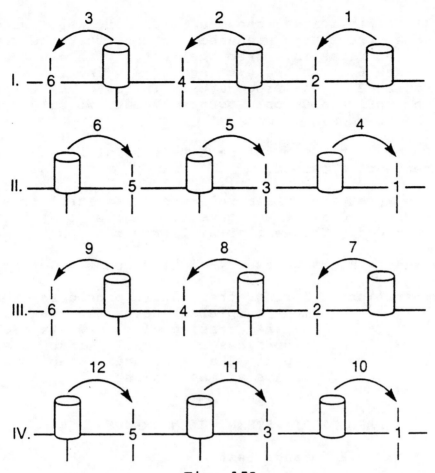

Fig. 15A

Graphic illustration of the "soda pop" coordination test

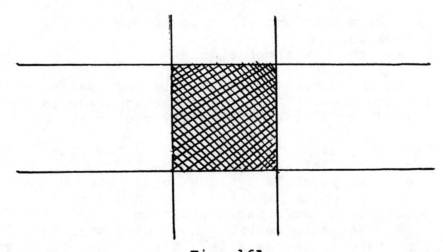

Fig. 16A

Shaded area illustrates the square that must be completely covered when turning the cans during the "soda pop" coordination test.

If a participant chooses to use the left hand, the same procedures are used, except that the cans are placed starting from the left, with can one over square 6, can two over square 4, and can three over square 2. The procedure is initiated by turning can one upside down onto square 5, can two onto square 3, and so on.

Scoring: Record the time of each test trial to the nearest tenth of a second.

Trials: Two practice trials followed by two test trials are given. Only the scores for the two test trials are recorded. The best trial is recorded as the score.

Approximate Range: Eight to twenty-eight seconds.

Special Considerations: During the entire procedure the cans must completely cover the squares formed by the crossing of the two tapes. If the person has a mistrial (misses a square), repeat the test until two successful trials are accomplished.

PARAMETER: STRENGTH/ENDURANCE

Test Item: Strength/Endurance test

Equipment: Four and eight pound weights (two quart plastic bottles with handles, for the four pound weight, or one gallon plastic milk bottle with handle, for the eight pound weight, can be filled with sand if unable to locate four and eight pound dumbbells).
Stopwatch
Normal chair without arms

Set Up: Weigh the dumbbells or the plastic bottles with sand for accuracy. A straight back chair with no arms is placed in an area with no obstructions.

Procedure: The subject is asked to sit in the chair with the back straight and against the back of the chair as much as possible. The eyes should be looking straight ahead and the feet should be flat on the floor in a comfortable position. The non-dominant hand should be resting in the lap with the dominant hand hanging to the side. The arm should be straight and relaxed.

The dumbbell is held in the dominant hand with the thumbs up and the arm extended toward the floor. (Fig. 17A). The four pound weight (quart container) should be used for women and the eight pound (one gallon container) should be used for men. The running stop watch should be placed in the non-dominant hand resting in the lap and facing the dominant side of the body. The administrator of the test should stand on the side of the dominant arm and place one hand on the dominant bicep and the other helping to support the weight. The hand helping to support the weight is then removed and the subject is asked to contract the bicep through the full range of motion until the lower arm touches the hand of the administrator of the test, which is on the bicep. This represents one total repetition (Fig. 18A). If the subject cannot bring the weight through the full range of motion, the test is terminated with a score of zero.

When the practice repetition is complete, the weight is placed on the floor for approximately one minute and again placed in the hand supported by the administrator of the test. The administrator then instructs the subject to make as many repetitions as possible in thirty seconds. The lower arm must touch the administrator's hand (on the bicep) for a complete repetition.

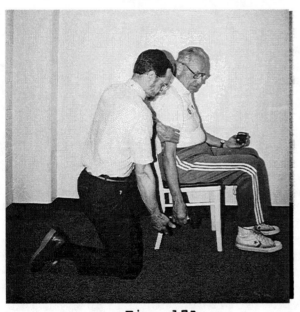
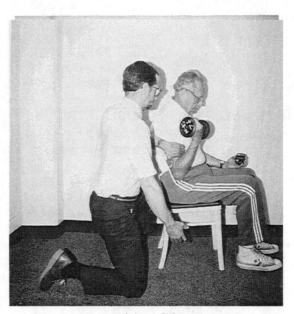

Fig. 17A   Fig. 18A

While watching the timepiece, the clinician instructs the subject to begin (unassisted) and counts the number of repetitions the subject can do in the thirty second period. The clinician starts and stops the time interval at a convenient time on the stopwatch.

Trials: One thirty second trial.

Scoring: Record the maximal number of complete repetitions in the thirty second interval.

Range of Scores: Zero to forty.

Special Considerations: If the subject cannot grasp the handle of the weight to hold it in place, this test should not be done.

Subjects should be instructed to breathe normally during the test.

The weight should not be bounced off the floor.   If this is the case elevate the chair.

Subjects should be instructed to stop the test if the subject experiences pain in the tested arm.   The administrator must determine if the pain is due to a structural condition or the lack of strength.   If the former, the test will be invalid and no score should be recorded.

PARAMETER: ENDURANCE

Test Item: Half mile (880 yard) walk

Equipment: Stopwatch
Measuring tape
Rubberized Cones or one gallon plastic bottles

Set Up: The test involves a continuous walk of 880 yards. The person will walk around a measured lap until he or she has walked a total of 880 yards. Using a measuring tape or similar device, measure an oval lap and compute the number of laps required to complete 880 yards. Mark the inside edges of the lap (oval or rectangle) with the cones or bottles. The lap should be designed with sufficient space to turn. The area should be well lit, the surface non-slippery and level. All obstacles should be removed from the path. People not taking the test should not be allowed to walk onto the course during the test.

Procedure: Instruct the participants to walk the course (X number of laps) as fast as they feel they comfortably can. The participants may not run. They should walk at their own pace independent of the other participants.   Do not allow people to walk in pairs or groups. It is important that they pace themselves so they are able to finish the distance and do not experience discomfort.   If a person is dizzy, lightheaded, nauseous, or experiences any pain, he or she should stop the test immediately and inform the administrator of the test. On the signal "Ready Go", the participants begin at a designated spot and walk the necessary laps until they reach the end of the half mile.

Trials: A single trial is used.

Score: Record the time in minutes and seconds to the nearest second as the score.

Approximate Range of Scores: 5 minutes 0 seconds to 14 minutes 30 seconds.

Special Considerations: Individuals should be screened for cardiovascular or orthopedic contraindications. (See the precautions and guidelines in this chapter).

Under the following circumstances the test administrator should either discourage or not allow the participant to perform this test without first consulting his or her physician:

Significant orthopedic problems that may be aggravated by prolonged continous walking (8-10 minutes).

History of cardiac problems (i.e., recent heart attack, frequent arrhythmia, valvular defects) that can be negatively influenced by exertion.

Lightheadedness upon activity or history of uncontrolled hypertension (high blood pressure).

The walk test should be administered last in the battery of tests. The warm-up session is left to the discretion of the test administrator.

Individuals should practice walking on several days prior to the test to determine their appropriate walking pace.

NOTE: *Norms are presently being established for these tests. If you wish to contribute to this project please contact Dr. Wayne Osness, Chairperson, Department of HPER and Director of the Fitness Clinic, University of Kansas, Lawrence, KS 66045.*

AAHPERD FUNCTIONAL FITNESS ASSESSMENT FOR ADULTS OVER 60 YEARS

Individual Data Collection Form

Name:_____ Testing Date_____

Sex: F M   Age (in years) _____   Location:_____

Test Administrator_____

- -

Administer the 6 item test battery in the suggested sequence. (Endurance walk and agility/dynamic balance tests should not be given consecutively).

Test Item	Test Trials/Score		Final Recorded Score
	Trial 1	Trial 2	
1. Ponderal Index (to nearest .1 of unit)			
Weight	[ ] [ ] [ ]. [ ] lb.		
Height	[ ] [ ]. [ ] in.		
Ponderal Index	[ ] [ ]. [ ] units		_____
2. Flexibility (Score to .5 in.) Practice given, not recorded	[ ] [ ].[ ]	[ ] [ ].[ ]	_____
3. Agility/Dynamic Balance Score seconds & tenths of sec. Practice given, not recorded	[ ] [ ].[ ]	[ ] [ ].[ ]	_____
4. Coordination Score seconds & tenths of sec. Practice given, not recorded	[ ] [ ].[ ]	[ ] [ ].[ ]	_____
5. Strength Score # of reps. in 30 sec. 4 lbs. women, 8 lbs. men Single lift practice			_____
6. Endurance Walk Time in minutes and seconds			_____

Warm-Up Exercises

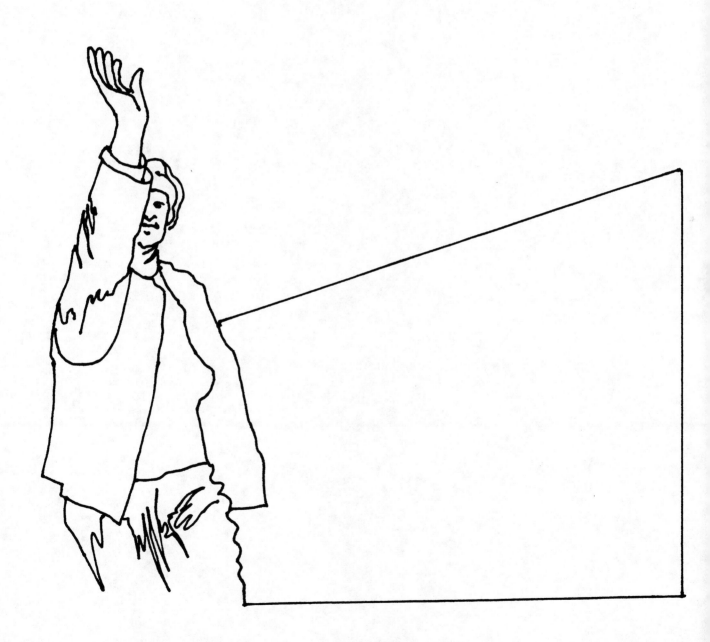

Chapter 6
Warm-Up Exercises

The purpose of warm-up exercises is to gradually stretch the muscles and to increase the body temperature so that as the activity becomes more intense or vigorous the body is prepared for the activity and consequently, injuries are less likely to occur.

There are many good ways to warm-up. This chapter describes many different exercises that we have found to be popular and effective. You may wish to alternate warm-up activities from day-to-day to keep them interesting or you may wish to stay with a routine of warm-ups that you enjoy or that you find particularly useful.

A warm-up session should last from 5 to 10 minutes. Certainly you would not do all of these warm-ups every time you exercise. We are merely presenting you with options. We do recommend that you chose 1 or 2 warm-ups from each of the four main sections.

Slow stretching warm-ups will help to release tension in the muscles. Noises you may hear in your joints as you move are not uncommon and they need not concern you. They occur in people of all ages.

Performing the warm-up exercises to music may help to keep your interest and make the exercises more pleasurable. We recommend it.

Many of the t'ai chi ch'uan and yoga exercises in Chapters 13 and 14 can also be used as warm-up exercises.

I. Head, Neck and Shoulder Warm-ups

All of the following warm-up exercises should be performed while sitting on a sturdy, well-balanced chair. The eyes should remain open and remember to keep breathing rhythmically while doing the exercises.

Head side tilt.

Tilt your head slowly to one side as far as it is comfortable, keeping your shoulders down. Repeat to the other side (3 or 4 times).

Head turn.

Turn your head in one direction to look over your shoulder then repeat, turning in the other direction. (Repeat 3 or 4 times).

Head and neck circles.

Circle the head slowly in one direction trying to bring the ear as close to the shoulder as possible then try to touch the chin to the chest and rotate the head to the other side trying to bring the ear as close to the other shoulder as possible. Repeat 3 times. Do not circle the head to the back as this movement places stress on the cervical (neck) vertebrae.

Extra Stretches for the Neck.

Tip the head slowly forward as far as it will go. Add to the stretch by lightly pushing the back of the top of the head forward with the index and middle finger--hold for 3 seconds.

Turn the head in one direction and with two fingers lightly push on the side of the chin to give an extra stretch--(Fig. 6.1) hold for 3 seconds then repeat to the other side.

Fig. 6.1

Shoulder Shrugs

Shrug your shoulders up toward your ears and hold for 3 seconds then relax. Then press the shoulders down while stretching the neck upward. Hold for 3 seconds then relax. Repeat 2 more times.

Shoulder stretch with finger grasp.

Raise one arm overhead, bending it at the elbow and place the palm between the shoulder blades. Place the other arm behind the back with the elbow bent and the elbow pointing down and the palm facing away from the back. Attempt to touch the fingers of both hands together or to grasp the fingers of both hands together. (Fig. 6.2) Hold the stretch for 5-10 seconds then repeat it on the other side.

Note: If you can't touch or clasp the fingers, you may grasp a hand towel between the hands using the towel to slowly bring the hands together.

Fig. 6.2

II. Finger, Hand and Arm Warm-ups

<u>Fist</u> <u>and</u> <u>open</u>.

Make your hands into fists then open your hands and spread your fingers wide apart. Repeat 5-8 times.

<u>Claw</u> <u>and</u> <u>open</u>.

Bend your fingers as if you are making a claw ready to scratch something, then open your hands and spread your fingers wide apart. Repeat 5-8 times.

<u>Finger</u> <u>fans</u>.

With your elbows bent and hands about one foot apart, face the palms away from you with the fingers tightly touching each other, then widely spread (or fan) your fingers (Fig. 6.3). Repeat 5-8 times.

Fig. 6.3

Next, separate only the index fingers from the rest of the fingers (3 times). Now try the little fingers only (3 times). Now try to separate the index and little fingers simultaneously while the middle fingers stay together (3 times). Try to separate the four fingers down the middle while keeping the two fingers on either side together (forming a "V") (3 times). Finally, try to separate the index and little fingers simultaneously on one hand while keeping the two fingers on either side together in a "V" on the other hand. Repeat the opposite pattern to the other side.

Hand shakes.

Bend your arms at the elbows and relax your hands. Now shake them briskly from the wrist for about 10 seconds.

Finger stretching.

With one palm facing away from the body use the other hand to gently stretch the index finger back towards the forearm. Continue doing each finger in succession. Repeat the same thing with the other hand. Next grasp one finger at a time with the thumb and first two fingers of the other hand and gently circle the finger you are grasping. Repeat this on each finger and then switch to the other side.

Wrist circles.

Bend at each wrist and circle the hands around 3 or 4 times in the same direction. Repeat 3 or 4 times circling in the other direction.

Arm and shoulder stretch.

Interlace the fingers and straighten the arms in front of the body with the palms of the hands facing away from the body. Now extend the hands up and over the head as far as you can go without letting the fingers come apart. Make sure you do not hold your breath during the exercise or that you do not arch the back. Repeat 3-4 more times.

Thumbs up and down.

Start with the arms stretched out in front of the body at shoulder height. Make fists and extend the thumbs up. Now rotate the arms inwardly so that the thumbs are pointing down. Rotate the arms making the thumbs point to the sides with the insides of the arms facing up. Repeat the full rotation 3-4 times.

Card player's exercise.

Place each hand with the palms facing up on the thigh of the each leg. Bend the thumb and each finger one at a time until all are bent on one hand then straighten each finger one at a time. Repeat twice with each hand.

<u>Jazz</u> <u>arm</u> <u>isolation</u> <u>sequence</u>.

This exercise helps to develop coordination and memory. It can be performed while seated, while standing or while walking.

Jazz Arm Isolation Sequence

Fig. 6.4

Fig. 6.5

Fig. 6.6

Fig. 6.7

Jazz Arm Isolation Sequence (continued)

Fig. 6.8

Fig. 6.9

Fig. 6.10

Fig. 6.11

When learning the sequence, hold each position for 8 counts before continuing to the next position. Continue practicing, holding each position for a slightly shorter period of time--4 counts, then 2 counts, then 1 count. (See Figs. 6.4-6.11).

III.   Torso Warm-Ups

Elbow to knee.

While seated in a sturdy chair bring one elbow across the chest while bringing the opposite knee up (with bent leg) and touch the elbow to the knee. Repeat with the other elbow and knee (3 or 4 times per side).

Trunk twister.

Sit up straight in your chair and grasp the back of the chair by bringing your arm across your body. Pull with your arm while twisting your body and head toward the hand that is holding the chair. Keep your feet on the floor directly in front of you. Repeat in the other direction with the opposite arm (3 times each direction).

Forehead to knee.

Grasp under one knee with both hands and pull the knee slowly toward your forehead. See if you can touch your head to your knee. Hold the stretch for about 3 seconds then do this on the other side. Repeat 3 times on each side.

Side stretchers.

Sit upright in your chair with both feet flat on the floor in front of you. Firmly grasp the chair on one side with the hand on that same side. Now lean your head and body away from the side you are grasping while reaching the opposite hand down toward the floor as you feel the side stretch. (Fig. 6.12). Do the exercise to the other side. Repeat 3 times per side.

Fig. 6.12

Back stretcher.

Sit up straight in your chair and hold on to the seat of the chair with both hands. Now bend forward from the waist as far as you can and hold that pose for 5-10 seconds. Now very slowly unroll the spine, starting at the lower back and working up the spine one vertebra at a time until the head is upright. Repeat one more time. Do not perform this exercise if you are prone to dizziness.

Rib Cage Isolations.

Sit with good posture, arms at sides, hands holding onto sides of chair. Slide rib cage sidewards and return to center. Slide rib cage to other side and return to center.

VARIATION: Continuously slide rib cage from right to left without stopping in center. This exercise can also be done with rib cage moving forward and backward.

IV. Leg, Feet and Toe Warm-Ups--Seated Position

Leg extensions.

Sit up straight in your chair and lift one leg straight out in front of you then place the foot back on the floor. Now do the same thing with the other leg. Alternate back and forth 3 or 4 times.

Foot shakes.

Sit up straight in your chair then extend one leg straight out in front of you. Now relax your foot and shake it briskly from the ankle, for about 10 seconds. Repeat the same exercise with the other foot.

Toe bends (Should be done without shoes on).

While sitting down, extend the legs in front of the body. Bend the toes as far forward as you can and then straighten them. Repeat this 8-10 times. (Fig. 6.13).

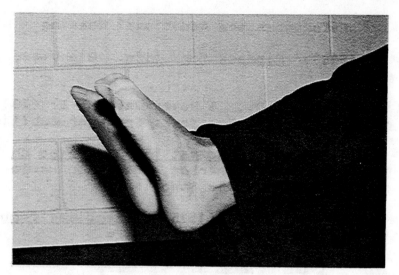

Fig. 6.13

V. Leg, Feet and Toe Warm-ups--Standing Position

Modified Knee Bends.

Stand behind your chair, holding on for support when necessary. The feet are shoulder width apart pointing straight ahead. Bend the knees as far as you can without lifting the heels from the floor and then straighten the knees. Make sure that the knees stay in line with the center of each foot during the bend and also make sure that the back remains straight. Repeat 6-8 times. To assist with balancing, focus on an object while doing the exercise.

Heel Raises.

Stand behind your chair, holding on for support when necessary. The feet are shoulder width apart pointing straight ahead. Raise the body by lifting the heels from the floor going on to the balls of the feet. Return to starting position. Repeat 6-8 times.

Leg Extensions.

Stand beside your chair, holding on with the left hand. Bend and lift the right knee to waist height, then extend the leg. Then touch the ball of the foot to the floor and then return it to starting position. Repeat 4 times and then reverse to the other side.

Toe Points.

Stand beside your chair holding on with the left hand. The feet are slightly apart. Point the right foot forward and close to starting position for 4 times. Then point the right foot to the side (keep the knee facing the front) for 4 times and then to the back 4 times. Repeat on the other side.

References and Additional Reading

Berland, T. (1986). <u>Fitness for life</u>. Glenview, IL: Scott, Foresman and Co.

Flatten, K., Wilhite, B., & Reyes-Watson, E. (1988). <u>Exercise activities for the elderly</u>. New York: Springer Publishing Co.

Forsythe, K.D. (1980). <u>Sit and get fit: Modified chair exercises for the older adult</u>. Ann Arbor, MI: Ann Arbor Recreation Department and Ann Arbor Public Schools.

Leslie, D.K., & McLure, J.W. (1975). <u>Exercises for the elderly</u>. Iowa City, IA: University of Iowa.

<u>Pep up your life: A fitness book for seniors</u>. Marketing Services Department, The Travelers Insurance Companies, One Tower Square, Hartford, CT 06115.

Schultz, S. (1980). <u>Let's get moving: A fitness program developed for those over sixty</u>. Mayville, ND: Mayville State College.

Chapter **7**

Exercises with Bicycle Innertubes
(or Other Types of Stretch Bands)

Chapter 7
Exercises with Bicycle Innertubes
(or Other Types of Stretch Bands)

We are devoting a long illustrated chapter to exercises done with old bicycle tubes because they have become such a popular part of our exercise programs. Inner tubes have become a focal point of many exercise programs throughout the country because:

1) they can be obtained for free at most bicycle shops,

2) they can be used as exercisers for people of all ages and,

3) they can be used as exercisers for people with a wide range of physical capabilities--the physically able, those confined to wheelchairs and even to the bedridden.

To obtain the bike inner tubes simply go to your local bike shop and ask them to save their old bike inner tubes for you. Normally they throw away several inner tubes every day (especially in the warm weather months when they are doing most of their tire repairs). The larger English or racing bike inner tubes are best suited for exercises for most older adults.

After you have obtained the inner tubes, cut the stems off them with an old pair of scissors. Simply cut across the whole tube on either side of the stem. Wash or wipe off the inner tube, then tie a square knot with the two loose ends of the tube. You now have a circular tube (like a giant rubber band) that is an excellent exercise apparatus. Exercises can be performed while standing, sitting or lying down. The resistance offered by the inner tube can be varied from exercise to exercise, from person to person and from one part of the body to another by varying how or where the tube is held or by re-tying the ends of the tube to make the tube circle smaller (for greater resistance) or larger (for less resistance).

Currently, there are many commercial elastic or stretch-type bands on the market. Some people prefer to use surgical tubing that they tie to make bands. Some people prefer Dyna-Bands (see the address at the end of the chapter). Each has its own advantages and disadvantages. Bike inner tubes are free, but they may not be available in some areas in the quantities that are needed. Products like Dyna-Bands come in different colors with different resistances. Dyna-Band is a registered trademark.

These exercises can be done individually at home while watching TV or they can be performed to music in large or small groups. Any music with a strong, steady beat is suitable. Some groups put a different person in charge of bringing the music each week. This helps to provide a variety of music and it gives the participants an opportunity to share favorite songs from their personal record collections.

Before doing the following exercises, it is recommended that the participants become familiar with the guidelines and precautions in Chapter 5 and that the participants are sufficiently warmed up (see Chapter 6). Remember that you need not do all of the exercises each time you exercise. Some of the exercises are more difficult than others. Don't strain to do an exercise. Progress gradually toward the more difficult exercises and remember to breathe rhythmically as you execute each movement.

In our exercise and dance programs we do not exclude anyone. If a person cannot do a particular exercise or dance, they may choose to sit that one out or they may choose to perform the exercise or dance in a modified way. It is rare that a person would not be able to do at least some of the exercises or dances in any given session. We urge people to do only what they can do or what they want to do, but people should never feel they have to participate on an all or none basis.

Sitting Exercises

These exercises should be performed while sitting in a sturdy, well-balanced armless chair. If the participants are doing the exercises in a group setting, they need to be sure that the chairs are well spaced so that the participants do not hit or bump into each other.

#1 - Arm forward and back

Grasp one end of the inner tube with one hand and the other end with the other hand--the closer together the hands are, the greater the resistance. Extend the arm forward at shoulder height and anchor the other hand by placing it against the chest. (Fig. 7.1) Swing the forward arm slowly back as far as it will go and rotate the head so that you are looking at the extended hand. (Fig. 7.2) Repeat this 5 times, then do the same on the other side.

Fig. 7.1

Fig. 7.2

#2 - <u>360 Degree Shoulder Circles</u>

Grasp one end of the inner tube with one hand and the other end with the other hand. Extend the arm forward at shoulder height anchoring the other hand near the shoulder. Now circle your extended arm up over your head. (Fig. 7.3) Keep circling 360 until you have past the starting point 3 times. Now reverse the direction and repeat 3 times. Do the same exercises with the other arm.

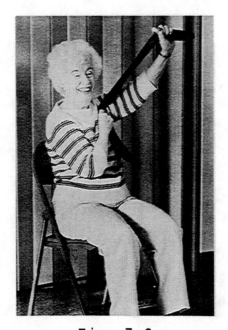

Fig. 7.3

#3 - <u>Pull</u> <u>downs</u>

Hook the tube on each thumb and extend the arms overhead
(Fig. 7.4).   Pull down while stretching the tube across the
chest. (Fig. 7.5) Return to starting position.   Repeat 5-8
times.   Next (from the same starting position) pull down behind
the head instead of across the chest. (Fig. 7.6)   Return to
starting position.   Repeat 5-8 times.

Fig. 7.4

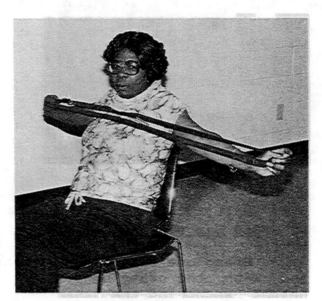

Fig. 7.5

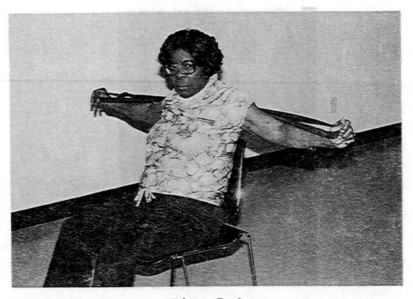

Fig. 7.6

#4 - Overhead Press

Hold the tube with both hands apart, one hand near each end of the tube. (Fig. 7.7) The closer the hands are together, the more difficult the exercise. Extend and press one hand straight up toward the ceiling while holding the other hand hugged tightly to your chest. (Fig. 7.8) Repeat 5-8 times, then switch sides.

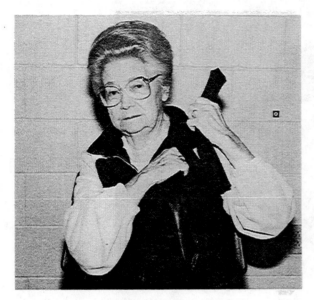
Fig. 7.7

Fig. 7.8

#5 - Curls

Hook one end of the tube under both feet with the heels anchored to the floor. Grasp the other end of the tube with both hands, palms facing up. Bend the arms and curl the hands toward the body. (Fig. 7.9). Repeat 5-8 times.

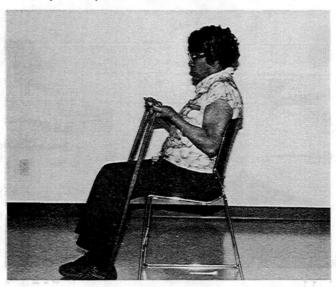
Fig. 7.9

#6 - <u>Rowing</u>

Hook one end of the tube under both feet with the heels anchored to the floor. Grasp the other end of the tube in an overgrip with both hands. Pull the tube toward the chin in a rowing motion. (Fig. 7.10). Repeat 5-8 times.

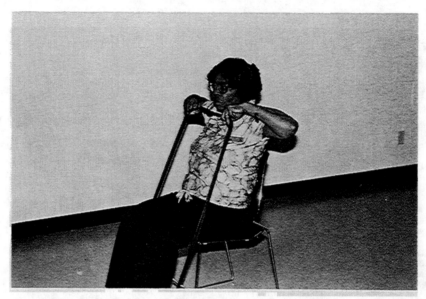

Fig. 7.10

#7 - <u>Punch swings</u>

Place the tube behind the back and hook both thumbs in the ends of the tube. Swing the arm across the body in a punching fashion. (Fig. 7.11). Alternate punch swings from arm to arm. (Fig. 7.12) Repeat 5-8 times per side. Back view. (Fig. 7.13).

Fig. 7.11

Fig. 7.12

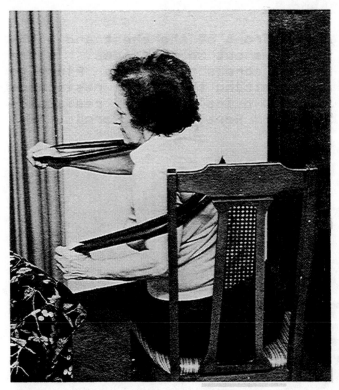

Fig. 7.13

#8 - <u>Wringing the tube</u>

    Double the tube over and then double it over again.   Grab
the tube with both hands and wring it back and forth keeping the
elbows high.   You should feel as if you are wringing the water
out of a wet washcloth. (Fig. 7.14).

Fig. 7.14

#9 - <u>Chest</u> <u>Strengthener</u>

Hold the tube in front of the chest and with the hands close together and the elbows out to the sides. Alternately stretch and release inner tube across the chest. Place your hands on the tube so that you are getting the proper resistance for your level of strength. You should feel that the resistance is challenging but not too difficult. Repeat this exercise 10-12 times. (Fig. 7.15).

Fig. 7.15

#10 - <u>Foot</u> <u>Flex</u> <u>and</u> <u>Point--Foot</u> <u>Circles</u>

Loop one end of the inner tube under one foot (leg extended in front of the body) keeping the other foot flat on the floor. Hold the other end of the tube in both hands, squeezing the tube together hand over hand (the closer the grip is to the foot, the greater the resistance). Alternately flex (Fig. 7.16) and point (Fig. 7.17) the foot 5-8 times, then circle the foot from the ankle (not the hip or the knee) for 3 or 4 circles. Reverse the circles. Do the same exercise on the other foot.

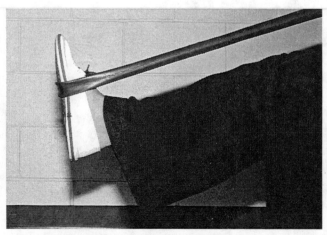

Fig. 7.16

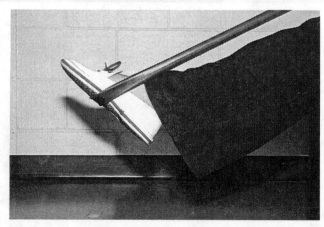

Fig. 7.17

#11 - <u>Tube jogging</u> (or "going nowhere fast")

Loop one end of the inner tube over both feet keeping the feet slightly apart. Hold the other end of the tube with both hands about 18 inches apart. (Fig. 7.18) Move the feet in a jogging motion making sure to sit on the forward part of the chair while leaning heavily on the chair back. The abdominal muscles should be contracted so that the back is supported. Continue the jogging motion for 1 minute. Eventually you can increase the time up to 5 minutes. This will serve as a good warm-up to a long, brisk walk. If this exercise puts too much strain on the back muscles, leave the heels on the floor and alternately point and flex the feet instead of the knees.

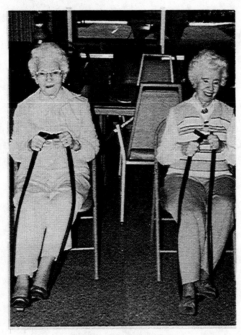

Fig. 7.18

#12 - <u>Single Leg Tuck</u>

Loop one end of the inner tube over one foot and extend that leg forward with the heel touching the floor. Hold the other end of the tube with both hands squeezing the tube together, one hand over the other. (Fig. 7.19) While pulling with the arms, lift the knee toward the chest as far as you can (Fig. 7.20) Repeat 5-8 times on each leg.

Fig. 7.19

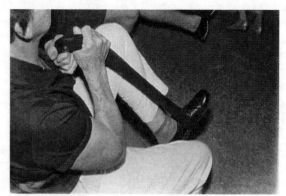

Fig. 7.20

#13 - <u>Knee</u> <u>Bends</u>

With the inner tube around one foot while holding the other end of the tube with both hands, alternately bend (Fig. 7.21) and straighten (Fig. 7.22) the leg. Repeat 5-8 times per leg.

Fig. 7.21

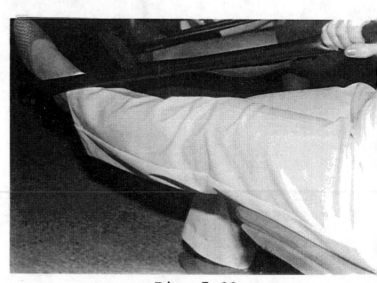

Fig. 7.22

Standing Exercises

Many of the sitting exercises can also be done in a standing position. It is strongly recommended that in the initial stages of performing the standing exercises, that you have a sturdy chair or something to hold on to, to help you keep your balance while exercising.

#14 - Behind the back stretcher

Hook both thumbs in the inner tube with the rest of the tube stretched diagonally across the back.   One hand should be above the head and the other should be near the hip. Stretch the tube across the back by extending one arm up and the other arm down. (Fig. 7.23) Repeat 5-8 times then switch so that the arm positions are reversed.   Do the exercise 5 to 8 times in this position.

Fig. 7.23

#15 - Arm pulls

Locate a sturdy handle or something similar that is secured to a wall. Then loop one end of the inner tube through the other so that the tube is securely fastened on one end. (Fig. 7.24) Hold the loose end of the tube in one hand and pull forward. (Fig. 7.25) Repeat 5-8 times then change arms. If the resistance is too great, you can loop two tubes together and this will make the exercise easier.   You can also do over the head pulls (using a throwing motion) while you have the tubes assembled as described above. (Fig. 7.26)

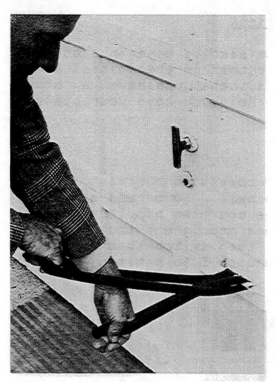

Fig. 7.24

Fig. 7.25

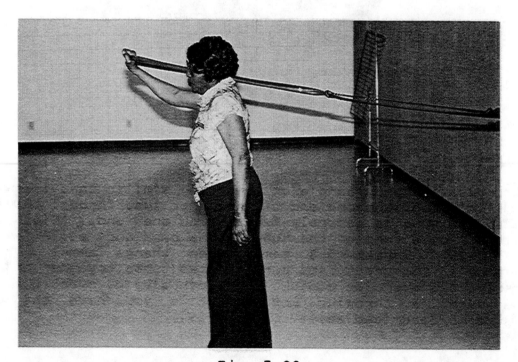

Fig. 7.26

#16 - <u>Shoulder cross-pulls</u>

Hold one end of the tube with one hand and anchor it to the hip on the same side of the body. Hold the other end of the tube with the other hand and lift that arm up across the chest with the elbow extended out from the body. Alternately bend and straighten the arm. Repeat 5-8 times on each arm.

#17 - <u>Behind the back exercise</u>

Grasp the tube with both hands behind the back so that the hands are about 3-8" apart.   Stretch the tube while keeping the arms straight and close to the buttocks. Continue the exercise by alternately stretching and releasing the tube.   If you are using a Dyna-Band or other shorter band you can hook your thumbs in the loops of the bands and then alternately stretch and release the band. (Fig. 7.27)

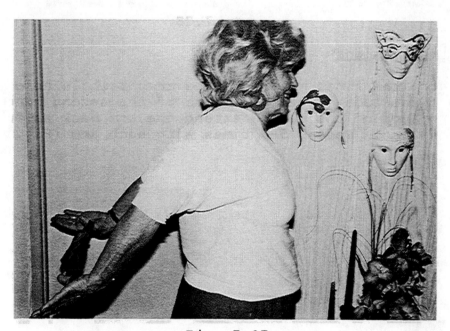

Fig. 7.27

#18 - <u>Overhead pull-downs</u>

Hold the inner tube over the head and grip the tube on both ends with both arms extended. Alternately pull the hands down toward the shoulder on the same side.   Do 5-8 exercises on each side. (Fig. 7.28).

Fig. 7.28

#19 - <u>Arm extensions</u>

Anchor the first hand near the armpit while holding on to one end of the tube. With the thumb of the second hand looped in the other end of the tube, extend the arm back as far as you comfortably can. Repeat 5-8 times with each arm (Fig. 7.29)

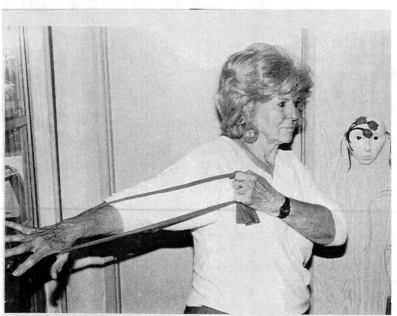

Fig. 7.29

#20 - <u>Chest exerciser</u>

Bend the knees slightly and lean slightly forward from the waist. Loop the tube around the thumb of each hand and cross the arms in front of the body. Press the arms away from each other and then release. Repeat 8-10 times. (Fig. 7.30).

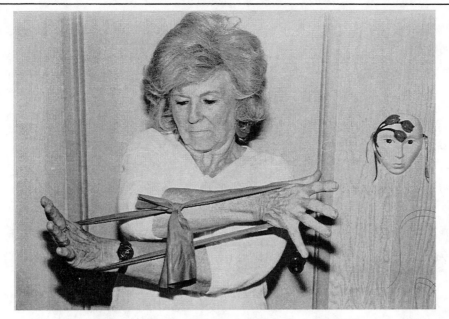

Fig. 7.30

#21 - <u>Standing leg combination</u> (use a wall or chair for
                                    added balance)

    Loop one end of the tube underneath one foot with the hand
on that same side holding the other end of the tube.   Stand with
your weight balanced on the opposite foot. (Fig. 7.31) Keeping
the free leg straight, swing it forward. (Fig. 7.32) Now return
to the starting position then swing the leg out to the side with
·the knee facing forward (Fig. 7.33).   Return to   the starting
position,   then swing the leg back (Fig. 7.34).   Return to the
starting position.   This is the whole combination.   Repeat it 3-5
times, then do the exercises with the other leg.

Fig. 7.31

Fig. 7.32

Fig. 7.33

Fig. 7.34

Floor Exercises

You may wish to perform these exercises on a mat or a carpeted surface to ensure more comfort.

#22 - Single leg lift

Lie down on the back and loop one end of the tube over one foot. Bend the knee of the other leg and place the foot flat on the floor. Hold the other end of the tube with both hands squeezing the tube together hand over hand. (Fig. 7.35) Lift up the leg (keeping it straight) as far as is comfortable while pulling up with the hands. (Fig. 7.36) Return slowly to the starting position. Repeat the exercise 5 to 8 times then switch legs.

Fig. 7.35

Fig. 7.36

#23 - <u>Side leg lift</u> (variation one)

Lie down on one side with one end of the tube looped over the top foot. Hold the other end of the tube with the top hand. (Fig. 7.37) Slowly lift the top leg up and apart from the other leg on the floor. Return to the starting position. Repeat 5-8 times then do the exercise on the other side.

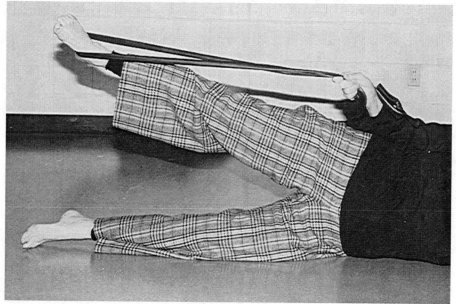

Fig. 7.37

#24 - <u>Side leg lift</u> (variation two)

Place a short inner tube or Dyna-Band around both feet and place the tube or band above the knees. Lie on one side then lift the top leg up while leaving the bottom leg in contact with the floor. Repeat 8-10 times on each side. (Fig. 7.38).

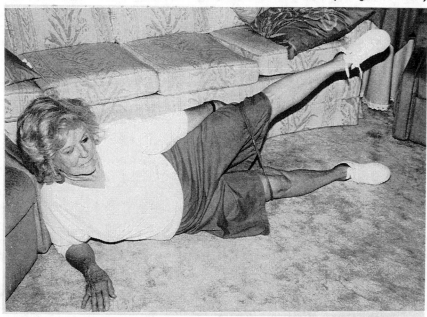

Fig. 7.38

#25 - <u>Leg</u> <u>curls</u>

With a short tube or band around the ankles, lie down on
your stomach.   Place one loop of the tube around the toe of one
foot.   Keeping the bottom leg on the floor bend the other knee
toward the buttocks as far as you can. Repeat 8-10 times on each
leg. To prevent strain on the lower back place a folded towel or
pillow under the hips. (Fig. 7.39).

Fig. 7.39

#26 - <u>Leg</u> <u>press</u>

Lie down on the back and loop one end of the tube over one
foot.   Bend the knee of the other leg and place the foot flat on
the floor.   Hold the other end of the tube with both hands
squeezing the tube together hand over hand.   Lift the leg up so
that the knee is close to the chest. (Fig. 7.40). Extend and
press the leg out at about a 45 degree angle with the floor.
(Fig. 7.41) The closer your hand grip is to the foot, the more
difficult the exercise. Repeat 5-8 times then do the exercise on
the other side.   (A variation is to alternately extend and flex
the foot after you have extended the leg).

Fig. 7.40

Fig. 7.41

#27 - <u>Ankle strengthener</u>

Sit on the floor with the legs extended in front of the body and a short tube or band looped over the toes of each foot. Spread the legs apart to achieve the desired resistance then rotate the feet out against the resistance of the tube. Repeat 8-10 times. (Fig. 7.42).

Fig. 7.42

#28 - <u>Ankle crossovers</u>

Sit on the floor with the legs outstretched in front of the body. Loop a short tube or Dyna-Band around the toes of each foot then cross one leg over the other leg. Rotate the feet outward against the resistance of the tube. After 8-10 repetitions then cross the other leg on top and repeat. (Fig. 7.43).

Fig. 7.43

#29 - Shin strengthener

Sit on the floor with the legs extended in front of the body. Place one loop of a short tube or band under one foot then place the other loop over the toe of the other foot. Place a folded towel on the shin or knee of the leg with the band under the foot. Bend the knee and place it on the folded towel. Now alternately flex and extend the foot. Do 10-15 repetitions on one foot then switch and repeat the exercise on the other foot. (Fig. 7.44).

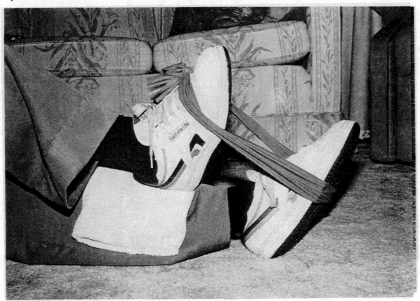

Fig. 7.44

#30 - "Bench" press

Lie down on your back with the inner tube behind the back and the hands grasping each end of the tube. Alternately press up, extending each arm. (Fig. 7.45) Repeat 5-8 times with each arm.

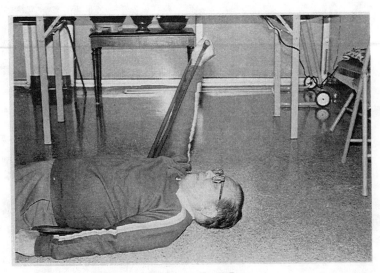

Fig. 7.45

As mentioned earlier in this chapter, many of these inner tube exercises can be adapted for people in wheelchairs.   The picture below shows one such exercise.   The tube is looped through the arm of the wheelchair and the other end of the tube is grasped with one hand.   The arm is then extended across the front of the body or above the head. (Fig. 7.46).

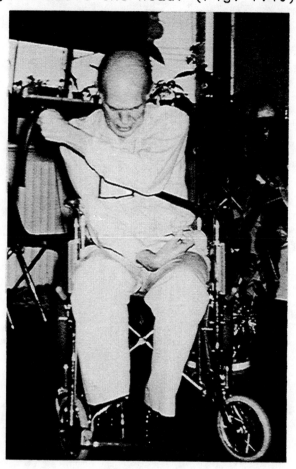

Fig. 7.46

Resources

Dyna-Bands are available from Future Dynamics, Inc., 3064 West Edgerton, Silver Lake, OH 44224, (800) 537-5512.

Dance in Chairs

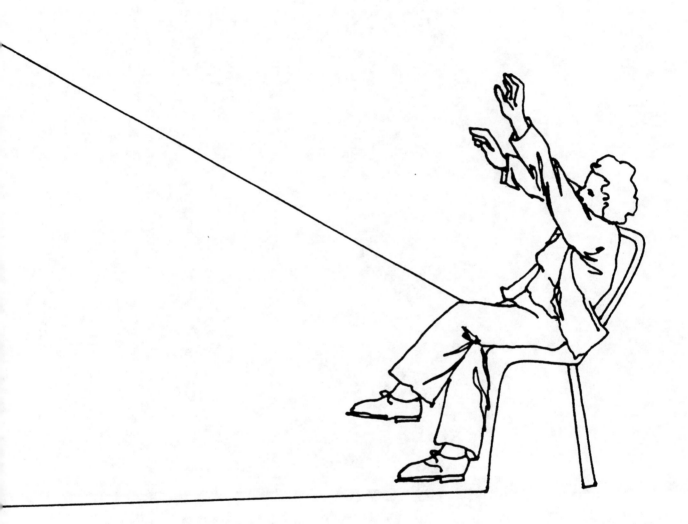

Chapter 8
Dance in Chairs

The dance activities in this chapter and in Chapters 9 and 10 require a leader. Ideally, this person will be a dance educator, physical educator, recreation leader or someone who will have enough dance background to lead the group through the dance sequences and be able to break down and explain the various steps and patterns. If none of these people are available, then the leadership may be shared by several of the members of the group so that no one person has all the responsibilities for learning and teaching all of the dances.

Many of the physical and social benefits derived from dancing can be experienced while sitting and moving in chairs. The activities that we present in this chapter adapt traditional dance steps and movements so that they can be performed while seated, making accommodations for various chronic health problems. Participants should be strongly urged to recognize their own limitations and should self-monitor their own physical performance, whenever appropriate. Spectators or those with very limited movement capacities can be included by providing maracas or homemade percussion instruments so that they may "accompany" the dancers. The primary goal of DANCE IN CHAIRS is to involve everyone in the spirit of the dance rather than emphasizing the technique of each separate movement. The leader serves as a guide, allowing ample opportunity for participants to interpret the pattern in their own way. The emphasis is on having fun and experiencing comfort while moving.

The DANCE IN CHAIRS patterns presented in this chapter are based on traditional dance steps from tap, ballet, modern, jazz, folk and social dance forms. They serve merely as a guideline for this type of activity. It is hoped that dance leaders will use these patterns as a basis for creating their own choreography. The music listed for each dance is offered as a suggested source of accompaniment. Certainly, the patterns can be executed without a recording or with simple accompaniment provided by voices or rhythm instruments.

For each dance, the patterns and the number of times it should be done are described. Most of the dance patterns presented are explained in the GLOSSARY at the end of this chapter. Some patterns are self-explanatory. Right and left will be indicated by "R" and "L."

The first part of this chapter describes nine sitting dances. The second part describes seven dances that can be done while either sitting or standing. If the standing variation is tried, the chair may be used for support. Armless, stable,

straight-backed   chairs are best for either method as they allow
for more freedom of movement.   It is recommended that the leader
and participants arrange themselves in a large circle so that the
leader can visually communicate with everyone and so that all
participants can offer encouragement to one another.

Remember to follow the precautions listed in Chapter 5.

SITTING DANCES

DANCE #1:   "FEETS TOO BIG"
            Ain't Misbehavin', RCA CBL2-2965

Measures (Meter 4/4)   Patterns

INTRO   JOIN HANDS
 (16 counts)

                              TORSO SWAY

                              TOE HEEL with fingers snapping

                              STEP KICK
Each of these
patterns is danced
for 8 measures   SNAP FINGERS or SHAKE HANDS at
(or 32 counts)   WRISTS
before continuing
on to the next
pattern.   CRAMP ROLL

                              SHOULDER THIGH HIT

                              TAP DANCE

                              SHAKE FEET

                              TAP DANCE or JOG

VARIATION: At the end of a phrase or certain measure,
                  add a "freeze" where everyone holds their
                  position for a moment and focuses on their
                  feet, which can be held in amusing poses.

DANCE #2: "OH SUSANNAH/CAMPTOWN RACES"
          <u>Happy</u> <u>Time</u> <u>Sing</u> <u>Along</u>, Kimbo 1225 or any lively
          marching music

<u>Measures</u> (Meter 4/4)   **Patterns**

INTRO (8 counts)   NO ACTION

    1 - 4   FRONT TOUCH/SIDE TOUCH

    5 - 6   KNEE SWAY or FOOT CIRCLE

    7 - 10   OUT OUT/IN IN

   11 - 12   KNEE SWAY

      13   STAND UP, TURN AROUND IN PLACE
                                     (See Box 9)

   14 - 17   CROSS AND HIT

   18 - 19   KNEE SWAY or FOOT CIRCLE

      20   STAND UP, TURN AROUND IN PLACE

   21 - 24   FRONT TOUCH/SIDE TOUCH

   25 - 28   ELBOW FLAP

Box 9

Remember to help individuals
adapt movements to meet their
needs. For example, if they
are unable to stand and turn
around, suggest other ways
that the body or body parts
can "turn around" while they
remain seated.

DANCE #3: "COMIN' 'ROUND THE MOUNTAIN"
        A Children's Disco Sing Along, Kimbo 1220
        or any lively marching music.

Measures (Meter 4/4)	Patterns
1 - 4	STEP TOUCH
5 - 8	ARM REACH (R and L)
9 - 12	STEP KICK
13 - 16	ARM CIRCLE
17 - 20	MARCH IN PLACE

DANCE #4:   "HAND JIVE"
This can be a sing-a-long dance that is
accompanied by the group singing familiar songs
such as:
"Heard It Through the Grapevine," "Ain't She
Sweet," "Five Foot Two,""Pennies from Heaven"

Sequence	Patterns
Do each pattern 8 times and then 4 times and then 2 times. Repeat sequence until song is finished.	SLAP THIGHS (R hand to R thigh, L hand to L thigh) at the same time.
	CLAP HANDS
	DOUBLE HIT WITH FISTS (right hand on top)
	DOUBLE HIT WITH FISTS (left hand on top)
	CROSS AND HIT
	WIND THE BOBBIN
	SNAP FINGERS (right hand)
	SNAP FINGERS (left hand)
	SNAP FINGERS ON BOTH HANDS

DANCE #5:   "MILLER'S REEL"
          Folkraft 1261BX45 or any Irish jig or reel
          music.

<u>Measures</u> (Meter 4/4)   <u>Patterns</u>

          1 - 4   BLEKING

          5 - 8   HEEL BOUNCE

          9 - 12   OUT OUT/IN IN

          13 - 16   ROW THE BOAT

Can repeat 1 - 16 or add the following:

          17 - 20   CLOG

          21 - 24   ARM REACH

          25 - 28   CROSS AND OPEN

          29 - 30   CLIMB ROPE

DANCE #6:   "DON'T WORRY, BE HAPPY"
          From Bobby McFerrin, <u>Simple Pleasures</u>
          EMI-Manhattan Records, E4-48059

<u>Sequence</u>	<u>Patterns</u>
DO EACH PATTERN 8 TIMES AND THEN 4 TIMES. REPEAT SEQUENCE UNTIL SONG IS FINISHED.	1. HAND CIRCLES , Right hand moves clockwise,CW
	2. HAND CIRCLES , Left hand moves CW
	3. Repeat Pattern #1 Moving right hand counter-clockwise (CCW)
	4. Repeat Pattern #2 Moving left hand CCW
	5. Move BOTH HANDS CW
	6. Move BOTH HANDS CCW
	7. FOOT CIRCLE, Right foot moving CW
	8. FOOT CIRCLE, Left foot moving CW
	9. Repeat Pattern #7 with Right foot moving CCW
	10. Repeat Pattern #8 with Left foot moving CCW
	11. Move BOTH FEET in circles CW
	12. Move BOTH FEET in circles CCW
	13. JAZZ ARMS (See Chapter 6 for directions, Fig.6.4 - 6.11)

DANCE #7: "SCARF DANCE"*
         "She Wore a Yellow Ribbon" from <u>Mitch</u> <u>Miller</u> <u>and</u>
         <u>the</u> <u>Gang</u>: <u>Sing</u> <u>Along</u> <u>with</u> <u>Mitch</u>, CBS PCT8004

Begin this dance by holding a chiffon scarf in each hand.
There is a different movement pattern for each verse. The chorus
pattern is repeated after each verse.

<u>Pattern</u>	<u>Directions</u>
A "Swing" Verse 1	Swing R arm across to L side at hip level (2X) Swing L arm across to R side at hip level (2X) Repeat the entire "swing" pattern
CHORUS ("Far away . . .") "Flicking"	Flick R hand forward and up and return hand to side (2X) Flick L hand forward and up and return hand to side (2X) Flick R L R L (Double time) R L R L R L R L Repeat all the above "flicking" pattern

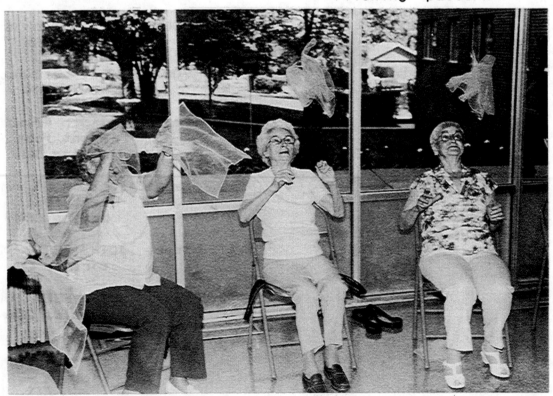

Fig. 8.1 -- Throwing and catching the scarves

B "Figure 8s" Verse 2	Swing both arms in FIGURE EIGHTS throughout this verse
CHORUS	"Flicking pattern" (see above)
C "Throw and catch" Verse 3	Throw R scarf up and catch it Throw L scarf up and catch it Keep alternating R and L catches throughout this verse
CHORUS	"Flicking pattern"
D "Stir" Verse 4	R arm circles scarf (CW) in a stirring motion at hip level L arm circles scarf (CW) in a stirring motion at hip level Alternate R and L "stirring" throughout this verse (Can be varied by stirring CCW)
CHORUS	"Flicking pattern"

All wave good-bye with their scarves at the end of the song.

Scarves can be purchased from:

Gopher Athletics
P.O. Box 0
Owatonna, MN 55060
1-800-535-0446

*This dance is based on movements created by Edith Clarke, a tutor/teacher for the EXTEND (Exercise Training for the Elderly and/or Disabled) program in Burton-on-Trent, England.

DANCE #8: "BATON DANCE"*
         "Don't Fence Me In" from <u>Mitch Miller and the Gang:</u>
         <u>Sing Along with Mitch</u>, CBS PCT 8004

     Everyone is seated in a circle.   Begin by resting the baton on
the right knee holding on to one end with the right hand.

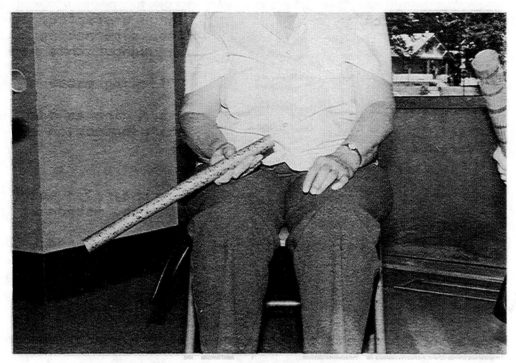

Fig. 8.2 --Starting position

Pattern	Directions
A	Swing L end of baton over to R side and return (2X) (change hand and knee)
	Swing R end of baton over to L side and return (2X)
	Repeat all of Pattern A
B	Swing R arm forward and back and lift R arm to L diagonal and change baton to L hand
	Swing L arm forward and back and lift L arm to R diagonal and change baton to R hand
	Repeat all of Pattern B

              C
       Pass baton around
       the circle to the L

Holding baton in R hand,
swing R arm forward and
back and forward again
and change baton to L
hand and then pass it to
to the next person's R
hand

Repeat 4X and then pause
with baton in L hand

Fig. 8.3 --Pattern C -- Passing the baton around to the right

              D   Reverse Pattern C
       Pass baton around
       the circle to the R

       Repeat Patterns A & B

   On the final refrain of the song,   shake the baton in the L hand
until the song ends.

   *Use cardboard tubes from rolls of waxpaper, wrapping paper,
foil, paper towels, etc. If you wish to make the batons stronger,
then stuff them with old newspaper and tape the ends to prevent the
paper from coming out. You may wish to cover the batons with wrapping
paper or decorate them with colored marking pens.

       *This dance is based on movements created by Edith
       Clarke, a tutor/teacher for the EXTEND (Exercise
       Training for the Elderly and/or Disabled) program
       in Burton-on-Trent, England.

DANCE #9: HOOP DANCE*

"You Are My Sunshine," <u>Mitch</u> <u>Miller</u> <u>and</u> <u>the</u> <u>Gang:</u>
<u>Sing</u> <u>Along</u> <u>with</u> <u>Mitch</u>, CBS PCT 8004

Formation: Two parallel lines (Line A and Line B) facing with pairs sitting across from one another (see illustration). Each pair holds a hoop between them and each pair is numbered 1, 2, 3, 4, etc.

Fig. 8.4 -- Hoop Dance Formation

Teaching Hint: The leader should designate a "front" and "back" of the room to assist with the following directions.

Begin by pairs holding the hoop, resting on their laps. There is a different movement pattern for each verse. The chorus pattern is repeated after each verse.

Pattern	Directions
A "Seesaw" Verse 1	Line A leans forward while Line B leans back, bending their elbows producing a "seesaw" effect
	Line B leans forward while Line A leans back with elbows bent

CHORUS "Swing, swing, all the way 'round"	Partners swing hoop toward front of room and then toward the back of room and then make a complete circle with the hoop returning it to their laps. Repeat, moving hoops in a reverse pattern going to the back first. Keep repeating these patterns throughout the chorus.
B "Wave" Verse 2	Each pair lifts and holds its hoop up on a designated count (1, 2, 3, 4, etc.). Then as the counting is repeated, each pair brings its hoop back down to knee level so that a "wave" effect is created.
CHORUS	"Swing, swing, all the way 'round" pattern (see above)
C "Hand Pass" Verse 3 (while humming)	Each pair holds the hoop parallel to the floor and then allows the hoop to slip through their hands moving it in a CW direction. Add variety by reversing the hand pass in a CCW direction.
CHORUS	"Swing, swing, all the way 'round" pattern

*Hoops may be purchased from:

> Things from Bell
> 230 Mechanic St.
> Princeton, WI 54968
> 1-800-543-1458

*This dance is based on movements created by Edith Clarke, a tutor/teacher for the EXTEND (Exercise Training for the Elderly and/Disabled) program in Burton-on-Trent, England.

SITTING AND STANDING DANCES

These dances allow dancers to participate at their own level. Those who are unable to stand and move around the chairs can continue to do the sitting patterns while the others stand and try variations of these patterns.

DANCE #1:   "LATE IN THE EVENING"
              Paul Simon's <u>One Trick Pony</u>
              Warner Bros. HS 3472 or any Samba recording.

<u>Measures</u> (Meter 4/4)		<u>Pattern</u> <u>(Sitting)</u>
	1 - 8	ISOLATED BOUNCING
	9 - 16	CUBAN WALK
Sequence A	17 - 24	TOUCH-SIDE, STEP IN PLACE
	25 - 32	SNAP FINGERS
	33 - 40	WIND THE BOBBIN
	41 - 48	ISOLATED BOUNCING
Sequence B	49 - 56	CUBAN WALK
	57 - 64	HOLD HANDS AND SWAY

Continue by repeating sequence "A" and "B" while moving in a sitting or standing position.

Standing participants join hands and follow the leader in a large serpentine formation around the outside of the seated participants. Then they weave into the center of the circle and around the chairs until the end of the music.

DANCE #2:   "CHARLESTON"
            Folkraft MCA 60092

<u>Measures</u> (Meter 2/4)   <u>Patterns</u> <u>(Sitting)</u>

INTRO	TILT HEAD SIDE TO SIDE
1 - 8	CHARLESTON
9 - 16	KNEE SLAP
17 - 24	WINDSHIELD WIPER HANDS
25 - 32	KNEE EXCHANGE
33 - 40	CHUG
41 - 48	ARM PUSH
49 - 56	TOE IN/TOE OUT
57 - 64	ARM PUSH

Repeat either sitting or standing. Those who stand
may use their chair as a support as they dance the
patterns.

Fig. 8.5 - Charleston Knee Slap

DANCE #3: "STEP IN TIME"
          from the Original Sound Track of "Mary Poppins"
          RCA-Victor CSO-111 (RPRS-4365)

The lyrics in each verse of this song cue the participants on what action (pattern) to do. Keep repeating the pattern until the lyrics change, then move on to the next verse and pattern.

Key Lyrics	Patterns
"STEP IN TIME"	STEP KICKS IN PLACE
"KICK YOUR KNEES UP"	MARCH IN PLACE, LIFTING KNEES AS HIGH AS POSSIBLE.
"ROUND THE CHIMNEY"	FOOT CIRCLES
"FLAP LIKE A BIRDIE"	ELBOW FLAPS
"UP ON THE RAILING"	STAND UP SLOWLY, LIFTING ARMS TO THE CEILING AND THEN SIT DOWN RETURNING ARMS TO SIDES OF BODY.
"OVER THE ROOFTOPS"	TORSO SWAY
"CLICK YOUR ELBOWS"	WITH HANDS HELD IN FRONT OF SHOULDERS, MOVE L HAND TO R ELBOW AND SNAP FINGERS OF BOTH HANDS. REPEAT TO OTHER SIDE.
"STEP IN TIME"	STEP KICKS IN PLACE.

After this verse, there is an instrumental section until the end of the dance. There is time to repeat all of the patterns three times. End the dance by having everyone join hands and lift arms to the ceiling.

"Step in Time" dance developed by Mary Horihan Adolph.

DANCE #4:   "MACNAMARRA'S BAND"/Folkraft FTC 32006
             This can be a sing-a-long dance with
             participants providing the accompaniment. Any
             lively march, square dance tune or two-step
             would also be appropriate.

Measures (Meter 4/4)   **Patterns** **(Sitting)**

       1 - 4   MARCH IN PLACE

       5 - 8   STEP KICK

       9 - 12   SALUTE FLAG and SIT TALL "AT
                             ATTENTION" (Keep repeating 4X)

      13 - 16   CLAP HANDS REACHING UP HIGH AND
                             THEN LOW ON A RIGHT DIAGONAL (2
                             CLAPS AT EACH POINT)

                             STAND UP

    Continue dance - standing participants dance all of
    the above patterns while marching around the
    outside of the seated participants.

DANCE #5:   "CRUISIN' DOWN THE RIVER"/Folkraft 1483
            This can be a sing-a-long dance with
            participants providing the accompaniment. Any
            slow to moderate waltz would also be appropriate.

<u>Measures</u> (Meter 3/4)   <u>Patterns</u> <u>(Sitting)</u>

     1 - 8   JOIN HANDS AND SWAY SIDE TO
                                    SIDE

     9 - 16   DROP HANDS - DO FIGURE EIGHTS

    17 - 24   KNEE SWAY

    25 - 32   JOIN HANDS AND SWING ARMS INTO
                                    CIRCLE AND OUT OF CIRCLE

                                    STAND UP

Those seated continue above patterns.

Those standing join hands with another person/s and
sway or waltz with a partner on the inside of the
circle of chairs.

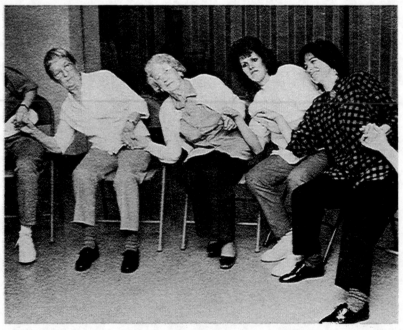

Fig. 8.6 -Join hands and sway side to side

DANCE #6: "SEVEN JUMPS" (A SEQUENCE DANCE)
          RCA The Folk Dance Orchestra
          41-6172A from Dance Record Distributor

FORMATION: This is a traditional Danish dance that has been
          adapted to allow the participants to create their
          own dance patterns. This dance may be done sitting
          or standing. It is very good for practicing memory
          skills.

          Begin the dance with the Chorus and return to it
          after each of the seven Figures.

CHORUS: STEP TOUCH (Do this pattern R,L,R,L)

          STEP KICK (R,L,R,L)

FIGURES: Seven participants each demonstrate one movement
          pattern. These patterns will be incorporated into
          the dance as the seven "figures" and they will be
          referred to as Figure #1, Figure #2, Figure #3,
          Figure #4, Figure #5, Figure #6, and Figure #7.

     1. On the first sustained note, the first figure is
        done by all dancers. Hold this movement until the
        second note and then sit motionless throughout the
        third note.

        NOTE: Stay motionless each time only to the last
               sustained note of music in each Figure.

                    REPEAT CHORUS

     2. Repeat Figure #1 and add Figure #2. REPEAT CHORUS.

     3. Repeat Figures #1 and #2 and then add Figure #3.
        REPEAT CHORUS.

     4. Repeat Figures #1, #2, #3 and then add Figure #4.
        REPEAT CHORUS.

     5. Repeat Figures #1, #2, #3, #4 and then add Figure #5.

     6. Repeat Figures #1, #2, #3, #4, #5 and then add
        Figure #6. REPEAT CHORUS.

     7. Repeat Figures #1, #2, #3, #4, #5, #6 and then add
        Figure #7. Finish the dance with a final CHORUS.

          Another sequence dance is "The Twelve Days of
          Christmas." In this dance, participants can sing
          along and create movements. There should be one
          movement created that is done at the end
          of each line of the song.

DANCE   #7:   "ELVIRA"* or any country-Western song in 4/4 time
              Oak Ridge Boys Greatest Hits 2
              MCA Records MCAC 5496

SEQUENCE	PATTERNS
DO EACH PATTERN 8 TIMES AND THEN 4 TIMES. REPEAT THIS SEQUENCE UNTIL THE SONG IS FINISHED.	OUT OUT/ IN IN
	CRAMP ROLL
	STEP KICK
	"ROPE" YOUR HORSE (Swing one arm overhead as if you are roping a horse)
	"RIDE" YOUR HORSE (Do the HEEL BOUNCE step "holding your hands on the reins"
	CHUG
	FRONT TOUCH/SIDE TOUCH
	"PUT ON YOUR BOOTS" (Do the STEP KICK while pretending to put on boots).

*Parts of "Elvira" were developed by Cindy Kugler.

DANCE IN CHAIRS GLOSSARY

ARM CIRCLE   Circle the arm from the shoulder in a
                   clockwise or counterclockwise direction.

ARM PUSH   With arms bent, hands at shoulders,
                   palms facing upward, push arm up to full
                   extension above head and return. Repeat
                   on other side. This movement can also be
                   done pushing the arms out to the side as
                   well as pushing them down from the
                   shoulders.

ARM REACH   Begin with hands on knees. Lift one arm
                   overhead and return. Repeat on other
                   side.

BLEKING   In this step the feet move simulta-
                   neously. Jut R heel forward either
                   raising heel in the air (Fig. 8.7) or
                   touching heel to floor. As R foot is
                   returning to place, L heel juts forward.
                   As L heel is returning to place, R heel
                   juts forward and the pattern continues
                   for the desired counts. This step is
                   similar to the "Mexican Hat Dance" (La
                   Raspa) step and is done very quickly.

Fig. 8.7 -- Bleking Step

CHARLESTON BASIC   Begin with feet together. Touch ball of
     STEP   R foot forward and return. Touch ball
                        of L foot back and return. (Touch forward
                        may be replaced by a kick.)

CHUG	Knees and feet are together and hands are holding onto sides of chair. With one bounce, feet move diagonally R and return to place and then move diagonally L and return to place.
CLIMB THE ROPE	Imagine a rope hanging overhead. Reach up with R hand, then L hand reaches over R. Continue as if climbing a rope. movement.
CLOG	The clog is made up of a SHUFFLE STEP movement. Brush the ball o the foot on the floor, forward and back (SHUFFLE) and then STEP on the whole foot. Repeat on other side.
CRAMP ROLL	The cue for this step is TOE TOE HEEL HEEL. Step onto R ball of foot (TOE). Step onto L ball of foot (TOE). Press heel of R foot down (HEEL). Press heel of L foot down (HEEL).
CROSS AND HIT	Cross arms at wrist with hands resting on thighs. Uncross hands to hit thighs. Cross wrists to hit opposite thighs.
CUBAN WALK	With feet and knees together begin very short walking steps (R and L) away from chair until legs are extended forward. Then return feet to place with short walking steps alternating R and L feet.
DOUBLE HIT WITH FISTS	Make a fist with R and L hands (thumb side up) in front of chest. Then hit the R fist to the L fist 2 times and then reverse.
ELBOW FLAP	Tuck thumbs under arms and flap elbows vigorously.
FIGURE EIGHTS	Extend arms in front of the body. Moving both arms at the same time in a rolling motion, make horizontal figure eights.
FOOT CIRCLE	Draw a large circle (clockwise) on the floor with the ball of the R foot. Repeat with L foot counter-clockwise.

FRONT TOUCH/ With knees and feet together, slide or
  SIDE TOUCH lift the feet forward and slide or lift
       them back (FRONT TOUCH). Keep knees together
       and separate R and L foot by sliding or
       lifting them out to the R and L sides and
       return to place (SIDE TOUCH). (Fig. 8.8)

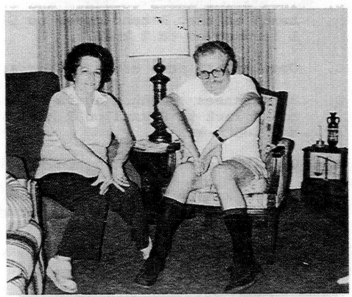

Fig. 8.8 -- Front touch/side touch

HAND CIRCLE   Hold palm of hand flat(as if pressing it
       against a window) and move it in a circular
       motion.

HEEL BOUNCE   With feet and knees together, lift heels
       from floor and bounce them to the rhythm
       of the music.

ISOLATED BOUNCING Isolate body parts (shoulders, head,
       hips, hands, feet, etc.) and bounce them
       to the rhythm of the music. Bounces may
       take the body parts in many directions--
       up, down, side to side, forward and
       backward.

JOG   Holding on to the sides of the chair,
       lift knees and feet and "jog" in place.
       Keep the abdominals contracted and
       support the back.

KNEE EXCHANGE   A continuous pattern moving through
                       parts A - E.

        Part A.   With knees apart, place R hand on R knee
                       and L hand on L knee.

            B.   Then bring knees together and cross
                       hands so that R hand moves to L knee and
                       L hand moves to R knee.

            C.   Open knees (arms are still crossed).

            D.   Bring knees together again and move
                       hands back to R hand on R knee and L
                       hand on L knee.

            E.   Open knees and begin again from Part A.

KNEE SLAP   Slap R knee with both hands and then
                       L knee with both hands. (Feet may be
                       lifted from the floor). (Fig. 8.9)

Fig. 8.9 -- Knee slap

KNEE SWAY   With knees and feet together, place
                       hands on knees and sway knees from side
                       to side. May vary by moving torso in
                       opposition to direction of knees.

OUT OUT/IN IN   With knees and feet together touch R
                       foot out to side (count 1), touch L foot
                       out to side (count 2), return R foot to
                       place (count 3), return L foot to place
                       (count 4).

ROW THE BOAT	Hands are in fists, elbows lifted to sides at shoulder height. Extend arms out in front of body and lean forward from the waist. Return hands and body to starting position and continue pattern in a rowing motion.
SHAKE FEET	Lift feet (or 1 foot at a time) from floor and shake vigorously.
SHOULDER, THIGH HIT	Hit L shoulder with R hand (count 1) Hit R shoulder with L hand (count 2) (arms are now crossed) Hit R thigh with R hand (count 3) Hit L thigh with L hand (count 4)
SLAP, CLAP, SNAP	Slap both knees with hands (R to R and L to L) Clap hands together Snap fingers of both hands simultaneously.
STEP KICK	Step R in place, kick L leg forward. Step L in place, kick R leg forward.
STEP TOUCH	Step sideward R with R foot. Touch ball of L foot by R instep. Reverse to move to L.
TAP DANCE	Participants do their own version of a tap dance.
TOE HEEL	Place weight on ball of R foot. Press down heel of R foot. Repeat to L.
TOE IN, TOE OUT	Place toes of feet together with heels apart (pigeon-toed). Then, place heels together with toes apart (duck-footed).
TORSO SWAY	Moving from the waist or from the hips, sway body side to side or front to back.
TOUCH-SIDE, STEP IN PLACE	Touch R foot out to R side. Return to place. Reverse for L.
WINDSHIELD WIPER	Bend elbows, palms facing away from body with fingers spread. Using elbows as pivot points, move forearms from side to side in a sweeping motion.
WIND THE BOBBIN	With elbows bent and hands (in fists) in front of chest, move the forearms around each other in a winding motion. Reverse the motion.

Chapter **9**

Line, Circle and Group Dances

Chapter 9
Line, Circle and Group Dances

The dance activities in this chapter require a leader. (See Chapter 8 for basic criteria for selecting a leader). The dances presented include adaptations of traditional folk, social and recreational dance forms. Two original choreographed dances have also been included. The use of familiar dance forms can help to make participants feel comfortable and at ease. The music and rhythms may evoke past memories of previous dance experiences that allow many to feel an immediate sense of comfort through recognition.

Until a solid group rapport has been established, it is suggested that line, circle and group dances, rather than partner dances, be presented. These dance forms eliminate the pressure or embarrassment that may often be felt in a one-to-one partner arrangement. However, if available, the use of volunteers or assistants as "escorts" (working arm-in-arm or hand-in-hand) can be a great source of encouragement to the less ambulatory individual who wishes to participate in the walking dances.

Adapting popular social, folk and recreational dances to the needs of the older adult, may involve any or all of the following: adjusting the tempo of the steps executed; altering the dynamics of the arm, torso or foot movements; and limiting or simplifying the number of variations or sequencing patterns. These adaptations need not sacrifice the etiquette of social dance, the style and exuberance that are characteristic of folk dance or the fun and spontaneity that often accompany recreational or party dances. Depending on the abilities of the participants, dances may not have to be modified at all. The basic goal of the dances is to provide opportunities for sharing in the spirit of the dance through the communal experience of moving together.

Once the basic form of the dance has been learned, the introduction of variations will enhance the dance. The participants should be invited to share any variations that they might have learned in their past. If a piano is available, some participants may be willing to play some of the familiar tunes that accompany folk, social and recreational dance forms.

The more traditional dance forms presented in this chapter can serve as a lead-up and foundation for the introduction of expressive group movement. Once the participants are familiar with one another and with the dance steps and patterns, they will be more willing to venture into the exploration of a new dance vocabulary--one that involves elements of improvisation and expressive movement. "Friends" (in the Group section of this chapter) is an example of a dance that incorporates elements of traditional dance with basic contact improvisational designs.

> NOTE: In the following dances, right and
> left will be indicated by "R" and "L."

LINE DANCES

DANCE #1:   "STAYIN' ALIVE" Music from the sound track of "Saturday Night Fever," RSO Records RS-2-4001 or any hustle or disco record.

Formation: Dancers are arranged in lines, all facing the same direction. Hands are not joined. This dance uses a basic "hustle" pattern.

Measures (Meter 4/4)	Patterns
1	Walk backward (R, L, R, L)
2	Walk forward (R, L, R, L)
3	Step Together, Step Touch (Step sidewards R, close L to R, Step sidewards R, Touch L foot to instep of R)
4	Repeat Step Together, Step Touch to L
5	Jump Forward, Jump Backward (Take 2 counts to jump forward and 2 counts to jump back to place)
6	Click Heels together 4 times
7	Touch Front, Touch in Place (Touch R foot front - 2 counts, Touch R foot in place by L heel - 2 counts)
8	Touch Side, Kick/Turn (Touch R foot out to side - 2 counts, execute a 1/4 turn to the L as you kick the R foot across the body to face a new line of direction - 2 counts) Repeat dance until the end of the music. Each 1/4 turn at the end of the dance places the group facing a new line of direction.

DANCE #2:   "WINCHESTER CATHEDRAL" Folkraft F1562 or
              "Nola" Folkraft OT-8151

Formation: Dancers are arranged in lines, all facing the
              same direction. Hands are not joined.

<u>Measures</u> (Meter 4/4)   <u>Patterns</u>

1   Step Close, Step Swing
                           (Step R on R foot, Close L to
                           R, Step R, Swing L leg across
                           in front of R leg and clap
                           once)

2   Repeat to L

3 & 4   Take 8 walking steps in your
                           own small circle (moving
                           clockwise) beginning with R
                           foot or march in place for
                           8 counts.

5 & 6   Repeat measure 1 and 2

7 & 8   SLAP, CLAP, SNAP, TURN

                           Slap knees with both hands
                           twice (2 counts)

                           Clap hands together twice (2
                           counts)

                           Snap fingers of both hands
                           twice (2 counts)

                           With a small jump, make a 1/4
                           turn to the R (2 counts)

Continue the dance facing a new line of direction after each 1/4
turn is done.

DANCE #3:   VIRGINIA REEL* (An adaptation of the traditional
dance). RCA Victor 45-6178

Formation: Contra lines of four couples facing each other.

Pattern	Directions
A	Walk forward R L R L Walk backward R L R L REPEAT
B	R Arm Swing - Couples join R elbows and walk around each other and then return to original places
C	L Arm Swing - Reverse Pattern B
D	Two Handed Swing - Couples join both hands and walk around each other.
E	Do-Sa-Do - Couples move forward towards one another, then pass R shoulders, back-to-back, and then L shoulders returning to their place.
F	Head couple stands side by side holding hands and walks to the foot of the contra line and then walks back to their place at the head of the line (Fig. 9.1)

Fig. 9.1

G

Cast off - Head couple separates and walks down the outside of their side of the contra line to the foot of the line where the couple meets again and forms an arch (Fig. 9.2) with their arms. Each having followed their leader, meet their partner and pass under the arch and walk to the starting formation with the second couple now as lead couple. The former lead couple is now at the foot of the formation. The dance continues until all of the couples have had a chance to be the lead couple.

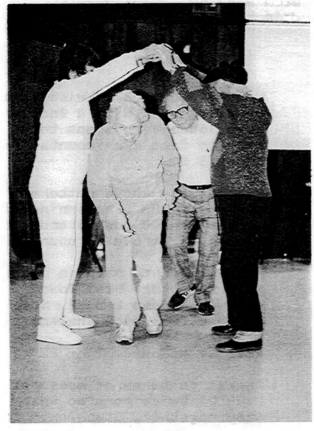

Fig. 9.2

*This adaptation is by Vicki Roitman of the Jewish Community Center of Greater Kansas City and former director of the "Silver Streak Dancers."

CIRCLE DANCES

DANCE #1:   "SAVILA SE BELA LOZA"
            Folkraft 45 rpm 1496x45 B

Formation: Traditionally this Serbian dance is done in a
            line with vigorous running and schottische
            steps. It has been adapted to a slower moving
            circle dance. Join hands and begin moving to
            the R.

<u>Measures</u> (Meter 2/4)   <u>Patterns</u>

   1 - 10   Moving counterclockwise in the
                                  circle, begin with R foot and
                                  take 16 walking steps then
                                  turn to face L on counts 17-20.
                                  (Fig. 9.3)

  11 - 20   Reverse the above pattern
                                  moving to the L beginning with
                                  L foot for 16 counts and face
                                  center of circle on count 17-20.

  21 - 22   Moving side to side in place,
                                  Step together, Step Touch
                                  (Step R, Close L to R, Step R,
                                  Touch L foot by R instep).

  23 - 24   Reverse measures 21 - 22 to L

  25 - 32   Repeat patterns of measures
                                  21 - 24 twice more so that
                                  Step together, Step Touch to
                                  the R and to the L is executed
                                  3 times in all.

     Keep repeating patterns of measures 1 - 32 until
     the end of the music.

Fig. 9.3

DANCE #2:   "I DON'T WANT TO WALK WITHOUT YOU'
             Barry Manilow, Paramount Records 45 rpm
             AS 0501 - SA

Formation: Dancers join hands in a circle and begin moving
             to R.

<u>Measures</u> (Meter 4/4)	<u>Patterns</u>
Introduction	Sway together in place
1 - 4	Take 15 Steps to R beginning with R foot (or if working with dancers that are less ambulatory - take 2 counts for each step, 8 walks in all). Turn to face L on count 16
5 - 8	Reverse to L for 15 counts Face center on count 16
9 & 10	Everyone walk forward into center of circle (8 counts) with arms leading upward beginning on R foot.
11 & 12	Sway 4 times in place (8 counts)
13 & 14	Walk backward to outside of circle lowering arms (8 counts) Begin on R foot.
15 & 16	Sway 4 times (8 counts)
17 - 24	Repeat patterns of measures #1-8
25 - 28	Drop hands, walk away from circle (8 counts). Return to circle (8 counts). Encourage participants to add arm or body gestures as they walk. Begin each part with R foot.
29 - 32	8 Step kicks in place (16 counts) Begin stepping with R foot and kick L foot into center of circle. Then step L and kick R foot into circle. Alternate for 8 step kicks in all.

Repeat entire dance beginning with sways and continuing through measures 1 - 16. The leader then creates an open circle by dropping the hand of the person to his/her right and moves in weaving patterns leading the group around the room in a serpentine design (Fig. 9.4) until the end of the music. Encourage participants to make eye contact with one another as they pass during the weaving segment of this dance.

Fig. 9.4

DANCE #3:   "PLJESKAVAC KOLO" Folkraft 1548

This dance is an adaptation of the traditional "Pljeskavac Kolo" using walking steps rather than step hops.

Formation: Form a circle with the hands joined and held down at sides. The circle moves counterclockwise.

Dancers should do a small bounce with each walking step to add to the style of this Yugoslavian dance.

<u>Measures</u> (Meter 4/4)   <u>Patterns</u>

PART A

1 - 2	Beginning with the R foot. Take 2 walking steps (slow, slow) then do 3 walking steps (quick, quick, slow)
3 - 4	Repeat measures #1 and 2 beginning with L foot
5 - 8	Repeat patterns of measures #1 - 4

PART B

1 - 2	Beginning with the R foot. Walk into the center of the circle with 2 walking steps (slow, slow) then do 3 stamping steps (quick, quick, slow).
3 - 4	Beginning with the L foot, walk backwards away from the center of circle with 2 walks (slow, slow) and then do 3 claps in place (quick, quick, slow).
5 - 8	Repeat patterns of measures #1 - 4

Repeat Parts A and B until the end of the dance.

DANCE #4: "BIRDIE DANCE" Fun Dance UR3397 from Dance Record Distributors

This dance was introduced by Malcom Davis at the 31st National Square Dance Convention.

Formation: Form an open circle or a square. This dance can also be done with dancers scattered randomly in the room.

PART A

1.   With your forearms up and hands facing another, make a bird's beak with your fingers. (open and close the hands, touching fingers to thumbs), three times.

2.   With your arms in bird wing position, (thumbs under or near your armpits and elbows lifted), flap your "wings" three times.

3.   Bend your knees and shake your "tail feathers" (wiggle your hips) three times.

4.   Clap your hands three times.

Repeat Part A three times.

PART B

Execute a right hand star or a right elbow swing with a partner turning for eight steps, and then reverse with a left hand star or swing for eight steps. Repeat this sequence twice and then go back to PART A.

OR

You may wish to make up your own steps to PART B.

The entire Birdie Song is repeated three and a half times until the final "Cheep."

GROUP DANCES

DANCE #1:   "JESSIE POLKA" Folkraft 1093 or any good polka.
             Adapted from the traditional dance.

Formation: Groups of 2's, 3's or 4's randomly scattered.
             Dancers in each group stand side by side holding
             hands or with arms around each other's waists.
             Groups may move counterclockwise around the room. If
             groups are skilled enough, they may move in any
             direction paying close attention to others moving in
             the space and making adjustments in the size of their
             step patterns to avoid collisions.

<u>Measures</u> (Meter 2/4)   <u>Patterns</u>

1   HEEL, STEP
                          (Beginning with L foot, touch
                          heel in front, then return L foot
                          to place)

2   HEEL, STEP (Fig. 9.5)
                          (Repeat measure #1 on R foot)

3   TOE, STEP
                          (Touch L toe to the back, then
                          return L foot to place)

4   TOE, STEP
                          (Repeat measure #3 on R foot)

5   POLKA STEP (Hop R, step L forward,
                          close R to L, step forward L).

6   Repeat Measure #5 beginning hop on L

7 - 8   Repeat patterns of measures 5 and
                          6 (4 polka steps in all, moving
                          forward). Continue patterns until
                          the end of the music.

                          Fig. 9.5

DANCE #2:   "FRIENDS" Recorded by Bette Midler
             Atlantic 45 rpm (45-2980)

This dance incorporates walking patterns with some
contact improvisational experiences.

Formation: The dancers take a space on the floor focusing in any
            direction they choose.   They move slowly in place
            (sways, bends, stretches, arm gestures) with the
            introduction of the music.   Dancers are encouraged to
            explore the space above, below and immediately around
            them.

When the tempo of the music picks up, they begin
moving through the entire space of the activity area
guided by the leader calling the following directions:

1. Make eye contact with everyone in the room as you
    walk through the space.

2. Move to a person and gently make contact with that
    person. (Contact may be made with any body part--a
    hand, an elbow, a hip, the head, a leg, etc.)

3. Move away from that person and walk in the space.
    Be aware of the people around you.

4. Move to another person and make contact. Stay
    connected and continue to walk with the rhythm of
    the music.

5. Disconnect and continue to walk in the space.

6. Move to another person. Make a connection.

7. Stay connected and move to another connected pair.
    Join with them so that 4 people are connected and
    moving.

8. Move your group in a circle. Move your group
    sideways without becoming disconnected.

9. Break away and move individually to the music. Let
    your hand lead you around the room as it moves
    rhythmically with the music.

10. Follow your hand into a large circle and connect it
    to another person's hand.

11. Hug the person on either side of you.

12. Join hands in a large circle and walk into center
    of the circle to end the dance in a tight cluster.

Before doing this dance, it is a good idea to talk with the participants about the kinds of movements they will be asked to do and to demonstrate ways of making gentle contact and connections.

A traditional pioneer dance performed by the Sod Busters of Council Bluffs, Iowa

Chapter **10**

Expressive Movement and Improvisational Activities

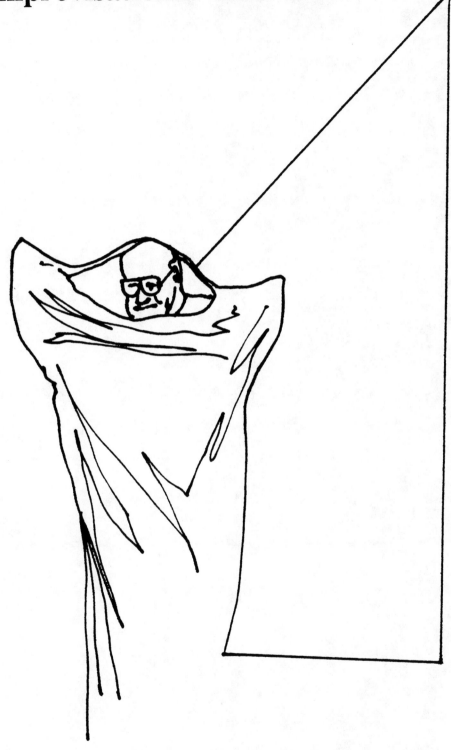

Chapter 10
Expressive Movement and Improvisational Activities

This chapter presents expressive movement and improvisational activities that can lead participants to discover their own body's natural and unique movement style. In addition to providing opportunities for older adults to bring their life experiences and emotions to the movements, improvisational and expressive dance activities offer the following benefits:

Benefits

1. **They may be the first chance for creative experiences since childhood.** As observed by expressive arts consultant Edward Lilley, we live in an age where we do not get "social credit" for expressing ourselves. Our "muscles" of expression are disappearing. Perhaps it is time to get back into the language of the body and remove the social presssure of communicating only through words. We need to use the body in non-verbal communication. Through dance, it may be possible to discover that we possess a wider range of expression than we thought we ever had.

2. **No matter what age, we can all benefit from interaction with others.** Expressive movement and improvisational activities can allow us to share a past experience, a present feeling or a future desire. Movement interaction can help us to better relate to one another--to find common ground for social interaction and mutual support.

3. **Expressive movement for older adults helps to promote self-esteem by providing a worthwhile activity**. Sometimes the loss of a job or meaningful responsibilities can create stress and cause depresssion or anxiety. The positive feelings that often accompany a dance experience can assist individuals in improving their attitude and outlook, thus making life seem worthwhile. Dance can help motivate people away from sedentary life.

4. **Observing dance movements allows us to look at things in many different ways**. By watching different movement interpretations on the same theme, we learn to see other points of view. Group improvisational activities can be a microcosm of the problems of the world, of living and working together in society. A group improv-

isational study can teach us to tolerate other points of view and to observe without being judgmental.

5.   <u>Participation in group improvisation can help to improve older adults' self-image by helping them to feel needed within the group</u>. Too often the older adult adopts the image that society has of older people, i.e., frail, inept, inactive. Through observing one another doing expresssive movements, the discovery is made that older persons, as well as young people, have a living, moving, expressive body that has the ability and power to create and stimulate. There is a great deal of energy and excitement generated in group movement activities.

6.   <u>Through improvisation and expressive movement, we can rediscover the joy of moving merely for the sake of moving</u>. Movement is basic to all humans. When executing a satisfying movement, we feel emotional as well as physical exhilaration.

Leadership

It should be noted that the leader of expressive and improvisational movement activities does not need to be a dance educator or a dance therapist in order for participants to derive some or all of the benefits listed above. Although these professionals are the preferred leaders, it is certainly possible that a lay person with a dance background can effectively lead the activities described in this chapter.

Following are some leadership suggestions:

General Guidelines for Leading Expressive Movement and Improvisational Activities

1.   Introduce improvisational activities <u>gradually</u> into the dance sessions. Participants will be more willing to express themselves through creative movement after they have experienced success with familiar dance forms such as those presented in Chapters 8 and 9. Their involvement with structured dances will provide a vocabulary of movement that they can draw from when asked to improvise or express themselves.

2.   Begin improvisational activities <u>en masse</u> or in relatively large groups so that individuals who may feel shy or embarrassed will feel secure because of the the anonymity inherent in a group arrangement. The leader should plan to be a participant in at least some of the activities.

3. Frequently remind participants that there is no right or wrong way to respond. Encourage them to focus on the enjoyment of the movement without worrying about technique.

4. Be advised that not all participants will be immediately responsive. Some may need more time than others to feel comfortable in expressive activities. Suggesting that movements be explored with eyes closed, may put some at ease.

5. It needs to be pointed out that improvisation is a skill that involves learning to break down barriers that restrict free movement. It takes time and effort and there is no set formula.

6. Encourage participants to try new ways of moving without falling back on established patterns that they have previously tried. Urge them to give in to their movement impulses and not to imitate others or become too "literal" (non-imaginative) with their movements or gestures. Be adventurous!

7. Many participants will try to predict what sequence their movements will take. Discourage advance planning as it may destroy the spontaneity of the movement.

8. The exact format of the expressive movement or improvisational activity may happen out of the situation. It cannot be predicted. The leader should prepare an outline or a list of movement questions that will be used to guide the activity. For example, lead the participants through the activity by providing a focus with such phrases as "Have you tried moving in a new direction? On a Different level? At a different tempo?" Call upon modern dance techniques for guidance in creating movement, problems, studies, challenges. (See the resources at the end of this chapter).

9. Do not ask participants do "Do your own thing." Most people will feel self-conscious and at a loss.

10. Most importantly, try to create a non-threatening atmosphere where each person is accepted regardless of ability and experience. Make it clear that each person makes a unique contribution to the dance by participating at his or her own level. Be supportive and have fun!

Activities

The resources for expressive movement or improvisational activities are unlimited. They may include a specific movement problem, a study with a theme, a free form dance to music, a movement to poetry or a sequence with props.

The following suggested activities are divided into three categories:

1. Exploring and Discovering - Introductory activities that present basic elements of modern dance and development of self and group awareness.

2. Shapes - Activities that foster individual improvisation and group expressive movement studies with shapes.

3. Wordplay and Poetry - Activities that allow the participants to use words and imagery as motivation for expresssive movement.

If some older adults are hesitant to participate in any of the following activities, the leader may suggest modifications or the leader may encourage the individual to be an active observer helping to comment on or direct some of the group activities.

EXPLORING AND DISCOVERING: CONTRACTIONS AND EXTENSIONS

1. As part of an exercise or dance session warm-up, include contractions and extensions of the whole body and of body parts as a starting point for expresssive movement.

    A. Begin by sitting in chairs and using sustained (slow motion) movements.

    B. Ask participants to stretch and extend the body parts away from the center of the body (extension) (Fig. 10.1) and then bring the body parts together, i.e., an arm to a leg, head to knee, etc. (contraction) (Fig. 10.2).

    C. Repeat slow contraction and extension movements until arms, legs and torso have been adequately warmed-up.

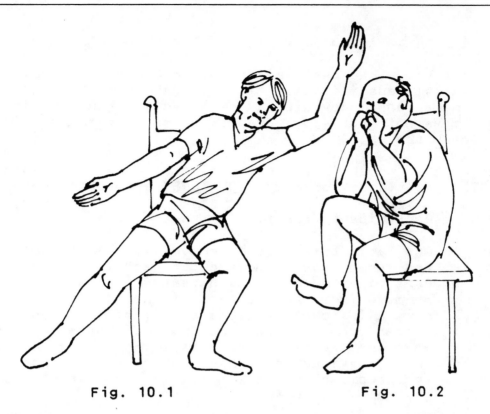

Fig. 10.1   Fig. 10.2

Initially, it may be helpful if the leader demonstrates a contraction and extension and then the participants "echo" those movements while the leader watches.

Another format that is effective is to direct the group to "follow along" and imitate what the leader is doing as he or she executes the motions. (See mirroring in this chapter).

To add variety and expressive elements to this activity, vary the dynamics (the flow of energy) of the movement. For example ask: Can you do contractions and extensions as if you were moving underwater? Try executing the movements as if you were in outer space without the force of gravity. Can you do the movements as you would if you were very tired? Very bored? Very strong and energetic?

This last question can be used to introduce percussive (striking, sharp, clear, strong) movement quality. Exploring the different amounts of force involved in percussive contractions and extensions will add variety and a better understanding of dynamics and energy flow.

CAUTION: Be sure that there is adequate space between the chairs to allow for safe, unhampered movement exploration.

Parts or all of this activity can also be done while standing. Whether sitting or standing, other elements of dance such as level, focus, space, shape, and time can be incorporated gradually into the movement sequences.

EXPLORING AND DISCOVERING: BODY SIGNATURES

This activity has been well-received by older adults of various physical capabilities. It helps everyone to learn one another's name and provides a relatively non-intimidating expressive movement activity even for persons with a limited movement vocabulary.

Arrange the group in a large circle so that everyone is visible. The directions for <u>BODY SIGNATURES</u> are as follows:

Formation: Participants are sitting in a circle.

Directions: One at a time, each person says his or her name and then does a movement to accompany the name. Participants can remain seated or they can stand or move from their chairs. The signatures can be a small movement like a tilt of the head or a large movement like punching into space or even no movement at all -- just assuming a pose. After the individual says his or her name and has done the accompanying movememt, all participants repeat the name and motion.

The above activity continues around the circle in a counterclockwise (CCW) pattern until all participants have created a movement for their name with the group immediately echoing the individual's name and body signature.

Because this activity will challenge the memories of all participants, it is helpful to frequently review names and motions. This can be done after every three names or you can start from the first person and review everyone's name and signature before each new person presents his or her name and movement.

Several variations that can be tried to further challenge the group follow:

1. After going around the circle CCW, reverse and do the names and signatures in a CW pattern.

2. Try the movements CCW and then CW without saying the names. Use only the movements.

3. Add music to #2 variation. "Moonlight Serenade" and "Pachebel Canon" work well.

4. Instead of using names and signatures, use a gesture or motion that indicates a profession, a hobby or specific task that is or was a part of the participant's life.

In Body Signatures, each person has a chance to make a creative contribution to the completed piece of choreography.

EXPLORING AND DISCOVERING: MIRRORING

The following improvisational activities help the beginner to develop new patterns of movement, to expand his or her expressive dance vocabulary, and to develop his or her awareness of others. These activities may be done with or without musical accompaniment.

#1 GROUP MIRRORING

Formation: The participants are sitting or standing, depending on their individual needs. They are scattered in front of the leader so that all have a clear view of the leader.

Directions: The leader uses professional right and left. (If the leader is facing the group, he or she will demonstrate with the R arm if he or she wants the group to move with the L arm). The leader tries to incorporate the use of many levels and a variety of contractions and extensions as he or she moves in a continuous sequence. The group tries to follow.

Remind those participants with physical limitations that they should feel free to modify the movements done by the leader.

#2 PARTNER MIRRORING (No Contact)

Formation: Partners should be sitting or standing face-to-face.

Directions: One person in each pair will be the initial leader and the other will follow. Encourage "leaders" to move slowly and continuously and to explore the space in front of them, to the sides, and overhead using different levels. "Followers" try to exactly imitate the movements done by their partner. After a few minutes, change leading and following roles.

In each activity described above, it is important that the movement of the leader be slowly and clearly stated so that it can be effectively followed without confusion.

#3 PARTNER MIRRORING: (Fingertip Contact)

Formation: Partners should be sitting or standing face-to-face.

Directions: Partners start with their hands at shoulder height, with fingers spread. They maintain a <u>very light</u> and <u>gentle fingertip contact</u> throughout the movement. <u>There is no leader or follower</u>. They try to move in harmony

allowing the movement to initiate from the
shared energy of their contact.   Eyes may be
closed.

Fig. 10.3

This activity always delights and amazes the participants in
that they can move so well together without any advanced
planning. (Fig. 10.3).

EXPLORING AND DISCOVERING: SMALL GROUP DANCES

DANCE #1

Formation: Small groups of 3-5 people are seated in
various arrangements--

```
   X X          X X          X          X          X X
    X            X          X X          X          X   X
                X X          X X          X            X
                                          X
                                          X
```

Directions: All groups are instructed to create a movement
phrase such as:

CONTRACT for 4 counts

EXTEND for 4 counts   Executed very
                           slowly (sustained)

CONTRACT for 4 counts

EXTEND for 1 count   Executed very
                           strongly (percussive)
EXTEND for 1

The group should move in unison once it has cooperatively decided on its motions. After each group has an opportunity to demonstrate its "dance," then a discussion follows regarding the <u>variety</u> of shapes and levels and motions used by each group even though all participants were given the <u>same</u> instructions. These observations are valuable for increasing the participants' awareness of movement possibilities.

Variation: Once each group has choreographed its movement pattern, ask the participants to provide sounds to accompany its dance. (Sounds can range from "oohhs" and "aahhs," to humming, to using instruments or body parts to create accompaniment).

DANCE #2

Formation: Each small group should be in a circle or in various arrangements as in DANCE #1.

Directions: Within every group, each person creates a movement and teaches it to the others in his or her group. All the individual movements are then put together to create a movement phrase. Each group must decide the order of the movements. Smooth transitions should be discussed and encouraged. Each group will execute the movements in the planned order and then reverse the order to complete its movement phrase. After each group has rehearsed its movement phrase then all group phrases are put together in the following way to create a dance.

Group 1 performs its phrase forward and backwards. As they finish the last movement, Group 2 begins its movement phrase, and so on around the room until all groups have contributed. If music is being used, the groups may keep alternating and repeating their phrases until the end of the song.

SHAPES

The following ideas may be used to explore shapes using sounds, props, and pictures.

SHAPES/SLIDE WHISTLE DANCE

Participants should be seated. The leader plays the slide whistle. As participants hear the crescendos and decrescendos of

the instrument, they move into shapes that reflect a gradual
rising and falling. This activity can be done sitting, or
standing, using a chair or support. If the participants' range
of whole body movements is limited, ask them to move to the sound
making different shapes using only a single body part or two body
parts. In addition to the rising and falling sounds, short
musical pieces for participants to dance to may be improvised by
the leader on the slide whistle.

SHAPES: STRETCH BAG DANCE*

Using "stretch bags," four to six participants assume a
starting pose at a level of their choice. (Fig. 10.4). Everyone
else slowly and deliberately chants the words "change your shape,
change your shape." Those in the stretch bags improvise, finding
ways to shape and reshape their contours to the rhythm of the
chant. After a few minutes of the "change your shape, " the
dancers hold their last shape for a few moments before relaxing.
The images that were evoked by the changing shapes are then
discussed by the group.

For safety there should be volunteers or assistants to
escort and move with the people in the bags so that they feel
secure.

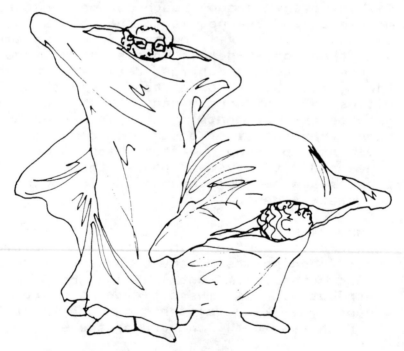

Fig. 10.4

*A "stretch bag" is made from two rectangular
pieces of stretch fabric (jersey, milliskin, etc.)
sewn together on three sides with an opening either
for the head or for the feet. The fabric is cut
large enough so that there is enough stretch in the
material for an average size adult to extend his or
her arms overhead.

SHAPES: SHAPES IN MOTION

Use Fig. 10.5 for the basis of this movement study of "shapes in motion." Arrange participants into small groups (3-5 people) and ask them to select 4 poses for their group. They will find many creative ways to adapt some of the seemingly impossible poses. After selecting the poses, they create a dance using simple transitions such as walking, turning, or twisting to move from one position to the next. Each group should have the opportunity to perform while the others observe.

VARIATIONS:

1. Once the group members have established its movement sequence, ask them to provide a <u>sound</u> to accompany its dance.

2. Ask each group to add the element of <u>focus</u> to its movement study.

Fig. 10.5 -- Shapes in Motion

3.   Before selecting the poses, have each group select an <u>emotion</u> that will be portrayed by the poses.   Emphasize that not only should the participants' bodies reflect the emotion but their facial expressions should, too.

A discussion should follow each presentation, i.e., what movement problems did you experience with the poses? With the transitions? Provide suggestions and solutions. What did you like or dislike about the dance study?

SHAPES: DESIGNS WITH RIBBONS

Each participant holds a crepe paper streamer or ribbon (about 3-7 feet long) in one hand.   Initially, the participants should be seated and then as the activity progresses they may stand and move through the space.   Direct them to discover ways of designing shapes in space with the ribbons.   The ribbons should be moving continuously, Provide suggestions such as:

1.   Write you name in space.

2.   Make figure eights.

3.   Find as many ways as you can to create a spiral shape.

4.   Change the ribbon from hand to hand while it is moving.

5.   Relate your ribbon movements to another person's ribbon movements.

It is fun to watch the movement of the brightly colored ribbons.   Divide the group in half and have each sub-group take turns observing and discussing the colors, designs, and shapes of the other sub-group.   Some common images that are usually mentioned include: kites flying, wind blowing, tornadoes, ticker tape parades, trees in the wind, celebrations, snakes, birds flying, and fish swimming. Some of these images may provide ideas for future movement studies.

VARIATIONS:

1.   Move with a ribbon in each hand.

2.   Have two people hold onto one ribbon and explore the ways they can move together, always maintaining contact with the ribbon.

SHAPES: GREAT MOMENT MONUMENT

This small group (4-6 people) activity involves "building a monument" to great moments in their lives. Before this activity is included in a dance session, the participants should have had many opportunities to discover how to make shapes and move through space, integrating focus and levels.

Each person in the group is asked to recall a great moment in his or her life. Perhaps it was a time when they had to take a stand on an issue, perhaps the birth of a first child, or a son or husband coming home from war. The participants are asked to share one great event from their life's journey.

This moment is to be portrayed by a single gesture or pose that for them reflects the event. Each person in the small group discusses his or her great moment and then decides on a pose. (Some people may prefer to help another member of the group express his or her great moment).

The next step is to put all of the great moments of each group into a monument. The members of each group arrange themselves into an interesting statue. They are reminded that their monument will be observed from the front, sides, and back.

Some participants may experience difficulty in expressing their great moment with a single gesture or pose. Asking them to think about the following questions may give them inspiration for this expresssive challenge:

1. What were your feelings during this event? What were you thinking about?

2. Should your pose reflect a sense of strength, sadness, excitement, or fear?

3. Should you be sitting, standing, or supported by others?

Each monument should be observed and discussed by the other groups. After walking around and discussing their thoughts on the monument, time should be reserved for each member of the monument to briefly share his or her moment with everyone.

This activity will usually produce a very literal interpretation of the great moment. As participants progress through more experiences with expressive dance and improvisational activities, the leader can guide them to abstract the idea or stylize the movement of their character or their event, so that the gesture or pose is extended into the realm of dance.

Liz Lerman, director of the Washington, D.C. based older adult dance troupe, "Dancers of the Third Age," uses an excellent activity that provides another way for older adults to share their life stories. She guides them to create "scripts" that are used for making dances about people's lives. In this activity, the stories for the scripts may come from real life, from books or they may be fantasized. Dancers are asked to select the key actions and gestures that will tell the story and then to create short dance phrases that can be connected to illustate the story.

After these dances are performed, observers are given an opportunity to discuss the dance, including some specific things that they especially liked about the dancer's movement. This positive reinforcement from others helps the individual to feel less inhibited in expressing his or her ideas through dance.

WORDPLAY AND POETRY

The use of words and poetry can be very effective sources for dance studies. Following are a few activities for improvisation using nonsense words and descriptive words plus two examples of expressive movement using poetry.

WORDS: NONSENSE DANCE

A selection of nonsense words are printed in large letters on 4" X 6" cards. Each group selects a word and then creates movements to accompany the word. As the dancers move, they repeat the word at least three times. Following are suggestions for nonsense words:

snickersnee	fiddle-di-dee
scrumpdillyishus	lickety-split
supercalifragilisticexpialidosius	jiggetty-jog
drumblehum	corlimbled
binlimular	strombulous

WORDS: ADJECTIVE DANCE

Participants are requested to bring an object to the dance session. As each person describes his or her object, the adjectives are written down. From this list of words, partners or small groups select six words and compose a movement for each word. When presenting this study, the participants say the word, perform the movement, and then walk for a few steps before saying the next word. Here are a few examples of words that have been used:

cuddly	ugly	smooth	slick
delicate	sharp	moist	heavy
lumpy	floppy	soft	warm
cool	squishy	skinny	bristly

POETRY: HAIKU DANCE

The use of expressive movement with Haiku poetry has proven to be a soothing, peaceful experience. It has been especially successful with older adults in nursing homes who have had limited exposure to movement activity of any kind.

Haiku (pronounced hi-coo) is an ancient form of Japanese poetry. The subject matter is usually about some aspect of nature or about humans in their relationship to nature. The poet expects the readers to use their imaginations and feelings to find meanings of the poems. The poems contain many beautiful moods and ideas and therefore, serve as an excellent basis for slow, graceful, expressive movements.

When interpreting Haiku poetry through movement, the leader may wish to create two or three motions to express the whole poem and then teach both the poem and movements to the group. Then the leader can print several pieces of Haiku on 4" X 6" cards and allow individuals or small groups to select one for interpretation.

Following are some examples of traditional Haiku poetry:

> The song of the bird!
> But the plum-tree in the grove
> Is not yet blooming.
> > Issa

> The Great Morning:
> Winds of long ago
> Blow through the pine tree.
> > Onitsura

> The moon beginning to fall
> On four or five people,
> Dancing!
> > Buson

POETRY: "DESIDERATA"

There are many poems that are suitable for expressive movement. "Desiderata" is especially appropriate for older adults because of its content, some of which deals with the wisdom of elders and the graceful surrendering of youth.

The activity should begin with the leader reading the entire poem to the group. Then the group is divided into seven smaller groups and each receives a paragraph of the poem to interpret through expressive movement.

Each section of the poem should be clearly printed on a large card. The groups discuss the meaning of their part of the poem and then create movements that express that meaning.

It should be pointed out to the groups that there are several ways of interpreting poetry through movement:

1. The movement can simultaneously accompany the words.

2.   The movement can be performed after a few words or
      a phrase has been read.

3.   The entire poem can be read and then the movement
      can follow as an interpretation to the complete
      thought behind the poem.

The leader should designate which form is to be followed so
that there is some continuity when the seven parts of the poem
are put together. If the poem seems too lengthy for a particular
group then the leader might excerpt certain parts of "Desiderata"
or decide to choreograph some of the parts and then teach them to
the group in unison.   Someone needs to serve as a narrator for
each section. This might be the leader or someone within each of
the small groups.

Following is the poem "Desiderata":

This poem is thought to have been written in the 16th or
17th century.   It was found in an old church in London, England
by Max Ehrmann in 1927.

DESIDERATA

Go placidly amidst the noise and haste, and remember what
peace there may be in silence.   As far as possible without
surrender be on good terms with all persons.   Speak your truth
quietly and clearly: And listen to others, even the dull and
ignorant: They too have their story.
Avoid loud and aggressive persons, they are vexations to the
spirit. If you compare yourself with others, you may become vain
and bitter; for always there will be greater and lesser persons
than yourself. Enjoy you achievements as well as your plans.

Keep interested in your own career, however humble; it is a
real possession in the changing fortunes of time.   Exercise
caution in your business affairs; for the world is full of
trickery.   But let this not blind you to what virtue there is;
many persons strive for high ideals; and everywhere life is full
of heroism.

Be yourself, especially, do not feign affection. Neither be
cynical about love; for in the face of all aridity and
disenchantment it is perennial as the grass.

Take kindly the counsel of years, gracefully surrendering
the things of youth. Nurture strength of spirit to shield you in
sudden misfortune. But do not distress yourself with imaginings.
Many fears are born of fatigue and loneliness.   Beyond a
wholesome discipline, be gentle with yourself.

You are a child of the universe, no less than the trees and
the stars; you have a right to be here. And whether or not it is
clear to you, no doubt the universe is unfolding as it should.

Therefore be at peace with God, whatever you conceive him to be, and whatever your labors and aspirations, in the noisy confusion of life keep peace with your soul.

With all its sham, drudgery and broken dreams, it is still a beautiful world. Be careful. Strive to be happy.

Resources

Beal, R.K. & Berryman-Miller, S.(Eds.). (1988). <u>Dance for the older adult</u>. Reston, VA: American Alliance for Health, Physical Education, Recreation, and Dance.

Caplow-Lindner, E., Harpaz, L. & Samberg, S. (1979). <u>Dance/movement: Expressive activities for adults</u>. New York: Human Sciences Press.

Lerman, L. (1984). <u>Teaching dance to senior adults</u>. Springield, IL: Charles C. Thomas.

Lockhart, A. & Pease, E. (1982). <u>Modern dance: Building and teaching lessons</u>. Dubuque, IA: Wm. C. Brown.

Minton, S. (1986). <u>Choreography: A basic approach to using improvisation</u>. Champaign, IL: Human Kinetics.

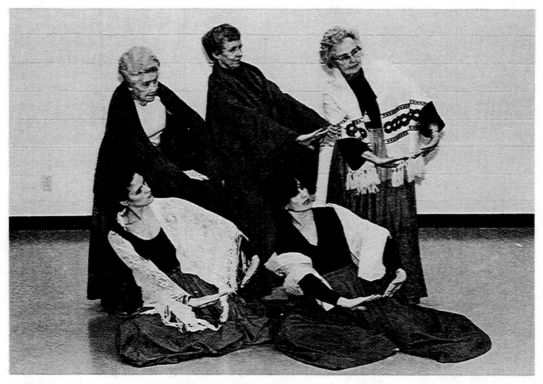

An Intergenerational Dance

Water Exercise
(by Vicki Roitman)

Vicki Roitman is the Sports and Fitness Director at the Jewish Community Center of Greater Kansas City. She directed the Aqua Therapy program at the Center for three years.

Photos in the chapter by Vicki Roitman

Chapter 11
Water Exercise
(by Vicki Roitman)

Introduction to Water Exercise

Water exercise, also known as hydro-aerobics, aqua-fitness, aqua-aerobics, etc. is a combination of exercises using the water as resistance to increase or maintain fitness. A series of movements are choreographed to music and cued by an instructor from the pool deck or in the water. Participants perform these exercises for 45-60 minutes in waist to shoulder depth water. Swimming skills are not required and almost everyone becomes comfortable in the water after a few sessions.

Benefits of Water Exercise

The benefits of a water exercise program can be the same as almost any other exercise program. By using the principles of proper flexibility, muscular strength and endurance, and cardiovascular endurance exercises, benefits can be achieved by participating regularly in a class of this type.

Additional benefits specific to exercise in water can also be gained. Water provides buoyancy for most people and will relieve some of the stress and strain of exercise on land where gravity is a greater influence. This can be especially beneficial to those with orthopedic problems in the lower extremities (legs, knees, and ankles), to those with weight problems that may prohibit vigorous exercise on land, and to those with arthritis, for whom movement may be irritating or painful. Body weight in water is less than 10% of its weight on land. The buoyant effect of the water allows for low-impact exercise.

If the temperature of the water is warm enough it will allow greater range of motion since muscles stretch better when they are warm. This is beneficial for people with arthritis, for those who have had joint replacement (knee or hip) and for post-mastectomy patients where range of motion in the shoulder joint may be a problem.

The social interaction common to most water exercise programs is another benefit. Increased self-esteem and decreased depression are also common outcomes of such programs.

Guidelines for Participating in or Leading a Water Exercise Program

1. Water temperature of the pool should be approximately 82-86 degrees F. Heart rate response to exercise depends on water temperature. It is difficult for the body to cool itself in high water temperatures and cooler water makes it difficult to maintain a normal body temperature. Participants with limited joint range of motion or arthritics require warmer temperatures.

2. Exercises should be performed in water depths of 4-6 feet (depending on the participant's height) for best use of the resistance of the water when exercising. The water surrounding the specific muscle group provides the opportunity for maximum resistance. Keeping the arms in the water helps with balance and direction changes as well as maintenance of buoyancy.

3. Movements should work all major muscle groups and allow opposing muscle groups to be exercised. This provides for proper muscle balance and development.

4. It is important to drink adequate fluid both before and after exercising in the water. Sweating does occur in the water but it is difficult to detect while submerged in the water.

5. Movements should be taught and performed at a low intensity level. Participants can individually adjust the resistance fo each exercise by increasing or decreasing the speed of a particular movement.

6. The use of target heart rate may be useful for determining the appropriate pace and for achieving cardiovascular benefits from water exercise. (See Chapter 5 for target heart rate information). Because of the hydrostatic pressure while in the water heart rates will not get as high as doing similar activities on land. For this reason aerobic exercises need only reach the lower limits of the target heart zone.

7. The cushioning effect of the water (buoyancy) allows for safe jumping and jogging without undue stress on the joints. Adding this type of movement will help keep heart rates at target levels.

8. Non-swimmers and participants who are uncomfortable in the water should be encouraged to exercise near the pool wall and should be permitted to hold onto the railing or gutter at the side of the pool.

9. Exercises should always be discontinued if pain, dizziness, or breathlessness develops. Participants should be advised to seek medical advice before continuing.

Designing a Water Exercise Program

A water exercise program should include stretching and range of motion of the major muscle groups and joints. An aerobic component is included to enhance cardiovascular conditioning. The remainder of the class is devoted to additional muscle-specific exercises as part of a cool down routine. The music should be in tempo with the activities being performed. Depending on the fitness level of the participant, other modes of water exercise may be incorporated into the session for variety.

A sample program follows:

1. Warm-up (10-15 minutes): Warm-up exercises raise the temperture of the muscles and the joints and slowly increase heart rate toward target levels. Exercises should begin at the shoulders and work toward the legs.

2. Aerobic conditioning (15-20 minutes): Continuous movement is sustained to maintain target heart rate. Movements should be repeated quickly using the resistance of the water. Large muscle groups of the arms, legs and torso should be used continuously for best results. If the group is very unfit this session should be much shorter initially and gradually the duration should be increased over a period of several months. If high intensity exercises cause for a high dropout rate, then ease off. As mentioned in Chapter 3, low intensity exercises can still be beneficial. It is better to exercise at a low level than to not exercise at a high level.

3. Cool down (5-10 minutes): Less vigorous, slower movements are used to return heart rate back to a normal level. Exercises should focus on stretching of the leg muscles.

4. Specialized exercises (10-15 minutes): Other modes of water exercises may be introduced for participants who wish an additional or advanced workout.

The exercises that follow are examples of those used in a typical exercise class. Follow the sample program described above and combine these and other exercises into a complete program. The resources listed at the end of this section will assist in finding a greater variety of exercises.

<u>Exercises</u> <u>for</u> <u>the</u> <u>arms</u> <u>(with</u> <u>arms</u> <u>and</u> <u>shoulders</u> <u>in</u> <u>the</u> <u>water):</u>

1. Push and pull. Extend both arms in front of the body just at surface level (elbows straight). Place the palms down and push downward against the water until arms are extended behind the body. Turn the palms up and return arms to the beginning position. Repeat 5-10 times. Work for a good range of motion in the shoulder joint. Pushing against the resistance of the water with your palms is required. (Fig. 11.1).

Fig. 11.1

Fig. 11.2

Fig. 11.3

2. Big Birds.   Begin with the arms extended down at
    side.   Turn the palms to face outward; bring the
    arms away from the body to the surface forming a
    "T" position.   Turn the palms downward and push
    against the water returning to the beginning
    position.   Repeat 5-10 times.   Push the water on
    the way up and back to the starting position (Fig.
    11.2).

    Little birds.   Extend both arms in front to the
    water level (elbows straight). With the palms
    facing downward flutter the arms up and down
    quickly.   Repeat 5-10 with palms facing down and 5-
    10 times with the palms facing up (Fig. 11.3).

3. Door Knobs.   Extend the arms (elbows straight) in
    front of the body.   The hands imitate grasping a
    door knob.   Turn the wrists and arms quickly back
    and forth as if opening a door.   Repeat 5-10 times
    while moving arms out to form a "T" position and
    back to the front. (Fig. 11.4).

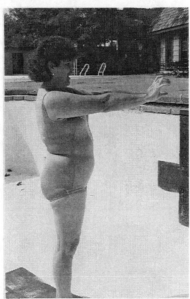

Fig. 11.4

Exercises for the Torso

1. Broomstick Arms.   Extend the arms at shoulder level
    in a "T" position. Twist at the waist keeping the
    arms extended.   Keep the feet firmly on the bottom
    of the pool.   Use the palms to push against the
    water as you twist.   The head should follow the
    path of the lead arm.   Repeat 5 -10 times.   (Fig.
    11.5).

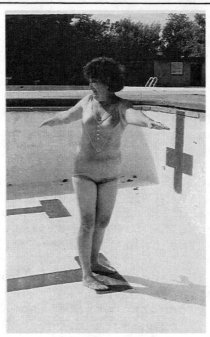

Fig. 11.5

2. Knee to Nose.   Face the wall of the pool.   Hold on
    to the side and bring the right knee up toward the
    nose.   Stretch the leg down and away from the wall.
    Repeat five times then repeat the exercise on the
    other side. (Fig. 11.6).

Fig. 11.6

3. Side Stretch.   Stand with the left side closest to
    the wall.   With the legs together extend the right
    arm up and over the head to touch the wall,
    stretching the right side. Return to the beginning
    position. Repeat five times, then switch direction
    using the left arm. (Fig. 11.7).

Fig. 11.7

Exercises for the Legs

1. Plies.   Face the wall of the pool.   The feet   are
    shoulder   width   apart   with   the   toes   pointing
    straight   ahead.   Keeping the back straight,   bend
    the   knees   and return to   the   starting   position.
    Repeat 10 times. (Fig. 11.8).

Fig. 11.8

2. Front and Side Kicks.   Stand with the back against
    the side of the pool.   Extend the right leg in
    front of the body, then push to the wall on the
    right side.   Return to the starting position by
    bringing leg directly down towards the left leg.
    Repeat five times then switch directions (side to
    front to standing position).   Repeat the entire
    exercise with the left leg. (Figs. 11.9 and 11.10).

Fig. 11.9

Fig. 11.10

3. Quick Kicks.   Stand at the side of the pool with
    the left side of the body closest to the wall.
    Bring the right leg up in front then back together
    quickly.   Repeat 10 times.   Bring the right leg
    back, then together quickly.   Repeat 10 times.
    Repeat using the left leg. (Fig. 11.11 and 11.12).

Fig. 11.11

Fig. 11.12

Exercises for Aerobics

1. Stride Jumps. Start with one foot in front and one foot in back in a stride position. Jump to switch the position of the legs. The arms move in opposition to the legs. Gradually work up to one minute as fitness level improves. (Fig. 11.13).

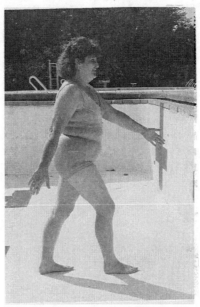
Fig. 11.13

2. Rocking Horses. Stand on the right leg with the left leg extended slightly toward the side. Bring the left leg quickly to touch the bottom of the pool, kicking the right leg out to the side. Switch the legs repeating for one minute. Alternate arms swinging from side to side to keep balance. (Fig. 11.14).

Fig. 11.14

3. Jumping Jacks. Start with the feet together. Jump to bring the feet shoulder width apart. Jump to bring the feet back together. Repeat quickly working up to one minute. The arms should swing out and in (do not bring them out of the water) in rhythm with the legs.

4. Tuck Jumps. Begin with the feet together. Jump up to bring the knees toward the chest in a tucked position and return to the standing position. The arms should be on the surface of the water to keep balanced. Repeat quickly working gradually up to one minute.

5. Hitch Kicks. Lean slightly back and alternately kick the legs (one at a time) four times (each leg) to the front of the body. Lean slightly forward and kick four times to the back. Repeat, working gradually up to one minute.

Single Kickboard Exercises

These exercises are performed in waist deep water using one kickboard as resistance against the water for an upper body workout.

1. Presses. Place the kickboard flat on top of the water and hold on to each end (with the elbows turned out). With the feet firmly on the bottom of the pool, push the kickboard down towards the bottom of the pool and allow it to freely come back to the surface. (Fig. 11.15 and 11.16).

   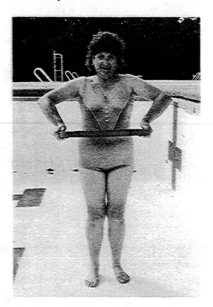

Fig. 11.15   Fig. 11.16

2. Backward Push-ups. Place the kickboard flat on the
    water behind your back. Grasp each end of the
    kickboard and push downward to extend the elbows.
    Flex the elbows to allow the kickboard to return to
    the starting position. (Fig. 11.17).

Fig. 11.17

3. Washing Machine Twists. Place the kickboard flat
    on the top of the water and hold on to the sides of
    the kickboard. The feet should be shoulder width
    apart. Twist at the waist to bring the kickboard
    around as far as is comfortably possible to the
    right side, then twist back to the left as far as
    possible. Repeat five times to each side. (Fig.
    11.18).

Fig. 11.18

Double Kickboard Exercises

These exercises are performed with a kickboard under each arm while supporting the body in deep water. Participants who have no fears of the water will feel comfortable executing these exercises.

1. Bicycles. Circle the legs to imitate the movement of pedaling a bicycle. The participant can use large range of motion or pedal with short but quick movements. Continue for about 30 seconds.

2. Straddle Stretches. Flex at the waist to bring the legs in an "L" position. Push the legs apart into a straddle position then close legs together to return to the starting position. Repeat 5 times.

3. Scissors Snap. With the body in a vertical position, begin with the right leg extended toward the front and the left leg extended toward the back. Switch the position of the legs keeping the legs in an extended position throughout the exercise. Repeat 10 times.

4. Do the Twist. With the arms extended, bring the body to a back float position with the legs extended and crossed at the ankles. Twist at the waist to bring the right hip out of the water. Repeat five times on each side.

References/Resources

Arthritis Foundation & YMCA of the USA. (1983). Arthritis aquatic program. Atlanta: Arthritis Foundation.

Conrad, C. (1985). Aqua dynamics. Washington, D.C.: National Fitness Foundation, President's Council on Physical Fitness and Sports.

Devarona, D. (1984). Hydro-aerobics. New York: Macmillan.

Jones, M.G. (1982). Swimnastics is fun. Reston, VA: American Alliance for Health, Physical Education, Recreation and Dance.

Katz, J. (1985). The water exercise techniques workout. New York: Facts on File Publications.

Koszuta, L. (1986). Water exercise causes ripples. The Physician and Sportsmedicine, 14, 10.

Krasevec, J. & Grimes, D. (1983). Hydrobics. Champaign, IL: Leisure Press.

Sova, R. (May, 1987). A workout that's all wet. Dance exercise today.

Weinstein, L. (1986). The benefits of aquatic activity. <u>Journal of Gerontological Nursing</u>, <u>12</u>, 2.

YMCA. (1983). <u>Physical</u> <u>fitness</u> <u>through</u> <u>water</u> <u>exercise</u>. Champaign, IL: Human Kinetics.

GOVERNING ORGANIZATION OF WATER EXERCISE

National Advisory Committee on Aquatic Exercise (NACAE)
Council for the National Cooperation in Aquatics (CNCA)
901 West New York Street
Indianapolis, IN 46223

Group Games and Activities

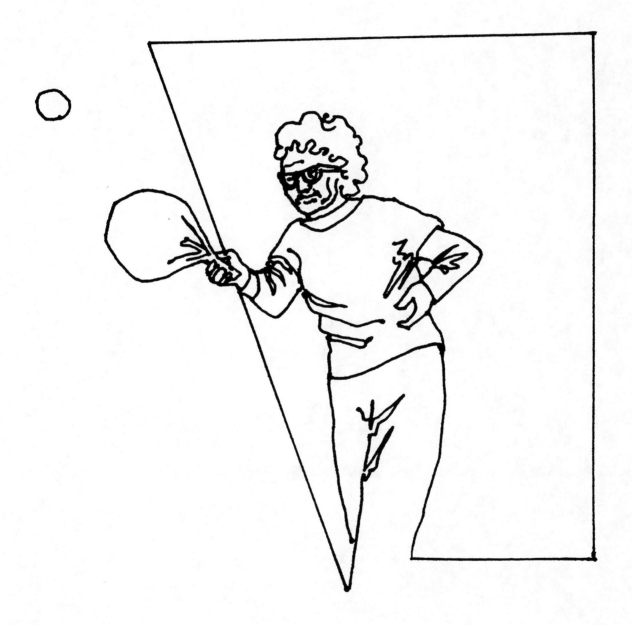

Chapter 12
Group Games and Activities

The activities in this chapter are recreational and group games that are fun, yet inexpensive. The emphasis is on fun and fitness, not competition. More often than not, they are games and activities that are interspersed into a regular fitness program to give it a change of pace or they are activities that are part of seasonal celebrations or "fitness festivals."

The activities in this chapter require homemade racquets and balls, milk dispenser bladders, parachutes, and bed sheets. Directions for making or obtaining these pieces of equipment precedes each activity.

HOMEMADE RACQUETS AND BALLS

To construct homemade racquets and balls you will need some old wire hangers, some old stockings or pantyhose, some string or rubber bands, and some plastic tape.

Bend the coat hanger into a circular shape, then insert it into the leg of an old stocking or pantyhose. Pull the stocking tight around the top and bottom of the wire circle. Tightly tape or tie the stocking at the top and bottom of the circle and clip off any excess material or string. Straighten the hanger hook and tape it so that it forms a grip for the racquet (be sure the end is securely taped so that the wire won't poke through and be a safety hazard). Now you have a racquet. (Fig. 12.1).

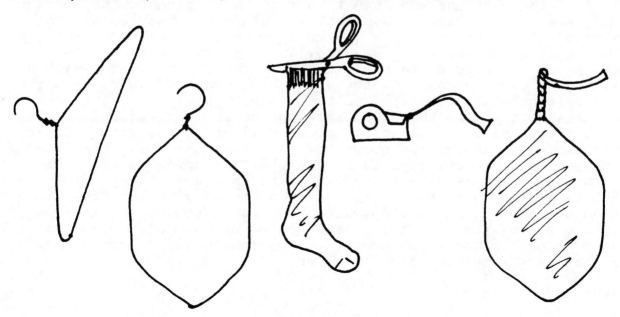

Fig. 12.1

To construct a ball, simply cut off the toe portion of stockings or pantyhose, and then stuff the toe with other material from the stockings or pantyhose. When you have the size of ball you want, tie off the toe with string or a rubber band. You now have a ball that is very soft and safe.

Another method of making a ball is to use yarn, cardboard, and string. Cut two large cardboard circles about 3 to 5 inches in diameter. Cut a hole about 1 1/2 to 2 inches in diameter in the center of the cardboard circles. Next place the two cardboard circles together (one on top of the other). Wrap yarn around the two circles until the holes are nearly full. Now, cut the yarn around the outside edge of the cardboard circle. Slide the two cardboard circles apart and then tightly tie the yarn in the center with string. Remove the cardboard circles and fluff the ball until it is round.

Memory Ball Game

The memory ball game is a good activity for cool down exercises at the end of an exercise class. Place a group of eight to twelve participants in a circle, seated in armless chairs. If you have a large group, then create as many circles as you need. Give one yarn ball to one of the participants to begin the play. This participant throws the ball to anyone in the circle he or she chooses, then the starter raises his or her hand. The next person throws the ball to another person in the circle and then raises his or her hand. The hands are raised so that subsequent players will know who has already had a turn. Each person in the circle throws the ball to a person who does not have his or her hand up until all people have caught the ball. The last person then throws the ball back to the person who started the game. Now that a pattern has been established, have the group try to throw the ball among the circle members in the exact same order as was previously established. Once the group is able to do this without dropping the ball or without having to be told where to throw the ball, then it is time to try the same game with the same pattern using two balls. The person who starts the game throws to the same person and waits for a few throws then he or she starts another ball using the same pattern. Now two balls are moving about the circle at the same time. If the group conquers this task then the same game can be played with up to five balls circulating at the same time. If the groups get so good that they find this too easy, then challenge them by letting them use only one hand for catching and throwing. If the group excels at this, then only let them play using their non-dominate hand. The groups can be monitored by keeping track of how many times the ball is dropped.

Racquet Activities

1) See how many times you can bounce the ball in the air with your homemade racquet without missing. (Fig. 12.2).

2) Suspend a ball from the ceiling (use other stockings or pantyhose legs to hang the ball). Hit the ball back and forth with a partner. (Fig. 12.3).

3) Hit a ball back and forth with a partner. See how many times you can hit the ball back and forth without missing.

4) If both partners desire, they can set up a net and court and play a game using badminton rules.

Fig. 12.2

Fig. 12.3

MILK DISPENSER BLADDERS

Many restaurants and cafeterias dispense milk or juice from machines where a metal knob is lifted to release the liquid through a rubber tube. The inner lining of these machines have a plastic bladder that can be fun to play with. Once you locate and obtain the bladders, they must be rinsed out with water several times before use. Next, blow up the bladder (being careful not to hyperventilate), bend the rubber tubing in half, and secure the bend by placing one or two rubber bands around the tubing. (Fig. 12.4) This "air pillow" is a very safe piece of equipment with which to play.

Activities for Milk Bladders

1) Seat a group of 5-10 people in a circle in sturdy, well-balanced chairs. Count the number of times the "air pillow" can be hit into the air without the pillow touching the ground and without anyone getting out of the chair to hit the pillow. (Fig. 12.5)

2) Play volleyball (either in chairs or standing) using the "air pillow" instead of a volleyball or a balloon.

Fig. 12.4   Fig. 12.5

PARACHUTE PLAY
(without jumping from airplanes, of course)

Parachutes are fun to play with for people of all ages. Before purchasing a parachute for your center or fitness group, check to see if you can borrow one from a local elementary school. Parachute activities are particularly spectacular on "field days" or "fitness days" when hundreds of people put on a demonstration using several multicolored parachutes. A source for purchasing parachutes is given in Chapter 20.

Parachute Activities (for 15-30 people per chute)

1) <u>The Bubble</u>. Stand in a circle around the chute with each person holding on with both hands facing down. On a "one, two, three, go" signal, simultaneously bend down extending the hands to the ground and then lift the chute up with the arms extended overhead. Step forward one step to allow the chute to make a full bubble.

2) <u>The Balloon</u>. Same as the bubble except the participants step forward three steps closing the bottom of the chute inward, thus making the chute "balloon."

3) <u>Fly Away</u>. (Best performed outside on a still day or in a large gymnasium). Perform the bubble and after the chute reaches its full height all

participants should release it simultaneously, letting the chute "fly away."

4) <u>Waves</u>. Pull the chute tight and hold it waist high. Raise and lower the hands rapidly causing waves in the chute.

5) <u>Popcorn</u>. Place tennis balls, yarn balls, or homemade stocking balls on the chute. Then make waves with the chute and watch the balls pop around and off the chute. Try a variation where you try to keep all of the balls on the chute. Try another variation where you try to pop all of the balls off the chute.

6) <u>Through the Hole</u>. Place tennis balls, yarn balls, or homemade stocking balls on the chute. Pull the chute tight trying to make the balls fall through the center hole in the parachute. (Fig. 12.6).

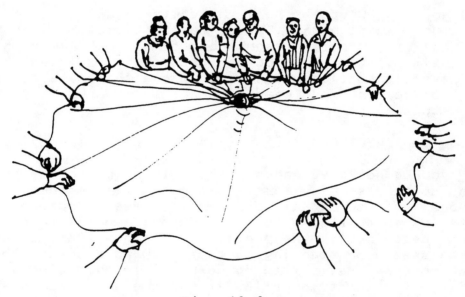

Fig. 12.6

7) <u>Under the Chute</u>. Form a bubble with the chute, then have a group leader call out different characteristics such as, "All people wearing blue." If the designated description fits the participant, then he or she must cross beneath the chute to the other side. The leader continues to call out different characteristics each time a bubble is formed. For safety reasons it is wise to have a tall person go to the middle of the chute to hold the center up to make sure the chute doesn't completely fall, until all designated participants have crossed to the other side of the chute. (Fig. 12.7).

Fig. 12.7

8) <u>Roll</u> <u>the</u> <u>Chute</u>.   Pull the chute tight and hold it
   about waist high. Divide the participants into two
   halves.   On "go" each group tries to roll up their
   half of the chute before the other.   (This is an
   excellent closing activity since the chute is now
   rolled up and ready to be put in a bag for
   storage).

SHEET PLAY* (for 8-14 people per sheet)

If you do not have enough people to do parachute play then
you can do many similar activities using flat sheets (double,
queen, or king size can all be used).   Waves, Popcorn, and Roll
the Chute (or in this case Roll the Sheet) can all be done with a
sheet as described in the previous section.   Participants can
either be seated or standing as they each hold on to the sheet
with two hands (palms facing down).   In addition to these
activities, the sheet lends itself to some other games as listed
below.

1) <u>Circle</u> <u>the</u> <u>Sheet</u>.   Pull the sheet tight and then
    place a soft yarn or stocking ball on the edge.
    Have the participants try to make the ball roll
    around the periphery of the sheet.   Reverse the
    direction to have it roll around the sheet in the
    opposite direction.

2) <u>V-Formation</u>.   With the sheet pulled taut, place a
    yarn ball on the sheet in one corner.   Have the
    participants try to make the letter V by rolling
    the ball to the center of the sheet on the opposite
    side then rolling the ball back to the opposite
    corner.   Start the activity from different corners
    of the sheet.

3) <u>X-Formation</u>. With the sheet pulled taut, place a yarn ball on the sheet in one corner. Have the participants try to make the ball roll to the opposite corner on the opposite side of the sheet. Let the ball roll straight across the end of the sheet to the other corner then complete the X by making the ball roll to the opposite corner on the opposite side of the sheet. Try the same formations using two balls of the sheet at the same time.

4) <u>Toss and Catch</u>. Place several yarn balls on the sheet. The group rhythmically makes the sheet go up and down three times as they count 1-2-3. On the count of 3 all the balls should be tossed in the air and then caught on the sheet. Try not to let any balls touch the floor.

Reference

Corbin, C.B. & Corbin, D.E. (1981). <u>Homemade play equipment</u>. Boston: American Press.

*Ideas for sheet activities are from Edith Clarke, teacher/tutor for the Exercise Training for the Elderly and/or Disabled (EXTEND) program from Great Britain.

T'ai Chi Ch'uan
(*by Frank Fong*)

Frank Fong studied T'ai Chi Ch'uan under three different masters in Hong Kong, where he was born. He has been practicing the art for over twenty-five years and teaching for over fifteen years.

Chapter 13
T'ai Chi Ch'uan
(by Frank Fong)

T'ai Chi Ch'uan* (pronounced Ti Chee Ch wan) is an ancient Chinese art through which attainment of rhythmic coordination, balance and harmony with nature can be developed through the practice of relaxed mental-physical exercises.

AS EXERCISE:

T'ai Chi Ch'uan is one of the best exercises for all ages. Those who practice it gain a healthy body as well as an alert mind. With the improvement to their health, they are able to concentrate better on their routine tasks and to make decisions more effectively.

The form of T'ai Chi Ch'uan, in performance, looks like a classical dance with graceful movements and alert actions. It also offers balanced exercises to the muscles and joints of the various parts of the body by way of complicated actions which, in turn, are regulated by the timing of deep breathing and the movement of the diaphragm. Furthermore, a tranquil state of mind and complete dedication to or spiritual concentration on all the movements, are required during the exercises. This concentration will insure that the central nervous system, including its fundamental components, is given sufficient training and is consequently toned as the exercise continues. It is quite logical to say that the efficiency of the various organs of the body depends largely on the soundness of the central nervous system. In other words, a strong central nervous system is the basic condition of a healthy body.

To the visceral, arterial and respiratory systems, T'ai Chi Ch'uan will bring forth the same beneficial effects. Besides exercising the muscles and the joints, it gives rise to harmonized and uniform breathing, especially in the movement of the diaphragm. Therefore, it can improve the circulation of the blood and the lymphatic fluids. The movement of the muscles exerts pressure on the veins, forcing the blood to flow towards the heart.

*Also known as T'ai Ji in modern Chinese parlance.

One of the characteristics of T'ai Chi Ch'uan is that breathing is brought into harmony with the actions. Since the breathing is so deep and the intake of air to the lungs is greater in quantity than usual, a greater amount of oxygen is available for consumption and thus, blood vessels carrying nourishment to the heart and the viscera are expanded.

T'ai Chi Ch'uan offers a good opportunity to exercise the stomach muscles. As a result, the function of the digestive system, including the stomach, is improved as evidenced by a better appetite and the prevention of constipation. This is advantageous to older adults in particular.

Because T'ai Chi Ch'uan serves the purposes of strengthening the central nervous system, improving the blood circulation, increasing nourishment to the heart and the viscera and promoting better digestion, it can help to prevent many kinds of diseases which are usually contracted by older adults.

T'ai Chi Ch'uan stresses the basic philosophy of Taoism-- "be natural." Let things develop and happen on their natural course. As in the opening of a rose, you only need to give it a little water every day and watch it bloom naturally. If you tried to help by pulling on the petals, which is totally unnatural, the result would be disastrous. The rose would die. T'ai Chi Ch'uan contains no extreme movements and emphasizes gentleness. When doing the exercises, called "forms," total relaxation of all parts of the body should be felt. All the forms move in a curving fashion, thus insuring that all parts of the body receive an equal amount of exercise, regardless of the duration of the form.

T'ai Chi Ch'uan contributes to health from still another viewpoint. In speaking of the way the human body works, doctors of Chinese medicine refer to a life force or vital energy called "chi" which flows through the body on specific pathways called psychic channels. Pressure points along these channels are used in acupuncture to correct an imbalance in the energy flow which has adversely affected the functioning of some internal organs. When you are doing the T'ai Chi Ch'uan forms in a correct, relaxed way, you are opening the channels along which this "chi" flows, thereby maintaining balance in the system. Acupuncture is a curing process. T'ai Chi Ch'uan is a preventive process which is far more beneficial for your health than just a gentle, graceful dance.

AS MEDITATION:

T'ai Chi Ch'uan, in addition to conferring the health benefits related to exercise, is also a type of moving meditation. It is different from Zazen meditation which is done sitting down. The flowing, slowly unfolding forms of T'ai Chi Ch'uan enhance the exchanging phenomenon of in and out, opening and closing, folding and unfolding which is a basic element of all forms of meditation. T'ai Chi Ch'uan is a physical expression of the philosophy of Taoism and has close relationships to the I-Ching (Book of Change). The different movements and positions open up various psychic channels in the body, releasing ordinarily untapped whole energy for creativity. Also, there is a general opening up of the different planes for growth. Taoists believe that everything flows in never-ending cycles, one after another continuously, as natural as night and day and the four seasons. They also believe that nothing in life is for certain, except that there are always changes. In other words, there are no constants but constant changes. Therefore, Taoists also believe that to harmonize best with the universe, which is constantly moving, a moving meditation as in T'ai Chi Ch'uan is highly satisfying philosophically.

Meditation helps to attain a state of mind in which thoughts are not jumping from some past events to events in the future, neither of which have any reality relative to the present moment. These moments are real life experiences and should be savored to the fullest instead of being diluted by fleeting thoughts of unreality of past and future. It is because of this distraction that more energy than necessary is often expended to accomplish a task. You can slowly learn to concentrate more and more on present moments by practicing the forms in T'ai Chi Ch'uan. All the forms are performed delicately and deliberately with total relaxation. In order to achieve this, you must give it your fullest attention. When you gradually learn to practice the forms correctly every day, you can slowly learn to concentrate fully on the forms for longer and longer periods without becoming distracted by all kinds of thoughts which have previously held your attention.

Therefore, T'ai Chi Ch'uan is a "centering" technique which provides a period every day to be quiet and calm. It reduces us from interaction with others and helps with physical and mental relaxation. If you can attain a few of these moments every day, then you will be renewed and recharged with energy. In addition, if you can practice diligently, then you can stay in the bliss of the moment longer and longer until a "still point" is reached. This training in energy conservation and life force recharging will enable you to focus your energy fully in desirable directions.

AS SELF-DEFENSE:

T'ai Chi Ch'uan contains different techniques of self-defense in all of its forms and movements. In order to use T'ai Chi Ch'uan as a self defense vehicle, you must devote a considerable amount of time to sensitivity training in a technique termed "push-hands." A beginner, however, is advised strongly to concentrate on the first two aspects of T'ai Chi Ch'uan, maintenance and conservation of physical and emotional energy.

A final word concerning the practice of T'ai Chi Ch'uan is that, as in so many other endeavors, there is no substitute for personal experience. You just have to do it for it to be meaningful.

Beginning Form ("Grasp Bird's Tail")

The traditional complete series of long forms contains 108 separate movements, one following another continuously. They flow as waves on the Yangtze River constantly moving. To prepare for starting anything, you should take a moment to just stand. Concentrate and allow every part of your body to let go. Stay totally relaxed and let your muscles "sink." Imagine that all your weight is concentrated around your heels and the bottom of your feet. Breath naturally and let your diaphragm drop. Even the muscles on your head and face should be relaxed. This total "letting go," surrendering or conscious relaxation, is termed "physical emptying." It is this emptying that allows you to use your power of suggestion to move your frame with the least amount of energy. Maintaining the physical relaxation allows the mental concentration to function, therefore allowing for the experience of the flow of your spirit. Hence, the paradoxical description of the forms. . ."the more you let it go, the more you have it."

Following is an explanation of one of the fundamental forms called "grasp bird's tail." There are four movements in this form, namely grasp, roll back, press and push.

1. Stand with feet parallel, head, shoulder, chest, solar plexus, hips and toes all pointing south.

2. Turn the left foot so that the toes are pointing southeast, with the toes of the still right foot pointing south.

3. Now turn the whole upper body, head, shoulders, chest and hips together until they all face the southeast direction and put all body weight on the left leg and foot. Bend the left knee. Place your right foot straight out to the south, heel touching the ground but no weight on the right foot. Form your arms and hands, left hand on top with right hand right beneath it as if you are holding an "energy ball." Shoulders and elbows should be dropped and rounded slightly to allow your upper back to relax. Be sure your hips do not stick out, keep your vertebrae vertical to the ground at all times. Now you have completed the "in" part of a cycle. (Fig. 13.1).

Front View   Side View

Fig. 13.1

4. To commence the "out" part of this cycle do the
   following:

   For the legs. Slowly straighten the left leg
   and at the same time bend the right leg at the
   knee. The weight of the body is also slowly
   being transferred from the left leg to the
   right. Keep both heels on the ground.

   For the body. Turn the head, shoulders chest
   and hips (HSCH) together starting from facing
   southeast and end up facing south. When turning
   the body, make sure that the head, shoulders,
   chest and hips turn together and at the same
   rate. This is to insure that the vertebrae are
   not twisted at any time.

   For the arms and hands. Bring the left hand
   slowly down and bring the right hand slowly up
   passing the inside of the left forearm so that
   it ends up in front of the face and left hand by
   the right elbow. At this point, the right foot
   should be pointing south with the knee bent,
   supporting about 2/3 of the body weight. The
   left foot should be pointing southeast with the
   knee still slightly bent, supporting about 1/3
   of the body weight. The head, shoulders, chest
   and hips should all be facing south. The hips
   should be collected in slightly, and the
   vertebrae should be perpendicular to the ground.
   This completes the grasp movement and the end of
   the "out" part of the cycle. (Fig. 13.3).

Move from Fig. 13.1 to Fig. 13.3 position very,
very slowly, evenly and smoothly. Synchronize
all parts of the body in the movement.
Synchronization means that all parts of the body
from the starting position to the ending
position should move and stop at the same time.
In other words, do not change weight with the
legs when the body is already turned, or do not
change the hands and arms to get to the end
position when the body is still turning.
Concentrate and move every part of the body at a
synchronized rate. Fig. 13.2 shows the half way
point between Fig. 13.1 and Fig. 13.3. At this
point the weight is evenly distributed between
the two legs and feet and the body is facing
southeast with the arms and hands just passing
one another.

Fig. 13.2

Front View   Side View

Fig. 13.3

5. At Fig. 13.3, we are at the end of the "grasp" movement and at the beginning of the "roll back" movement. We are also at the end of the "out" part of the cycle and the beginning of the "in" part of the cycle. Each cycle consists of an "in" and an "out" portion. Starting at this position, slowly shift the weight from the right leg to the left, straightening out the right knee and bending the left knee, ending up with all the body weight resting on the left foot and with no weight on the right foot. Turn body (HSCH) from facing south to the southeast. Pull both arms back and down as the body turns, and shift the weight as if you were pulling on the arm of someone who is standing in front of you. At the end of the movement, turn the right hand so that the right palm is facing you. Turn the left hand so that the left palm is facing and touching the right wrist. This whole movement is the "roll back." See Fig. 13.6. Fig. 13.4 and Fig. 13.5 show the intermediate part of going from Fig. 13.3 to Fig. 13.6. This completes the "in" portion of another cycle.

Fig. 13.4

Fig. 13.5

Fig. 13.6

6. From the position in Fig. 13.6, press the left palm on the right wrist, turn the body (HSCH) from southeast to south, then shift the body weight from the left foot to the right. Again move slowly, evenly and smoothly and end in the position shown in Fig. 13.7. The right foot should be supporting 2/3 of the body weight while pointing south. The hands should be directly in front of body, and the left foot should be pointing southeast while supporting 1/3 the of body weight. The hips should be collected and the vertebrae should be perpendicular to the ground. The whole body should remain relaxed. This completes the "out" portion of the cycle and completes the "press" movement.

Front View   Side View

Fig. 13.7

7. From the position in Fig. 13.7, release the left palm and press on the right wrist while withdrawing both arms slightly as in Fig. 13.8. At the same time, turn the body (HSCH) slowly to the left until it is facing the southeast. Shift the body weight from the right foot to the left until all weight is supported by the left foot and no weight is on the right foot. See Fig. 13.9. This completes the "in" portion of the "push" movement.

Front View   Side View

Fig. 13.8

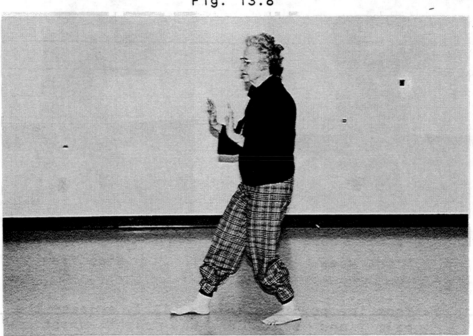

Fig. 13.9

8. From the position in Fig. 13.9, turn the body
   (HSCH) from facing southeast to south. Shift
   the weight from the left to the right foot and
   push both arms and palms forward, ending up as
   shown in Fig. 13.10. This completes the "out"
   portion of the "push" movement.

Front View   Side View

Fig. 13.10

To summarize the above movements:

MOVEMENTS	CYCLES	BREATHING	FIGURES
Preparation of grasp	in	in	13.1
Grasp	out	out	13.1 to 13.3
Roll back	in	in	13.3 to 13.6
Press	out	out	13.6 to 13.7
Preparation of press	in	in	13.7 to 13.9
Press	out	out	13.9 to 13.10

This completes the four movements of "grasp bird's tail." It is essential to concentrate fully on the "cleanness" of the movements while feeling relaxation all over the body. It is this complete mental concentration that tones up the nervous system. It is also necessary to go through the movements as slowly as possible, in order to check the "cleanness" of the correct positions and also to allow you to feel and sense all parts of the body. This will insure that all of the parts of the body are relaxed throughout. If your muscles feel tight somewhere, just concentrate on that part of your body and "let go."

For all who sincerely wish to enjoy the "bliss" of the "flow," remember that consistent daily practice of ten to fifteen minutes is better than two to three hours practiced once a week. Also, the quality of your practice is more important than the quantity. Remember, nothing should be forced. In order to realize the harmony of the body, mind and spirit, old ingrained habits must be unlearned and new habits formed. This takes a great degree of concentration, patience and acceptance and time should be given to practice. A new shoot on an old tree is delicate and must be allowed to develop at its own pace, "naturally."

References

Huang, A. (1987). Embrace tiger, return to mountain. Berkeley, CA: Celestial Arts.

Huang, W. (1979). Fundamentals of t'ai chi ch'uan. Seattle: South Sky Book Co.

Lee, Y. (1979). Lee's modified t'ai chi ch'uan for health. Honolulu: Unicorn Press.

Reid, H. (1988). The way of harmony. New York: Simon & Schuster.

Veith, I. (1973). The yellow emperor's classic of internal medicine. Berkeley, CA: University of California Press.

Watts, A. (1975). Tao: The watercourse way. New York: Pantheon.

Yoga
(by Judy Vann)

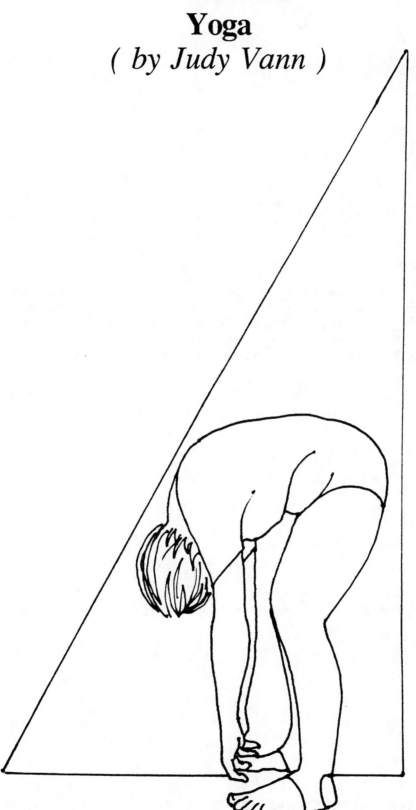

Judy Vann has taught yoga for almost twenty years. She has participated in yoga workshops in Tokyo, London, and Los Angeles and she is currently promoting yoga through her weekly classes and frequent television appearances in Omaha.

Photos in this chapter by: David Milder, Tom Vann, Judy Vann, and David Corbin.

Chapter 14
Yoga
(by Judy Vann)

Yoga, a word meaning "union" or "joining together," is a step-by-step technique which links body, emotions, and mind to function as one. The medical community acknowledges the mind's influence upon the body for good physical health, and vice versa. Weight control, a toning of the muscles, relaxation, improved health, and a positive mental outlook are experienced by those who practice Yoga.

Some additional benefits which may accrue include straight posture, grace, breath control, greater stamina, and resistance to illness. Exhilaration and fun are keynotes. Yoga exercises help develop self-confidence and reduce the tension of modern living.

<u>Points to Remember When Doing Yoga</u>

1. Move in slow motion for each posture.
2. Co-ordinate breath and movement.
3. Practice on an empty stomach for feelings of well-being.
4. Schedule your practice daily, so Yoga will become a healthy habit.
5. Wear loose clothing while you practice, so that circulation, breathing, and movement will be unrestricted.
6. Avoid comparing your postures with others. Individuals differ in their physical abilities. Compete only with yourself.

NOTE: The following exercises are not meant to be a panacea or a replacement treatment for medical therapy. If you have any questions, ask your physician before starting Yoga.

YOGA DAILY DOZEN

The first 4 postures are to be performed before getting out of bed in the morning. These movements are used as a transition between sleeping and alertness. If desired, these exercises can be practiced on the floor using a rug or mat.

1. <u>Side to Side Rock</u>

This is an excellent exercise for the lower back. Lie on your back with your arms spread out to the sides.

(Fig. 14.1) Bend your knees, keeping your feet flat on the bed. Now, drop your knees to the right as you turn and face left. (Fig. 14.2) Then, bring your knees to the center and your face to the center. Repeat these movements in the opposite direction. Repeat 2 more times to each side in a slow continuous motion. Inhale each time your knees and face are in the center position; exhale as your knees are dropped and your head is turned.

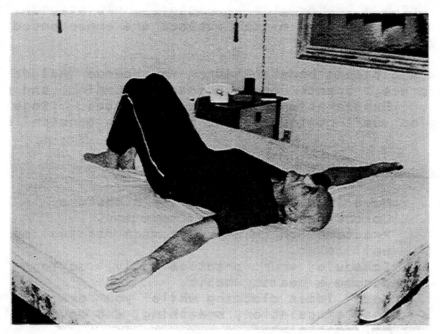

Fig. 14.1

Fig. 14.2

2.   <u>Knee</u> <u>Press</u> <u>with</u> <u>a</u> <u>Leg</u> <u>Lift</u>

This exercise helps remove excess gas and is good for lower back and hamstring flexibility. Lie on your back. Inhale, raising both legs to your chest. Reach behind your knees and lock both hands. (Fig. 14.3). Squeeze your knees to your chest, exhale and bring your forehead to your knees. Inhale as you release your knees slightly and lower your head to the bed. Repeat 3 times.

VARIATION: Breathing normally, slowly straighten your right leg on the bed. Lift and lower it three times while lifting the forehead toward your left knee. (Fig. 14.4). Repeat with other leg.

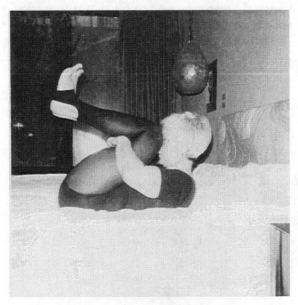

Fig. 14.3

Fig. 14.4

3.   <u>Bridge</u> <u>with</u> <u>Shoulder</u> <u>Rotation</u>

The Bridge relieves stress in the lower back, strengthens the buttocks and improves shoulder flexibility. Follow these steps.

1.   Lie on your back and bend your knees keeping them 8 - 12 inches apart, with the toes facing forward. (Fig. 14.5).

2.   Press the small of your back to the bed. Slowly, one vertebra at a time, raise your hips off the bed so that your body forms a slant board from knees to shoulder. Breathe normally.

3.   Lace your fingers together and slowly draw your shoulder blades together toward your spine. (Fig. 14.6) Tighten your buttocks.

4.   Unlace your fingers, inhale; then lower your spine to the bed as you exhale slowly. Repeat 3 times.

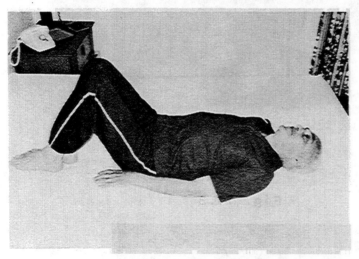

Fig. 14.5

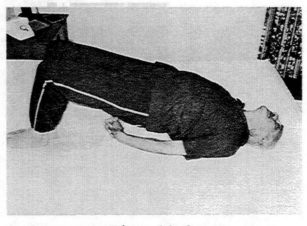

Fig. 14.6

4.   <u>Half</u> <u>Sit-Up</u>

This position is excellent for strengthening the abdominal muscles and the neck muscles.

Follow these steps:

1.   Lie on your back and bend your knees keeping them 8 - 12 inches apart with your toes facing forward. Place your arms along the sides of your body.

2.   Breathing normally, raise your head, shoulders, and arms off the bed. Contract your abdominal muscles and buttocks. Hold for 5 seconds. (Fig. 14.7)

3.   Slowly lower your head, shoulders, and arms. Relax your abdomen and your neck.

4.   Repeat 2 more times, increasing the hold to 10 seconds.

Fig. 14.7

The next 4 postures are to be performed while standing on the floor. If balance is a problem, use the wall for support.

5.   <u>Complete</u> <u>Breath-standing</u>

This exercise can have a positive effect on the entire body. It can help you to overcome fatigue. It can also help to strengthen the toes, feet, ankles, and legs, as well as increase blood circulation and improve balance.

Follow these steps.

1.   Stand comfortably with your arms at your sides and your chin at your chest. (Fig. 14.8).

2.   Exhale through your nose, and empty your lungs as completely as you can.

3.   Slowly inhale through your nose as you extend your abdomen and then your entire chest. While inhaling, slowly bring your arms overhead and rise on your toes. (Fig. 14.9). Hold for a moment. Use the wall for support, if needed.

4.   Slowly exhale, while making a quiet humming sound, as you lower your arms gracefully. Return your heels to the floor. Repeat 2 more times.

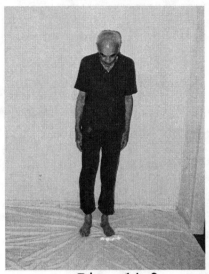

Fig. 14.8

Fig. 14.9

6.   <u>Bellows</u> <u>Breath</u>

The vigorous breathing in this exercise is ideal for cleansing the lungs. It renews energy by ventilating the respiratory system with oxygen.

Follow these steps:

1.   Stand comfortably, placing your hands on your hips.

2.   Slowly inhale through your nose as you extend your abdomen and then your entire chest.

3.   Quickly and forcefully exhale through your nose and contract your abdomen.

4.   Repeat 2 more times.

7.   <u>Chest</u> <u>Expansion</u> <u>with</u> <u>Shoulder</u> <u>Drop</u>

Chest Expansion improves posture and removes tension throughout the entire neck and shoulders.

Follow these steps:

1.   Clasp your hands behind your back with the arms straight. (Fig. 14.10).

2.   Breathe in deeply, then exhale slowly, bending at the waist and hips as far as possible. Use the wall for support as needed.

3.   As you bend, bring your arms up, and back away from your body, bending your knees slightly. (Fig. 14.11).

4.   Breathing normally, relax your neck and hold for a few seconds.

5.   Then inhale and come up slowly to a standing position. Unclasp the hands. Relax. Repeat 2 more times.

Shoulder Drop is a simple counter-movement to Chest Expansion.

Bring your shoulder upward toward your ears. Hold a few seconds. Then drop quickly. Repeat 2 more times.

NOTE: Chest Expansion can be performed while sitting in a chair if balance or dizziness are a problem. (Fig. 14.12).

Fig. 14.10

Fig. 14.11

Fig. 14.12

8.   <u>Cow</u>

This pose will limber up the back and legs. It is a standing relaxation pose, and it will help the body feel less fatigued. Use a wall for balance as needed. Stand upright letting your arms hang loosely at your sides; slowly bend forward at the waist and hips. (Fig. 14.13). Allow your head and arms to lower slowly toward the floor. Hold for a few seconds, relaxing the back of your neck and bending your knees slightly. (Fig. 14.14).

Slowly roll back up to a standing position. Concentrate on feeling each vertebra straighten up one at a time.

Remember to breathe out through your nose as you bend over, and breathe in as you roll up. Repeat 2 more times.

NOTE: Cow can be performed while sitting in a chair if balance or dizziness are a problem. (Fig. 14.15).

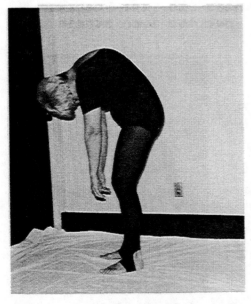

Fig. 14.13

Fig. 14.14

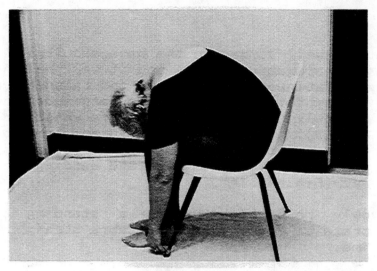

Fig. 14.15

The next 4 postures should be performed while sitting in a chair.

9.   <u>Neck</u> <u>Roll</u>

The benefits of the Neck Roll are the removal of tightness, stiffness, and tension throughout the neck.

While sitting straight, lower your chin toward your chest. Hold a few moments breathing normally. (Fig. 14.16).

Roll your head to one side (Fig. 14.17) then slowly roll towards the center. Now roll the head to the other side. Repeat the rolls 3 times to each side.

CAUTION: Do not roll the head to the backwards position. This position can put too much strain on the cervical vertebrae.

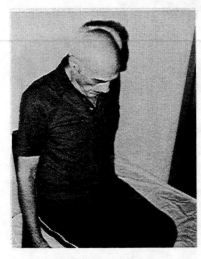

Fig. 14.16

Fig. 14.17

10.   Eye Exercises and Palming

This exercise helps to relieve tension in the eye muscles, and it also helps to relax tired eyes.

Look upward towards the ceiling, but do not move your head. Hold one second. (Fig. 14.18).

Roll your eyes to the extreme right. Hold one second.

Roll your eyes to the extreme bottom. Hold one second.

Roll your eyes to the extreme left. Hold one second.

After 3 repetitions, perform 3 identical movements counter-clockwise.

Palming

Briskly rub your palms together. Then place the soft pad below your thumb, on your closed eyes. Hold a few seconds. (Fig. 14.19).

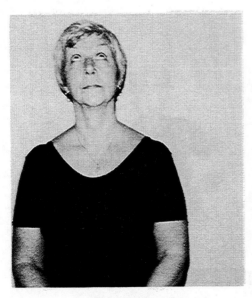

Fig. 14.18

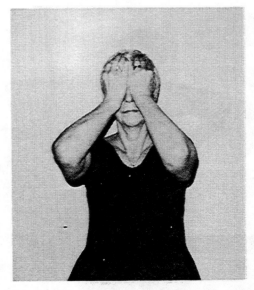

Fig. 14.19

11. <u>Spinal</u> <u>Twist</u>

This exercise promotes flexibility of the spine.

Follow these steps:

1. Sit in a chair with your knees together and feet flat on the floor.

2. Place your left hand on your right knee. Place your right hand on right side of the chair back. (Fig. 14.20).

3. Inhale; then, exhaling, slowly twist to the right. Start from the navel, then include the ribs, then the right shoulder, then the chin, then look over your right shoulder with the eyes. (Fig. 14.21).

4. Hold for 10 seconds while breathing normally.

5. Slowly return to the original position.

    Repeat in the opposite direction.

    Repeat 2 more times in each direction.

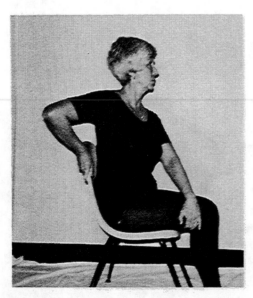 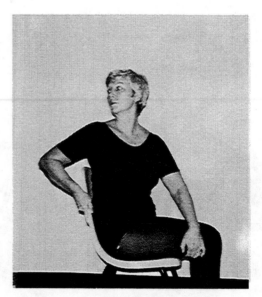

Fig. 14.20   Fig. 14.21

12.   <u>Alternate</u> <u>Nostril</u> <u>Breathing</u>

The breathing in this exercise helps to create a feeling of calmness and tranquility.

Follow these steps:

1.   Lightly touch the first two fingers of the right hand between your eyebrows. (Fig. 14.22).

2.   Press your right nostril closed with your thumb. Inhale slowly and quietly through your left nostril to the count of 8.

3.   Close both nostrils by pressing the left nostril closed with the third finger. Hold your breath for the count of 4. (Fig. 14.23).

4.   Release the right nostril (still holding the left closed) and exhale slowly and quietly through the right nostril for 8 counts.

5.   Still holding the left nostril closed, inhale for 8 counts through the right nostril; close both nostrils and hold the breath for 4 counts; exhale for 8 counts through the left nostril.

Repeat the whole sequence two more times.

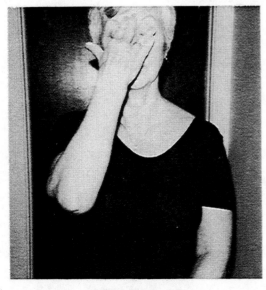

Fig. 14.22

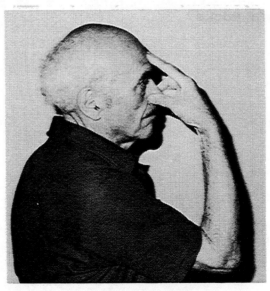

Fig. 14.23

References/ Resources

Ahuja, S. (1979). <u>Savitri's way to perfect fitness through hatha yoga</u>. New York: Simon & Schuster.

Bender, R. (1976). <u>Be young and flexible after 30, 40, 50, 60</u>. Avon, CT: Ruben Publishing Company.

Bender, R. (1975). <u>Yoga exercises for every body</u>. Avon, CT: Ruben Publishing Company.

Christensen, A., and Rankin, D. (1972). <u>The light of yoga society beginner's manual</u>. New York: Simon & Schuster.

Folan, L. (1976). <u>Lilias yoga, and you</u>. New York: Bantam Books, Inc.

Folan, L. (1981). <u>Lilias, yoga, and your life</u>. New York: MacMillan Publishing Co., Inc.

Hittleman, R. (1969). <u>Yoga 28 day exercise plan</u>. New York: Workman Publishing Co.

Iyengar, B.K.S. (1979). <u>Light on yoga</u>. New York: Schocken Books.

Iyengar, G.S. (1985). <u>Yoga: A gem for women</u>. New Delhi: Allied Publishers Private Ltd.

Lidell, L. (1983). <u>Sivananda companion to yoga</u>. New York: Simon & Schuster.

Smith, B. (1982). <u>Yoga: For a new age</u>. Englewood Cliffs, NJ: Prentice-Hall, Inc.

Van Lysebeth, A. (1968). <u>Yoga self-taught</u>. New York: Barnes & Noble Books.

A Walking Program

Chapter 15
A Walking Program

According to the President's Council on Physical Fitness there are some 50 million Americans who walk two or more times a week as part of an exercise program. Walking is one of the best all-around exercises. According to Dr. Kenneth Cooper, author of The New Aerobics, if you're over age 60, "avoid jogging, running, and vigorous competitive sports. Walking, swimming, and stationary cycling will do you a lot more good." Cooper further explains:

> However, there are exceptions for the over-60 bracket. If you have been keeping in shape by regular exercise for many years so that you have built up and maintained your aerobic capacity, you may safely participate in such vigorous activities as jogging, running, and stationary running. You're also free to engage in more strenuous activities if you do your exercise in a medically supervised group. (Cooper, 1970).

The reason we are devoting an entire chapter of this book to walking is because we feel that walking offers the greatest number of aerobic advantages to the greatest number of older adults.

> Walking offers several advantages over other forms of exercise; it requires no previous instruction, it can be done almost anywhere, it can be done at almost anytime, it costs nothing and it has the lowest rate of injury of any form of exercise (Pep Up Your Life, n.d.).

Another advantage of walking (as is also true for jogging, swimming, and cycling) is that the "milking" action of the leg muscles on the veins in the legs helps move the blood through the legs more efficiently, thus helping to eliminate the pooling of blood in the feet. Walking is also an enjoyable method for strengthening the muscles of the legs.

Although it may take longer to achieve aerobic conditioning through walking than through other more strenuous activities, the differences are not great. It has been observed, for example, that jogging a mile in 8 and one half minutes burns only 26 more calories than walking a mile in 12 minutes. The conditioning benefits from walking improve greatly if you increase the pace to faster than 20 minutes per mile.

Walkers burn an average of 66 calories per mile when walking 3 miles per hour (20 minutes per mile) but they burn 124 calories per mile when they increase their pace to 5 miles per hour. Keep in mind that a good aerobic fitness program requires at least 15-20 minutes of continuous exercises 3 or more days per week. Review the guidelines and precautions in Chapter 3 before you begin your walking program.

You may find it more enjoyable to walk with other people. If so, find a friend and walk with him or her, or start a walking club. This can provide not only aerobic training, but social and intellectual stimulation as well. You can discuss different topics each time you walk, i.e., current events, movies, art, etc. The Heritage of the Future is an excellent book that can help you select discussion topics for each group walk. (Bigelow, 1982). Remember, if you can't walk and talk at the same time because you are out of breath, then you're overdoing it!

In Great Britain cross-country walking is called rambling. They offer the following reasons for rambling:

> Walkers will tell you that it is the only way to appreciate the countryside, to learn to recognize bird songs, to spot wild flowers, to get to know our beautiful native trees. Perhaps even more important is the companionship that grows up within a group of walkers. Walking and talking is almost a therapy in itself. For promotion of positive and happy health in later years, walking offers much, exercising limbs, heart and lungs and generating a wonderful feeling of well-being. . . . Rambling is often particularly attractive to retired people, who can appreciate the sense of freedom generated in a mid-week walk, contrasting very pleasantly with the daily round of work now behind them. (Beth Johnson Foundation, n.d.).

Box 10 gives you some tips on how to walk and what to wear. An important addition to the "What to wear section" is to wear light-colored clothes or a reflecting band when it is dark so that drivers can easily see you. Always walk facing oncoming traffic and do not assume that drivers will notice you on the roadway (U.S. Dept. of Health & Human Services, 1981).

Box 10

HOW TO WALK

A good walking workout is a matter of stepping your pace, increasing your distance and wal more often. Here are some tips to help you get most out of walking:

Move at a steady clip, brisk enough to make your heart beat faster and cause you to breathe more deeply.

Hold your head erect, back straight and abdomen flat. Toes should point straight ahead and arms should swing loosely at your sides.

Land on your heel and roll forward to drive off the ball of your foot. Walking only on the ball of the foot or walking flatfooted may cause soreness.

Take long easy strides, but don't strain. When walking up hills or walking rapidly, lean forward slightly.

Breathe deeply, with your mouth open if that's more comfortable.

WHAT TO WEAR

Shoes that are comfortable, provide good support and don't cause blisters or calluses are the only special equipment necessary. They should have arch supports and should elevate the heel one-half to three-quarters of an inch above the sole. They should also have uppers made of materials that "breathe" such as leather or nylon mesh. Some examples are: especially manufactured walking shoes, light trail or hiking boots or casual shoes with thick rubber or crepe rubber soles.

Wear lighter clothing than the temperature would ordinarily dictate because walking generates a lot of body heat. In cold weather, wear several layers of light clothing. They trap body heat and are easy to shed if you get too warm. A woolen cap is important in very cold temperatures.

Adapted and reprinted from fitness program materials, courtesy of the Travelers Insurance Companies.

The following sample walking program is recommended by the National Heart, Lung, and Blood Institute. If you find that walking does not meet your needs or is unsuitable to you in some way, look for other aerobic exercise programs in pamphlets and books on aerobic exercise or sports medicine (See Chapter 20).

Do not feel compelled to go through the program in the exact sequence listed. If you find that you are too tired after any of the steps in the program then feel free to repeat one week's schedule or even go back to a less strenuous schedule until you feel ready to progress. There is nothing magical about this program; it is merely intended to be a guide for helping you to start gradually and to move progressively toward a good aerobic fitness program.

A SAMPLE WALKING PROGRAM (USDHHS, 1981)

	Warm up	Target zone exercising	Cool down	Total Time
WEEK 1 Session A	Walk slowly 5 min.	Then walk briskly 5 min.	Then walk slowly 5 min.	15 min.
Session B		Repeat above pattern		
Session C		Repeat above pattern		

Continue with at least three exercise sessions during each week of the program.

Week 2	Walk slowly 5 min.	Walk briskly 7 min.	Walk slowly 5 min.	17 min.
Week 3	Walk slowly 5 min.	Walk briskly 9 min.	Walk slowly 5 min.	19 min.
Week 4	Walk slowly 5 min.	Walk briskly 11 min.	Walk slowly 5 min.	21 min.
Week 5	Walk slowly 5 min.	Walk briskly 13 min.	Walk slowly 5 min.	23 min.
Week 6	Walk slowly 5 min.	Walk briskly 15 min.	Walk slowly 5 min.	25 min.

eek 7	Walk slowly 5 min.	Walk briskly 18 min.	Walk slowly 5 min.	28 min.
eek 8	Walk slowly 5 min.	Walk briskly 20 min.	Walk slowly 5 min.	30 min.
eek 9	Walk slowly 5 min.	Walk briskly 23 min.	Walk slowly 5 min.	33 min.
eek 10	Walk slowly 5 min.	Walk briskly 26 min.	Walk slowly 5 min.	36 min.
eek 11	Walk slowly 5 min.	Walk briskly 28 min.	Walk slowly 5 min.	38 min.
eek 12	Walk slowly 5 min.	Walk briskly 30 min.	Walk slowly 5 min.	40 min.

eek 13 on:
heck your pulse periodically to see if you are exercising within our target zone. As you get more in shape, try exercising within he upper range of your heart zone. Remember that your goal is to ontinue getting the benefits you are seeking and enjoying your ctivity.

Walking in shopping malls has become a very popular type of alking for a certain segment of American society. Avia nternational, a division of Reebok International (a major thletic shoe manufacturer) estimates that there may be as many s half a million mall walkers in the United States. Indeed, via has introduced a walking shoe designed specifically for mall alking. (Pereira, 1989). The British ramblers mentioned earlier n this chapter would probably miss the singing birds and the ommuning with nature but many mall walking advocates enjoy the limate controlled environment. Some malls have perks like free lood pressure screening, walkathons, and free refreshments. ome people have met their mates while mall walking (Pereira, 989).

Some of the same variations that are used for jogging can be sed for walking. Some of the more common variations are Corbin, 1988):

Walk for a specified time rather than for a specific distance.

Join a walking club (see addresses at the end of the chapter).

Walk to raise money for charity.

Pace walk by predicting the time it will take you
to walk a specified distance.   The closer you are
to your predicted time, the better. Make your walk
a dance where rhythm is more important than speed.

"I'm into Walking"-Drawing by Elizabeth Layton

Walk with a friend.

Vary your walking route to prevent boredom.

When you travel take walking tours rather than bus tours. Many hotels can give you maps of scenic, historic and safe walking routes. The Complete Book of Walking (Kuntzleman, 1979) gives route maps of walking tours of many American cities.

You can even walk on the deck of the ship if you go on a cruise.

Walk and sing. Perhaps you can pick a song that matches the rhythm of your breathing. You can use headphones or go a capella. For the more inhibited walkers, humming to yourself may be your forte.

Walk with your dog. It will benefit both of you and your dog will love you for it.

Walk to do errands or to commute. It's good for you and it kills two birds with one stone.

If you wish to be even more bizarre you can try walking while bouncing a tennis ball or try walking backwards every once in a while (as long as you look where you are going).

References/Resources

Beth Johnson Foundation (n.d.). Rambling for the over fifties. Stoke-on-Trent, England: A Beth Johnson Training Aid, 64 Princes Road, Hartshill, ST4 7JL.

Bigelow, B. (1982). The heritage of the future. Washington, D.C.: The National Council on the Aging, Inc.

Cooper, K.H. (1970). The new aerobics. New York: M. Evans & Co. Inc.

Corbin, D.E. (1988). Jogging. Glenview, IL: Scott, Foresman and Company.

Consumer Guide. (1988). Walking for health and fitness. Lincolnwood, IL: Publications International, Ltd.

Kuntzleman, C.T. & the Editors of Consumer Guide. (1979). The complete book of walking. New York: Pocket Books.

Pep up your life: A fitness book for seniors. (n.d.). Marketing Services Department, The Travelers Insurance Companies, One Tower Square, Hartford, CN 06115.

Pereira, J. (1989, February 15). Attention, shoppers: The 100-store walk is about to begin. The Wall Street Journal. pp. A1, A7.

U.S. Department of Health and Human Services. (1981). Exercise and your heart. (Publ. No. 81-1677). Bethesda, MD: National Heart, Lung and Blood Institute.

Walking for a healthy heart. (1984). Dallas: American Heart Association.

Walking Clubs and Organizations

American Mall Walkers Club and Walkers Club of America
P.O. Box 883
Westbury, NY 11590
(Send self-addressed, stamped envelope)

American Volkssport Association
1001 Pat Booker Road, Suite 203
Universal City, TX 78148
(512) 659-2112

American Walkers Association
6221 Robison Road
Cincinnati, OH 45213

Rockport Walking Institute
P.O. Box 480
Marlboro, MA 01752
(617) 485-2090
Attention: Debbie Kravetz

Walkabout International
835 Fith Avenue
San Diego, CA 92101
(619) 231-7463

The WalkWays Center
733 15th Street NW, Suite 427
Washington, D.C> 20005
(202) 737-9555

Hiking Clubs and Organizations

American Hiking Society
1015 31st Street, NW
Washington, D.C. 20007
(703) 385-3252

British Tourist Authority
40 W. 57th Street
New York, NY 10019
(212) 581-4708

National Audubon Society
950 Avenue
New York, NY 10022
(212) 756-9202

Sierra Club
930 Polk Street
San Francisco, CA 94109
(415) 776-2211

Wilderness Society
1400 I Street, NW
10th Floor
Washington, D.C. 20005
(202) 842-3400

Chapter **16**
Relaxation and Stress Reduction

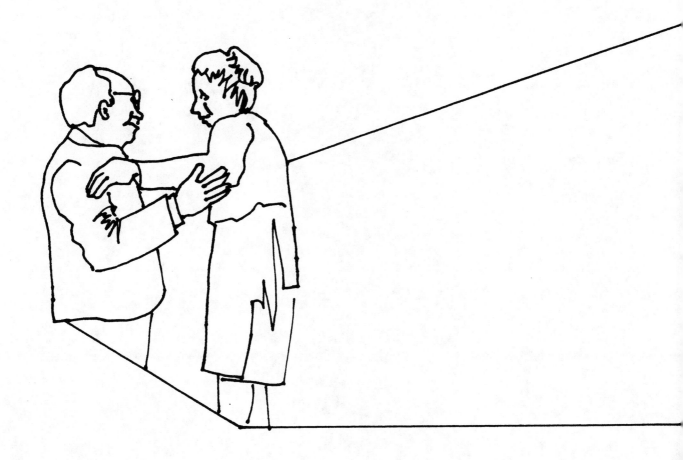

Chapter 16
Relaxation and Stress Reduction

In Chapter 3 it was pointed out that older people commonly have to deal with many more stressors than any other age group (Butler & Lewis, 1982). We have also pointed out in other chapters throughout the book that certain types of exercises are stress reducers.

"Successful aging may be defined as the ability to cope effectively with both major life events and chronic hassles, and to adapt to new situations. An individual who has survived to the age of 75 or older has proved to be adaptable to new situations. Hence, older people who continue to use coping strategies that have proved successful in the past will be likely to maintain their life satisfaction and well-being throughout the later years" (Hooyman & Kiyak, 1988). By the same token, older people who have learned to cope effectively with stress have probably accepted that new types of stressors may require new or different types of stress management skills and people are never too old to learn new things. Mark Twain once said that if the only tool you have is a hammer then everything starts looking like a nail. To deal with stress we need many different tools depending on the stressor. The question isn't which is the best stress management technique, but which is the best technique for which situation. A hammer is an excellent tool for pounding nails but not for turning a screw. In this chapter we will briefly summarize some popular, effective relaxation and stress management tools. As with exercise, stress management skills are something that must become a part of your whole lifestyle. You cannot learn a stress management technique, practice it once and then expect it to provide you with lifelong immunity to stress related diseases. Similarly, taking up walking for one week will not keep you fit for the rest of your life. Like brushing your teeth or bathing, stress management skills need to be learned and practiced at frequent intervals in order to provide the maximum health benefits. If this is done, the health payoffs can be large. Headaches, skin rashes, allergies, ulcers, hypertension and cardiovascular diseases are but a few of the diseases or disorders that might be stress related and therefore amenable to stress management skills. In addition, practicing stress management skills can help you to maintain a positive and realistic approach to life.

Technically, stress is neither good nor bad. Dr. Hans Selye (1974), the father of the scientific investigation of stress, was quick to point out that a person who has no stress is dead. Selye distinguished between "good" stress (eustress) and "bad" stress (distress). Whether or not a stimulus is eustress or distress depends upon two main factors: 1) how the person perceives the stress; and 2) how the person reacts to the stimulus.   Stress   management skills and techniques may approach stressors from either or both aspects.

Because of the wide range of personalities of older adults and because of the equally broad range of possible stressors, the problem of stress management is multi-faceted.   Today many older Americans are concerned about using drugs to "solve" stress-related problems.   They find that drugs do nothing to get at the underlying stress problems, and at the same time, drugs actually become   stressors,   especially   if   physical   or   psychological dependence develops (see Chapter 18).   More and more Americans are turning to non-drug methods for coping with stress and anxiety.   These methods often work, irrespective of a person's chronological age and despite the fact that the person may have never practiced the skills or techniques in his or her younger years. We urge you to read through the stress management techniques in this chapter to decide which are most suitable to your personality and needs, then you will need to learn more about the technique (see the references at the end of this chapter) and finally practice the techniques. Remember that some types of exercise and dance are stress reducing, and have been discussed elsewhere in this book (i.e., dance improvisation, T'ai Chi Ch'uan, yoga, and walking in Chapters 10,   13,   14, and 15, respectively).

Meditation

The two most popular types of meditation in the U.S. today are Transcendental Meditation (TM) and Relaxation Response. Transcendental Meditation is a trade name and can only be taught by a person who has completed training directly from the founder of the technique, Maharishi Mahesh Yogi.   TM involves the repetition of a secret word, while seated in a comfortable position.   This word, the mantra, is given to the meditator by a teacher. The meditator is to introspectively seek the source of thought, thereby allowing the mind to transcend superficial thought to arrive at a calm, peaceful and tranquil state.   The reduction in metabolic rate, heart rate, blood pressure and ventilation rate are well documented through scientific research (Wiswell, 1980).   TM is not a religion or dogma, but because of its ties and origins with Eastern culture, many people reject it as being non-secular.   Others find the cost of the TM program prohibitive despite the fact that it could be a preventative health practice that could pay for itself many times over in reduction of future health care costs.

Dr.   Herbert Benson, through his book <u>The Relaxation Response</u>, introduced to the American public, a meditation based on TM, that can be self-taught and practiced.   All that the meditator need do is meet these four criteria: 1) have a quiet environment in which to learn and practice;   2) be in a comfortable position; 3) have a passive attitude; and 4) have a mental device like a mantra or a prayer to repeat over and over. Dr. Benson described the benefits and details of the "Relaxation Response" in his book (Benson, 1975).

There are many other types of meditation and they are summarized in Lawrence LeShan's excellent book, How to Meditate (LeShan, 1974).

Progressive Relaxation

Progressive relaxation was developed by Dr. Edmund Jacobson (1934). In its pure form, it takes its practitioners through a step-by-step series of voluntary contractions and relaxations of the muscles, one muscle group at a time. It is Jacobson's belief that people can learn to reduce tension in the muscles by first learning to recognize the various degrees of muscular tension that exist.

Throughout the years, Jacobson's techniques have been modified in many different ways. An example of a modified progressive relaxation lesson follows:

Clench your fists as tightly as you can for 5 seconds. Now release. Notice the difference between the tense state and the relaxed state. Now clench your fists at 50% maximum. Hold for 5 seconds. Now relax. Tune in to the different levels of tension that you have just experienced in your hands. Now clench your fists at 25% of your maximum and hold for 5 seconds. Release and let all the tension flow out of your hands. Now just imagine clenching the fists at 100%, but don't actually clench them. Imagine for 5 seconds. Now release. Notice the difference in the tension levels you were able to produce and the lack of tension you are experiencing now.

The practitioner of this type of relaxation becomes more and more aware of, and in control of, his or her muscular tension as he or she practices the technique with different muscle groups. However, people with hypertension should consult with a physician before doing progressive relaxation since the isometric contractions may be contraindicated for this group.

Autogenics

Autogenics or autogenic training is a relaxation technique that consists of six mental exercises which are to be practiced several times a day. The practitioner is trained, through person-to-person contact or through audio tapes, to concentrate on the following feelings or sensations:

1. heaviness in the arms and legs
2. warmth in the arms and legs
3. cardiac control
4. breath control
5. warmth in the upper abdomen
6. coolness in the forehead (Wiswell, 1980).

The Relaxation and Stress Reduction Workbook (Davis, Eshelman & McKay, 1988) is an excellent source of practice exercises in autogenics and other stress management techniques.

Self-Hypnosis

Many of the so-called new techniques of relaxation are merely variations of hypnosis themes--imagery, autogenics, quieting response, and psychocybernetics. Self-hypnosis is an easy technique to master and can be learned in less than an hour. Self-hypnosis is the application of time honored techniques of hypnosis that have been used through the years in health related professions. One of the biggest barriers to self-hypnosis is the negative attitude many people have towards hypnosis because of its portrayal by the media as either a mystical experience, a malevolent force, or a comic diversion. When used properly though, self-hypnosis can be an excellent stress management technique. Once people are exposed to self-hypnosis they are more likely to view it positively (Corbin, 1984). Remember that stress management techniques have to be practiced regularly to gain maximum benefits. Don't expect to remedy all of your life's stressors in a few sessions.

If you are interested in more information about self-hypnosis read Self-Hypnotism: The Technique and Its Use in Daily Living (LeCron, 1964), Self-Hypnosis: A Conditioned-Response Technique (Sparks, 1962) or The Relaxation and Stress Reduction Workbook (Davis, Eshelman & McKay, 1988).

Massage

Hans Selye said the following about massage: "Not only can massage help to reduce distress, but it can be effective in producing favorable stress, eustress"(Hofer, 1976). Past and current European and Eastern cultures have long extolled the virtues of massage. Perhaps it is time for more Americans to realize, as Selye pointed out that : "Massage is one of the most ancient, effective means of obtaining relaxation from excessive stress in daily life" (Hofer, 1976).

Legitimate massage therapy should not be undermined because of the negative publicity surrounding "massage parlors" that are fronts for prostitution. One of the best ways to determine if a massage therapist is "legitimate" is to see if he or she is a member of the American Massage Therapy Association. If you can't afford the luxury of a professional massage, then read The Massage Book (Downing, 1976), Total Massage (Hofer, 1976) or some other massage book, and then practice with a partner.

We like to have a massage component to each exercise and dance class that we conduct. One person sits in a chair and a partner stands behind the seated person. The seated person leans forward in his or her chair so that the person behind can massage the back. Generally, a pattern or sequence is followed such as: kneading, finger tapping (with the pads of the fingers, as shown in Fig. 16.1, hacking (keeping the fingers loose to absorb the shock as shown in Fig. 16.2), cupping (making a cup with the thumbs and the hands) and feather strokes (very light swirling strokes on the back--not so light as to tickle the person as shown in Fig. 16.3). Each of the different strokes is done for about thirty seconds to a minute. All of these can be done wearing regular street clothing. Soothing music is suitable for background if desired. Massage is an excellent way to cool down after an exercise class. Make sure that the partners take turns in giving and receiving the massage.

Fig. 16.1

In addition to the relaxation and good feeling of receiving the massage, the giving of the massage is good exercise for the hands. A massage period added to a dance or exercise program often becomes one of the most popular segments of a total program. The importance of touch cannot be underestimated (Montagu, 1978).

The oils used in professional massages can help to keep the skin in good condition. The range of motion exercises common in massage and the increased blood flow to the muscles and joints may help to reduce pain due to certain types

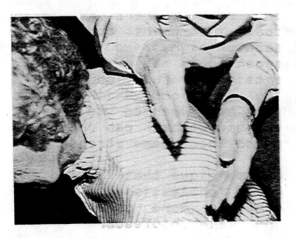

Fig. 16.2

of arthritis.   If the services of a massage therapist are too expensive then consider the possibility of asking friends and family to give gift certificates for massages or perhaps enrolling in a course on massage therapy with a partner would be a reasonable alternative. A videotape entitled "The Massage: Instruction for Beginners" by Steve Abraham is available from:

> The Bodymind Approach
> P.O. Box 6230
> Omaha, NE 68106

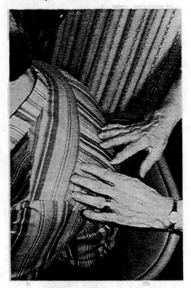

Fig. 16.3

<u>Biofeedback</u>

Biofeedback is basically a self-assessment tool.   Through the combined use of machinery and a clinician (registered nurse, physical therapist, health educator, psychologist or physician), the patient or client can monitor various bodily functions such as blood pressure, muscular tension, skin temperature, brain waves and heart rate.   The biofeedback instruments convert body processes into audio or visual feedback signals so that the patient or client knows what is happening in his or her body. Once a person learns to recognize certain body functions, then he or she can learn to control those functions which may be destructive to health.   If a person has learned to respond inappropriately to stressors, then biofeedback can help the person achieve new ways of responding to those same stressors.

Biofeedback is not a relaxation technique that is used very often by itself. Almost all health professionals who use biofeedback equipment also use one or more other stress management techniques in combination with biofeedback. Some types of health insurance cover biofeedback training that is administered by a physician or referred by a physician.   If interested in biofeedback check the terms of your insurance policy.   Nowadays there is a wide variety of biofeedback equipment available to the general public.   One company that sells handy and rather inexpensive yet sophisticated biofeedback equipment is:

Thought Technology, Ltd.
2180 Belgrave Ave.
Montreal, Canada

Simple finger mercury thermometers for temperature biofeedback are available for less than a dollar each from the Conscious Living Foundation (address is given in the imagery section). An excellent book about biofeedback is Stress and the Art of Biofeedback by Barbara Brown (1977).

Assertiveness Training

Assertiveness lies somewhere on a continuum between passivity and aggressiveness. If you find yourself to be either too passive or too aggressive in response to stressors involving other people, then you might want to consider taking classes or workshops in assertiveness training. Many older adults could use assertiveness training to combat the agism that exists in our society. Alex Comfort recommends the following:

> React to people who talk slightingly about seniors ("old duffer," "old biddy," "dirty old man," "old lady in tennis shoes"). . . . Tell them you don't appreciate that sort of language. Your reaction will give them a salutary shock. Usually they mean no harm, but need their heads changed, to see older people as people, and only incidentally or secondarily as old. Don't put up with being addressed by nurses, aides and others as "Granny," "Pop" or the like.

The above quote is just a brief example of assertive behavior. There are many community organizations that offer free or inexpensive workshops and classes in assertiveness training. For many older adults, learning to exhibit assertive behavior can be an effective way to to reduce interpersonal stressors.

Creative Visualization or Imagery

The popularity of such books as Mind as Healer, Mind as Slayer (Pelletier, 1977), Getting Well Again (Simonton & Matthews-Simonton, 1980), Creative Visualization (Gawain, 1985), Love, Medicine and Miracles (Siegel, 1986) and The Healing Brain (Ornstein & Sobel, 1987) have brought to millions of people's attention the power of imagery in healing and stress management processes. To over simplify, it all boils down to "you are what you think." According to Hanson (1986):

> Although it seems an unscientific approach, I can usually tell when an old person has given up. It's when he or she voluntarily stops buying new clothes!

Their attitude of depression and impending death seems to render such purchases pointless to them. Such negative thinking, mirrored in the shiny seat of their pants, is a classic signal that life is over. With alarming regularity, people who have given up on themselves in this way follow their depressed attitudes right into the grave.

Conversely, when people look at the positive side of life and when they can muster their imaginations to work for them instead of against them, then they have won much of the battle. A positive attitude is why placebos work.

The placebo, then, is not so much a pill as a process. The process begins with the patient's confidence in the doctor and extends through to the full functioning of his own immunological and healing system. The process works not because of any magic in the tablet but because the human body is its own best apothecary and because the most successful prescriptions are those that are filled by the body itself. (Cousins, 1979).

The knowledge that healing and relaxation are within us all is a powerful notion. Positive thoughts can, with practice, become self-fulfilling. If using the imagination and producing positive thoughts is difficult then he or she would do well to remember the saying "fake it till you make it." We can all learn to have more control over our bodies and we can all gain from the power of positive thinking. It is hypothesized that it is as important to know what kind of person has a disease as it is to know what kind of disease a person has.

Practice of creative visualization and imagery will help people to deal with anxieties and stessors that occur in everyday life. If major illnesses or stressors occur then the groundwork has already been laid for effectively dealing with these major events through creative visualization and imagery in combination with more traditional treatments. Audio and video tapes on creative visualization, imagery, and other techniques are listed at the end of this chapter.

Following is an example of an image used to help produce relaxation. Read it slowly into a tape recorder then play it back whenever you wish to relax.

The Featherbed

Imagine that you are suspended atop a large featherbed. All that it will take to make you sink into the big billowy bed is a slight push on the various parts of the body. One by one different body parts will be gently pushed until eventually your whole body will disappear into the featherbed. You will still have a breathing space and you will be able to breathe regularly and slowly. First imagine that a gentle downward pressure is applied to your right foot. It sinks down into the featherbed. It feels warm and limp. It will feel good to have the other foot feel the same way. A gentle downward pressure is applied to the left foot and it too, drifts down into the featherbed. It feels warm and limp. Next a gentle downward pressure is applied to your right leg (from your hip to your foot). It feels pleasantly warm and limp. It will feel good to have the other leg feel the same way, so a gentle downward pressure is applied to the left leg (from the hip to the foot). It too, feels warm, limp and relaxed. Your whole lower body from your hips to your feet feel warm, limp, and relaxed. Each time you breathe, you feel even more relaxed. As you exhale you feel tension leaving the body and as you inhale you feel relaxation entering your body. You are looking forward to the upper body feeling as relaxed as the lower body. A gentle downward pressure is applied to your right hand. It sinks into the featherbed and it feels warm, limp and relaxed. A gentle downward pressure is applied to the left hand and it too, sinks into the featherbed. It feels warm and limp. A gentle pressure is applied to the right arm (from the shoulder to the hand). It drifts into the featherbed and feels warm, limp and relaxed. A similar pressure is applied to your left arm (from the shoulder to the hand) and it drifts into the soft featherbed. It feels limp and warm and pleasantly suspended. A gentle downward pressure is applied to your upper torso (including your chest and abdominal cavities). Your torso feels pleasantly suspended, limp, warm and relaxed. Only your head and neck remain above the featherbed. It will feel good to have them join the rest of the body in comfort and warmth. A gentle downward pressure is applied to your head and neck and they sink into the featherbed. A breathing space remains but otherwise your body has disappeared into the soft, billowy featherbed. Your body feels pleasantly suspended, comfortable, warm, limp, and relaxed. Each time you breathe you feel even more relaxed. As you exhale your tensions and anxieties leave your body and as you inhale you breathe in relaxed feelings. You feel warm, comfortable, peaceful, serene, and relaxed. It is a great feeling. Now take a few minutes to enjoy your feelings of warm weightlessness. You deserve this session.

Other Techniques

This chapter by no means covers all of the stress management possibilities. Simply having someone to talk to is a very effective method of dealing with stress. Sometimes problems are so great that it is necessary to seek professional help from mental health professionals. Self-help and support groups are often helpful ways to cope with stress. Keeping diaries, practicing time management skills, and simply listening to soothing music can also be effective stress management methods. According to Teague (1987): "Stress is actually the effect of uncertainty, unsuccessful coping, and negative images that evoke body and mind tensions. Stress, however, is a unique and private phenomenon. Each person quite personally shapes expectations and solves psychological and social problems in special personal ways." The purpose of this chapter was to introduce the reader to some of the options that we have in determining our own personal methods of dealing with stress.

References/Resources

Benson, H. (1975). The relaxation response. New York: Avon Books.

Brown, B. B. (1977). Stress and the art of biofeedback. New York: Bantam Books.

Butler, R.N., & Lewis, M.I. (1982). Aging and mental health: Positive psychosocial and biomedical approaches. St.Louis: C.V. Mosby.

Comfort, Alex. (1976). A good age. New York: Crown Publishers.

Corbin, D.E. (1984). Attitudes toward hypnosis among university students before and after self-hypnosis classes in a stress management course. Journal of Hypnotherapy. 5, 1, 3-5.

Cousins, N. (1979). Anatomy of an illness. New York: W.W. Norton.

Davis, M., Eshelman, E.R., & McKay, M. (1988). The relaxation and stress reduction workbook. Oakland, CA: New Harbinger Publications.

Downing, G. (1976). The massage book. New York: Random House.

Gawain, S. (1985). Creative visualization. New York: Bantam.

Hanson, P.G. (1986). The joy of stress. Islington, Ontario: Hanson Stress Management Organization.

Hofer, J. (1976). Total massage. New York: Grosset and Dunlop.

Hooyman, N.R. & Kiyak, H.A. (1988). Social gerontology. Boston: Allyn & Bacon.

Jacobson, E. (1934). You must relax. New York: McGraw-Hill.

LeCron, L.M.   (1964). <u>Self-hypnotism: The technique and its use in daily living</u>. New York: Signet.

LeShan, L. (1974). <u>How to meditate</u>. New York: Bantam Books.

Montagu, A. (1978). <u>Touching: The human significance of the skin</u>. (2nd ed.). New York: Harper and Row.

Ornstein, R. & Sobel, D. (1987). <u>The healing brain</u>. New York: Touchstone.

Pelletier, K.R. (1977). <u>Mind as healer, mind as slayer</u>. New York: Dell Publishing Co.

Selye, H. (1974). <u>Stress without distress</u>. Philadelphia: J.B. Lippincott.

Siegel, B.S. (1986). <u>Love, medicine and miracles</u>. New York: Harper & Row.

Sparks, T. (1962). <u>Self-hypnosis: A conditioned-response technique</u>. North Hollywood, CA: Wilshire Book Co.

Teague, M.L. (1987). <u>Health promotion: Achieving high-level wellness in the later years</u>. Indianapolis: Benchmark Press.

Wiswell, R.A. (1980). Relaxation, exercise, and aging (Chapter 39). In J. Birren and B. Sloane (Eds.), <u>Handbook of mental health and aging</u>. Englewood Cliffs, NJ: Prentice-Hall.

Audiotapes

ARC Audiovisual Enterprises, Inc.
Dept. BSS
500 West End Avenue #58
New York, NY 10024

Conscious Living Foundation
P.O. Box 9
Drain, OR 97435
(503) 836-2358

Creative Audio
Department BSS
8751 Osborne
Highland, IN 46322

Effective Learning Systems, Inc.
5221 Edina Ind. Blvd.
Edina, MN 55435
(612) 893-1680

New Harbinger Publications
Dept. B
5674 Shattuck Ave.
Oakland, CA 94609

Source
P.O. Box W
Stanford, CA 94309
(415) 328-7171

Whatever Publishing
P.O. Box 137
Mill Valley, CA

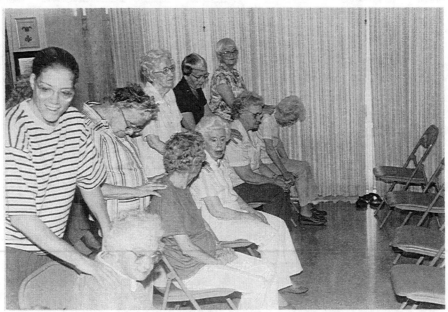

Massages at the end of an exercise class.

Chapter 17

Nutrition for the Older Adult
(by Rita Frickel, M.S., R.D.)

Rita A. Frickel, M.S., R.D., has worked as a registered dietician for the past eight years in various hospital out-patient and in-patient programs. She counsels all age groups in various aspects of diet and clinical nutrition.

Chapter 17
Nutrition for the Older Adult
(by Rita Frickel, M.S., R.D.)

For older adults, as for any age group, good nutrition is an important component in the maintenance of an optimal state of health. The focus of this chapter will be on the nutritional concerns of healthy, independent-living older adults rather than on the institutionalized or severely debilitated older adult.

In discussing the nutritional needs of this age group, it should be noted that nutritional needs are not the same for all older people. Instead, the nutritional status of each older adult is a unique product of the lifetime influences of heredity, environment, and culture, thus making this age group heterogeneous in regards to nutrition needs. The discussion and guidelines given are merely practical considerations from which most healthy, older adults could benefit.

Physiological Changes Affecting Nutritional Status

Despite the known heterogeneity of older adults, there are some generalizations which are valid in regards to the physiological changes that occur normally with the aging process (Fuller, 1986). It is important to review these since they may have profound effects on an individual's nutritional status and needs.

Sensory Changes: The senses of taste and smell are vital to the enjoyment of food. With aging, both of these senses gradually become less acute. For example, there is a loss in the number of taste buds. Sweet and salty tastes are lost first; thus, older adults frequently complain of foods tasting bitter or sour (Busse, 1978). The changes in taste and smell may contribute to a disinterest in eating and thus negatively affect an individual's nutritional status. Herbs and spices may be added to enhance flavors of foods since they are low in sodium and are generally allowed on most therapeutic diets.

Teeth: Approximately 50% of adults over the age of 65, and 60% over the age of 75 have lost most of their teeth and require dentures (Hickler and Wayne, 1984). Having missing teeth or having to wear dentures does not imply necessarily that eating must be impaired, as many older adults are still able to incorporate most foods into their diet regardless of texture. However, those who have poor fitting dentures or dental problems may need to modify texture to accommodate their dental status.

Texture can be modified without compromising the basics of a balanced diet. For example, if chewing meat is bothersome, softer protein sources such as cottage cheese, fish, eggs or casseroles with melted cheese, tender chunks of poultry or ground beef may be substituted. If raw fruits and vegetables cannot be chewed, they can be slightly cooked or juices may be used instead. Care should be taken not to let such a diet become too dependent on fatty or high cholesterol foods.

Gastrointestinal Changes: In general, aging is accompanied by a reduction in the body's secretion of digestive juices. These changes vary widely among individuals and for the most part, do not appear to affect the body's ability to absorb and utilize most nutrients, with the possible exceptions of iron and vitamin B12 which will be discussed later.

Another gastrointestinal change is the slowing of the intestinal muscles so that constipation frequently results. A high fiber diet to alleviate this will be discussed later. The benefits of exercise on constipation are discussed in Chapter 3.

Body Composition: With aging, the composition of the body changes, with the percentage of lean muscle tissue decreasing while the percentage of fatty tissue increases (Fuller, 1986). This change causes a decline in the basal metabolic rate, or the rate at which the body "burns" calories. This change in calorie needs will be discussed later.

Nutrient Needs: To date, only limited data exists as to the effects of aging on nutrient needs. The Recommended Dietary Allowances (RDAs) established by the Food and Nutrition Board are the most commonly used guideline for establishing nutrient needs for aged adults. However, these guidelines are currently receiving criticism as to their validity for older adults since they are based on extrapolation of data using young adults.

Until further research is completed in this area, it is assumed that the need for most nutrients remains unchanged with aging, with a few exceptions. These will be discussed later in this chapter.

Energy Needs: Research has indicated that the benefits of maintaining an ideal body weight throughout life includes a lowered risk of developing such diseases as hypertension, diabetes, and heart disease. Therefore, the ultimate goal in discussing energy needs is determining a caloric level that will help maintain weight and prevent excessive weight gain.

As mentioned previously, the most commonly used guidelines for nutrient recommendations for older adults is the RDA. The 1980 RDA separated calorie (or energy needs) of the older adults into two age groups: 51-75 years and 75 plus years (Food and Nutrition Board, 1980). According to these guidelines, persons 51-75 years of age require only about 90% of the calories required for younger adults while persons over 75 years require only 75-80% of the calories allowed for younger adults.

Several factors may contribute to this decrease in caloric needs of older adults. The most pronounced appears to be the shift in body composition (i.e., the proportion of body fat increases as muscle mass decreases). Lean muscle mass causes the metabolic rate to be increased, meaning the rate at which the body burns calories is faster. This change in body composition causes a lowering of the basal metabolic rate (BMR) by approximately 15-20% between the ages of 30 and 90 years old (Hickler and Wayne, 1984). This decrease in the BMR necessitates fewer calories be consumed to maintain the status quo.

The Expert Committee on Energy and Protein Requirements suggests that caloric needs of moderately active adults be decreased by 5% for each decade between ages 40 and 59 and 10% between ages 60 and 69 and another 10% after age 70 (NIH Concensus Conference, 1984).

To assure these lowered calorie diets are nutritionally adequate for older adults, the individual must be more careful in making his or her food selections. Following the "Basic Four Food Groups" guidelines is helpful in meeting these needs. (See Table 17.1).

Another factor which may cause a further decrease in calorie needs for older adults is a decrease in activity level. In the absence of major medical problems, it is advised that the older adult maintain an active lifestyle. See Chapters 6-15 for recommended activities.

<u>Protein:</u> In the past, it was suggested that protein requirements were higher for older adults than for younger people. Part of this speculation was based on knowledge that lean muscle mass decreases with age. It was thought that higher protein levels would prevent this decline of lean tissue. However, we now know that excess dietary protein has little effect on muscle mass. Rather, the combination of <u>adequate</u> calories and protein, along with appropriate exercise are the factors known to increase muscle tissue. Therefore, the majority of current research indicates that protein requirements do not change with age. The RDA for all adults suggests that 12% of total calories be derived from protein (Food and Nutrition Board, 1980). This can be met by following the Basic Four Food Groups Guidelines in Table 17.1. Most dietary surveys indicate that based on the RDAs, protein intake is one of the few nutrients found most frequently in adequate amounts in older adults (Garry, et al., 1987).

<u>Vitamins</u> <u>and</u> <u>Minerals:</u> The current RDAs indicate vitamin and mineral needs are the same for older adults as for younger adults. However, these recommendations are based on extremely limited research. More recently, research indicates that there may be changes in the nutrient needs for older adults for Vitamins A and D and the mineral calcium.

Vitamin A: In general, it appears that older adults consume Vitamin A in amounts exceeding the current RDAs (Munroe, 1985). In addition to a high prevalence of older adults taking vitamin supplements (48%), there is an increase in Vitamin A absorption with aging (Blumberg, 1986). These factors cause more concern of a toxicity of Vitamin A rather than a deficiency. Secondary to these concerns, the 1980-1985 RD Committee has proposed the RDAs of Vitamin A be lowered for older adults from 1000 RE to 900 RE for men and from 800 RE to 600 RE for women (Blumberg, 1986). This requirement can be met by including a dark yellow or green vegetable or fruit serving every other day, i.e., carrots, sweet potatoes, squash, spinach, broccoli, greens and apricots.

Vitamin D: Nutrition surveys indicate that 62-74% of free-living older adults consume less than two-thirds of the RDA of Vitamin D (Gulpa, Dworkin and Gambert, 1988). Factors contributing to inadequate Vitamin D intake include an inadequate diet as well as lack of exposure to the sun. Since Vitamin D is essential for the formation of normal bone (along with calcium), a deficiency state contributes to osteomalacia, a disease characterized by softening of the bones.

Because Vitamin D is found naturally in some fish, eggs, liver and butter as well as in fortified milk, inclusion of several servings of these foods daily can help achieve an adequate intake. Exposure to the sunlight twice a week for 15 minutes duration can also provide weekly Vitamin D needs. If you are on a low cholesterol diet skim milk is an excellent source of Vitamin D without the cholesterol. Note that very little sunlight is necessary. You need not risk skin cancer to get the Vitamin D that you need.

Calcium: Of all the nutrients studied to date, calcium has been found to be the one most deficient in diets of older adults (Freedman and Ahronheim, 1985). Furthermore, the body's ability to absorb calcium declines with age, subjecting the older adult to a greater risk of calcium deficiency. This calcium deficiency has been associated with the development of osteoporosis.

Because of this, many experts in the field of nutrition consider the current RDA for calcium (800 mg/day) to be inadequate for this age group. It is believed that the amount of calcium needed to maintain bone status increases with age. For example, men over the age of 51 may need 1000 mg/day and postmenopausal women need approximately 1500 mg/day (Hahn, Peck and Riggs, 1985). For women, this would require approximately five cups of milk a day. (Each cup provides 300 mg of calcium). At this level, this would account for approximately half of her calorie needs, making it difficult to obtain a balance of other nutrients. Therefore, calcium supplements, especially in the form of calcium carbonate, may be beneficial in addition to dietary sources. In addition to diet, a sound exercise program is recommended to maintain bone status.

Fiber: Although fiber is not regarded as an essential nutrient, it is an important constituent of the diet, especially for older adults. Fiber helps soften solid waste products (stools), helping to alleviate constipation, and thus hemorrhoids. Fiber has also been implicated in prevention of both diverticulosis and possibly colon cancer (Burkett, 1982). Recently, fiber has also been touted as a preventative measure in coronary heart disease. Oat bran and psyllium products (i.e., Metamucil) are thought to raise the HDLs (good cholesterols) and therefore lower total cholesterol levels.

Although a RDA has not been established for dietary fiber, a range of 25 to 30 grams daily is generally recommended (Burkitt, 1982). This level can be achieved by following the "Rule of Twos":

1. 2 tablespoons of unprocessed (raw) bran. (This can be sprinkled on cereals, soups, salads, etc.).

2. 2 slices of 100% whole wheat bread.

3. 2 servings of raw fruits and 2 servings of raw vegetables. (If raw foods are difficult to chew, they should be only slightly cooked, leaving skins on apples, pears, etc.).

To aid in the stool softening effects of fiber, plenty of fluid is needed. This is discussed in the next section.

Water: Sensitivity to thirst generally decreases in older adults (Fuller, 1986). This change often tends to result in inadequate amounts of water consumption. In extreme conditions, this can lead to dehydration or heat stroke since water plays an essential role in temperature regulation. The use of certain diuretics can compound this problem. Therefore, it is essential that regardless of thirst, the older adult should drink a minimum of six cups of fluid daily (consumption of some foods will supply some of the daily water needed). If the older adult is exercising or exposed to hot weather then fluid intake should be even greater.

Nutrition and Cancer: Diet may be an important aspect of cancer prevention. The American Cancer Society recommends the following dietary considerations to cut the risk of developing cancer:

1. Eat more cabbage-family (cruciferous) vegetables such as broccoli, cauliflower, brussels sprouts, cabbage and kale.

2. Eat more fiber.

3. Choose foods (not vitamin pills) with Vitamins A and C.

4. Trim the fat in your diet and control your weight.

5. Subtract salt-cured, smoked, nitrite-cured foods such as bacon, ham, hot dogs, and sausages.

6. If you drink alcohol, consume it only in small amounts.

Nutrition and Cholesterol: Elevated blood cholesterol is a major cause of atherosclerosis, which causes most heart attacks and strokes. As cholesterol levels drop the risks of heart attack and strokes drop. "In fact, for every one percent reduction in blood cholesterol, heart attack risk decreases two percent" (Byrne, 1988). Generally speaking, the lower your cholesterol the better. The American Heart Association recommends reducing total fat intake to 30 percent of total calories consumed. They also encourage the substitution of polyunsaturated and monosaturated fats whenever possible. These include oils from safflower and sunflower seeds, corn, soybeans, cottonseed, canola, and olive oil. To keep these oils within the guidelines of the 30 percent level, use no more than five teaspoons of oils per day for cooking, baking, salads, or as condiments.

To keep your intake of cholesterol to less than 300 mg/day and to keep fats to less than 30 percent of calories, limit your intake of meat, seafood, and poultry to no more than six ounces per day. (A three ounce portion is equivalent in size to a deck of cards). Also, remove the skin from poultry, trim all visible fats from meats, and buy extra lean cuts of meat. Limit the use of organ meats, such as liver, heart, and gizzards to no more than once per month. Limit egg yolks to less than three per week (American Heart Association, 1985). Substitute skim milk for whole milk.

In addition, Byrne (1988) suggests the following guidelines for reducing cholesterol:

1. Reduce saturated fat like those in red meat, whole milk, butter, cheeses, ice cream, lard, shortening, palm oil, coconut oil, and cocoa butter.

2. Reduce dietary cholesterol. Limit it to less than 300 mg/day.

3. Eat more soluble fiber such as that found in pectin in fruits and vegetables, oat bran and beans.

4. Eat more fish such as salmon, mackerel, tuna, white fish, herring, and trout. The omega-3 fatty acids in cold-water fish can reduce cholesterol and triglycerides. Try to obtain the omega-3 fatty acids through the fish listed above rather than through capsules. The capsules often contain additional saturated fats which would conteract any possible benefits.

5. Read food labels. Watch for hidden fats in processed foods.

6. Get regular exercise. (See Chapters 6-15).

7. Control your weight. If you have high blood pressure or high cholesterol, any extra pounds may increase your risk of heart disease.

8. If cholesterol levels are very high and they do not respond to the above, then it may be necessary for your physician to prescribe medications.

<u>Social and Physical Influences on Nutritional Status:</u>   Numerous social changes occur with aging which can affect an individual's nutritional status. Most noteworthy is the loss of a spouse. If the loss of a spouse results in an individual living alone, he or she often loses interest in the preparation and consumption of food for him or herself, resulting in an inadequate diet. Social support or professional counseling may be necessary for the person to work through his or her grief before a healthy appetite returns. Eating meals at Senior Citizens' Centers may fulfill some important social aspects of eating.

If there is difficulty in preparing food because of arthritis then it may be necessary to obtain self-care aids. The local Arthritis Foundation can be helpful in this regard. Local Area Agencies on Aging can provide information on other services such as Meals on Wheels and Senior Companions.

Summary

Adults over the age of 65 are a heterogeneous group regarding their nutritional status and thus, their nutritional needs. Changes in physical, social, and economic status all contribute to the quality of the older adult's diet.

The current RDAs for older adults are receiving critical analysis as to their appropriateness for this age group. The nutrients warranting the most attention for this age group are calories, Vitamins A and D, calcium, fiber, and water.

By following the Basic Four Food Group Guidelines, the American Cancer Society's steps to a healthier life, the American Heart Association's recommendations, and Dr. Byrne's guidelines for cutting cholesterol, in addition to adjusting calories according to activity level, older adults should be able to achieve an appropriate intake of most nutrients to aid in attaining an optimal state of health.

References

American Cancer Society. (1985). Taking control: 10 steps to a healthier life and reduced cancer risk.

American Heart Association. (1985). The American Heart Association diet: An eating plan for healthy Americans.

Blumberg, J. (November, 1986). Nutrient requirements for the healthy elderly. Boletin Asociacion Medica de Puerto Rico, 78, 494-496.

Burkitt, D. (1982). Dietary fiber: Is it really helpful? Geriatrics, 37, 119-126.

Busse, E.W. (1978). How mind, body and environment influence nutrition in the elderly. Postgraduate Medicine, 63, 118.

Byrne, K. (1988). Cut your cholesterol - Now! Medical Self-Care. 49, 26-31.

Food and Nutrition Board. (1980). Recommended dietary allowances (9th ed.). Washington, D.C.: National Academy of Sciences, National Research Council.

Freedman, M.J. & Ahronheim, J.C. (1985). Nutritional needs of the elderly: Debate and recommendations. Geriatrics. 40, 45-59.

Fuller, E. (1986). What's a "sound diet" for the elderly? Patient Care, 20, 90-106.

Garry, P.J., Hunt, W.C., Bandrofchak, J.L., VanderJagt, D. & Goodwin, J.S. (1987). Vitamin A intake and plasma retinol levels in healthy elderly men and women. American Journal of Clinical Nutrition, 46, 989.

Gupta, K., Dworkin, B. & Gambert, S.R. (1988). Common nutritional disorders in the elderly: Atypical manifestations. Geriatrics, 43, 87-97.

Hahn, B., Peck, W., & Riggs, L. (1985). Warding off osteoporosis. Patient Care, 19, 20-39.

Hickler, R. & Wayne, K. (1984). Nutrition in the elderly. American Family Physician, 137.

Munroe, H. (1985). Nutrient needs and nutritional status in relation to aging. Drug-Nutrient Interactions, 4, 55-74.

National Institute of Health Concensus Conference. (1984). Journal of the American Medical Association, 252, 799.

Chapter 18

Drugs and the Older Adult

Chapter 18
Drugs and the Older Adult

People over age 65 make up about 12% of the population, but they take almost a third, or $9 billion worth, of prescription medications. According to a Special Report done by the _Arizona Republic_, more than $2 billion of these prescriptions are unnecessary. Indeed, this same Special Report stated that nearly 2 million older Americans become ill each year due to misuse of prescription drugs. About 73,000 of these older Americans die each year from adverse reactions and interactions to improper medication (Masterson and Cook, 1988). The prescription drug problem among older adults has been deemed by the Department of Health and Human Services (DHHS) Inspector General Richard P. Kusserow to be the "nation's other drug problem" to distinguish it from the war on illegal drugs, primarily among younger adults.

A report by the DHHS inspector general indicated that:

1. In 1985, an estimated 243,000 older Americans were hospitalized because of adverse reactions to drugs.

2. Every year about 32,000 older adults fracture their hips in drug-induced falls.

3. Serious mental impairment is either caused by or made worse by prescription drugs in over 163,000 older adults.

4. Nearly 2 million older Americans are addicted or at risk of addiction to tranquilizers or sleeping pills because of daily use for at least one year (Elderly Called Most at Risk from Drugs, 1989).

Frank Whittington (1988) recently edited a special issue on "Alcohol and Drugs: Abuse and Misuse" in _Generations: Journal of the American Society on Aging_. In this issue he set the tenor of the situation in the following quotation:

> Drugs and alcohol have become established parts of everyday life in American society. We use both in our attempts to "make it better," and we are often successful. The many benefits of properly used drugs are so numerous that we often overlook them; they are so important that many of us, quite literally, could not live without them. Even alcohol, though certainly more of a problem, is as Robert Kastenbaum argues . . . not without its advantages.

Our use and acceptance, however, have led predictably to misuse and disaster. Of course, the paths we typically travel to arrive at the unfortunate destinations of alcoholism, drug dependency, medication-induced illness, or death are varied, and the constellation of problems and issues presented by the use of alcohol are certainly different from those of medical drugs. . . . Whether by drinking or by drugging, someone is attempting, usually without fully understanding the risks, to apply a chemical solution to a human problem. Tragically, the results of such efforts too often bring to mind the old saying about diseases and cures and which is worse (Whittington, 1988).

How the body reacts to drugs depends on many factors among which are: 1) gender; 2) race; 3) nutritional status; 4) physical condition; 5) expectations of the drug; 6) emotional state; 7) how drugs are combined; and 7) age. As with nutrition (see Chapter 17) as people age their capabilities of metabolizing drugs changes. So, at a time in life when people have more chronic conditions and are therefore more likely to be taking both over-the-counter and prescription drugs, they are also more vulnerable to the effects of drugs. They need to be doubly cautious. It is important to keep in mind that there is a lag between the professional preparation of medical personnel and the aging boom. Training in the medical professions has not nearly kept pace with the numbers of people who are growing older. According to Masterson and Cook (1988) 70% of physicians in a study in Pennsylvania failed a test on geriatric care and pharmacology and only 2% of medical students in the U.S. are required to take courses in geriatric medicine. There is a nationwide shortage of geriatric specialists and studies show that many doctors are biased against older patients and they spend less time with older patients than with younger ones.

What all of this means is that older patients need to be self-advocates. They should work in partnership with health care professionals and they should ask relevant questions about any medications they take. Using medicines wisely means using the right drugs in the right amounts at the right times. It can also mean avoiding the overuse of drugs or not using drugs at all. Many health problems can best be dealt with by non-drug therapies such as proper diet, exercise, and stress management or through the avoidance of smoking or drinking too much alcohol. Although medication is often seen as a "magic bullet" solution to a problem it has the potential of making matters worse. It is paramount that the process of aging is not treated with medication. As has been stated before in this book, aging is not a disease. One must beware of diagnoses based on the premise that "one has to expect this or that to happen as one grows older."

Guidelines for Taking Prescription Drugs

Following are some guidelines for taking prescription drugs compiled from Wise Use of Medicine for the Elderly (n.d.) and A Special Report: Drugging Our Elderly (1988).

1. Make certain that you understand why you are taking the drug. If the prescription makes sense to you then you will be more likely to conscientiously take the medication as directed.

2. Make sure you get complete instructions on how and when to take the medications. Don't be afraid to ask the doctor to repeat the instructions. If you can't read the instructions then ask for larger print. If you have trouble with "child proof" caps on bottles then ask for an alternative, but keep this medication out of the reach of children.

3. Know what the common side effects of your drug are. If you notice that conditions are getting worse, consider that you could be experiencing an adverse side effect. Consult with your physician immediately.

4. Always inform your physician of any other drug that you may be taking, including alcohol, tobacco, over-the-counter drugs, and illegal drugs. The combined effects of many drugs can be dangerous and sometimes fatal.

5. Follow the doctor's orders unless you are experiencing side effects. Do not stop taking a medication simply because your symptoms have lessened or disappeared. If you are concerned that a dosage is too high or that you are experiencing an adverse side effect, then discuss it with your physician. Some medication dosages should be less for older adults than for younger adults so your dosage or type of drug may need to be changed.

6. Do not double up dosages because you skipped a previous dose or because you think two doses will work twice as good as one dose. This could be setting yourself up for an overdose.

7. Never share prescriptions. This can be detrimental to your health and it is illegal.

8. Do not save old medications or use outdated prescriptons. Some medications become ineffective with age and others can become harmful.

9. Whether you must take one or several medications, organize a system or a chart to keep track of when the medications were taken.

10. Watch what you eat and drink when you are on medications. Some foods and beverages (especially alcohol) can react adversely with some medications. If you are asked to take medications with meals, ask if this presumes three meals a day. Inquire about what you should do if you eat more or fewer meals a day.

11. If you cannot afford a necessary medication then inquire about any subsidies for which you may qualify.

12. Above all, maintain a working relationship and open communications with your physician and pharmacist. Ask questions and seek satisfactory answers. Become skillful at listening to your body so that you can better describe any problems to health care professionals. The better the information you give, the more likely your treatment is to be well suited to your condition. Be prepared to tell your physician what's wrong: describe the wheres, whens, and hows of your condition. Vague complaints are likely to be treated with vague remedies.

Guidelines for Taking Over-the-Counter (OTC) Drugs

Over-the-counter (OTC) drugs are not without hazards and they should be taken with caution. When taking OTC drugs it is important that the patient correctly determines what is wrong and then use the OTC drug properly and cautiously. Following are some guidelines for taking OTC drugs (Stanley, Overman, Ponedal & Stickgold, n.d.).

1. Thoroughly read the labels and ask the pharmacist about warnings you do not understand. Follow the directions given.

2. Do not use OTC drugs for severe or persistent conditions. In these cases seek medical advise.

3. Never use OTC drugs for extended periods of time unless under a doctor's orders. Using OTC drugs could mask symptoms that require a doctor's attention and most OTC drugs are not intended for longterm use.

4. Don't buy OTC drugs in large quantities uless they can be used before their effectiveness date expires. Some medications can even become poisonous.

5.   Do not take several OTC drugs at the same time without consulting your physician or pharmacist.

6.   Always check with the pharmacist before buying OTC drugs if you are using prescription drugs or legal drugs (i.e., alcohol, nicotine, or caffeine). Even aspirin can be dangerous under some conditions.

Smoking

Smoking tobacco is thought to be related to one in six deaths among Americans. In terms of illness and disease, no other substance produces so much harm to so many. According to Robert Kastenbaum (1988): "No solid evidence has been presented for positive health effects at any level of use" of tobacco. Indeed, most health experts agree that no matter the person's age, the level or extent of tobacco use, and despite the presence of smoking- related disease, the best advice would still be to tell the tobacco user to stop. Corbin & Stacy (1988) showed that the grandparent group of never-smokers (mean age of 76) rated their health higher than their smoking grandchildren (mean age of 26). Smoking tobacco, as has been documented since the first U.S. Surgeon General's Report over 25 years ago, is a risk factor in a litany of diseases and disorders including lung cancer, bronchitis, emphysema, mouth cancers, throat cancer, bladder cancer, esophagus cancer, pancreas cancer, arteriosclerosis, heart disease and kidney disease (Ferguson, 1987).

Nicotine addiction is thought to be more addictive than heroin, but it <u>can</u> be beat as evidenced by the millions of former smokers in the United States. Excellent smoking cessation programs exist throughout the United States and are as near as your local affiliates of the American Cancer Society, the American Lung Association, American Heart Association, and the Seventh Day Adventist Church. For those who need the help of nicotine gum, a physician should be consulted. It should be kept in mind, however, that for best results, nicotine gum should be used in combination with another type of smoking cessation program like those mentioned above and the gum should be used only as directed. Smoking affects the results of numerous medical tests thus increasing the chances of improper diagnoses. In addition, smoking also alters the effect of many drugs and nutrients on the body (Ferguson, 1987).

Alcohol

Some studies have shown that consumption of small amounts of alcohol may have a protective effect on the formation of cardiovascular disease, but more recent studies done in England have called to question any helpful effects in terms of cardiovascular disease. Small amounts of alcohol can help to relax a person or stimulate his or her appetite but among older adults one of the biggest concerns is the mixing of alcohol with prescription or over-the-counter drugs. Many drugs when used in combination can produce untoward side effects and even death. Alcohol does not mix well with acetaminophen (Tylenol), arthritis medicines, aspirin, antidepressants, antihistamines, barbiturates, major tranquilizers, sedatives, sleeping pills, and pain killers.

As many as one in ten American drinkers has a serious problem with alcohol. These people need to seek help either through medical treatment, counseling, or through support groups such as Alcoholics Anonymous (AA) or a combination of any of these. Alanon is an organization that helps the family and friends of alcoholics and problem drinkers and Alateen is a support group for teenagers whose lives are affected by alcoholics or problem drinkers. Adult Children of Alcoholics is a more recent support group for people whose lives were affected by an alcoholic parent or parents. Mother's Against Drunk Drivers (MADD) is an organization that offers support to the families of victims and families of drunk driving accidents. In addition, MADD monitors the courts in drunk driving cases and it lobbies legislative bodies to pass laws that can help to diminish drunk driving accidents.

Caffeine

Caffeine is frequently consumed without consequence in such products as coffee, tea, cola drinks, cocoa (chocolate), and many OTC diet and pain relief medicines. Some people are sensitive to caffeine and it can endanger their cardiovascular system by causing hypertension or cardiac arrhythmias. People with hypertension (high blood pressure) would be wise to avoid caffeine containing products. In addition, caffeine is related to anxiety and insomnia because it increases adrenalin which increases nervousness, restlessness, and breathing rate. Caffeine is also a diuretic so it increases the frequency of urination, which during the night, will disrupt sleep. Some people develop a dependence on caffeine and suffer withdrawal if they are deprived of it.

Although caffeine can contribute to alertness and a delaying of fatigue, it may not be worth consuming considering the above mentioned risks (Piscopo, 1985). Caffeine contributes to a small decrease in calcium absorption. So if you are a heavy user of caffeine containing products it could contribute to osteoporosis (Brittle Bones, 1985).

Summary

Drugs can be a boon or a bust. It depends on how and when they are used. Jean Mayer, renowned nutritionist, said: "There are no toxic substances, only toxic amounts." An analogy can be made to fire. When uncontrolled, it can destroy a home or a whole city; when controlled it can heat our homes and cook our food. Drugs have contributed to the control of many diseases but they have also caused many illnesses and deaths. Whether the drugs are prescription, over-the-counter, legal, or illegal, they should be respected for their potential for harm. It is imperative that consumers of drugs become knowledgeable about how and when they should be used.

References

Brittle Bones. (1985). <u>Nutrition Action</u>, <u>12</u>, 6.

Cook, C. & Masterson, M. (1988, June 26-July 2). Special report: Drugging our elderly. <u>The Arizona Republic</u>.

Corbin, D.E. & Stacy, R.D. (1988). A three-generation study of smoking behavior. <u>Wellness Perspectives: Journal of Individual, Family, and Community Wellness</u>, <u>5</u>, 4, 33-36.

Elderly called most at risk from drugs. (Feb. 16, 1989). <u>Omaha World-Herald</u>.

Ferguson, T. (1987). <u>The smoker's book of health</u>. New York: G.P. Putnam's Sons.

Piscopo, J. (1985). <u>Fitness and aging</u>. New York: Macmillan.

Stanley, E., Overman, S., Ponedal, S., & Stickgold, A. (n.d.). <u>Wise use of medicine for the elderly</u>. Gardena, CA: Behavioral Health Services, Inc.

Sexuality and Aging

Chapter 19
Sexuality and Aging

According to Alex Comfort, author of the best selling book The Joy of Sex: "In our experience, old folks stop having sex for the same reasons they stop riding a bicycle -- general infirmity, thinking it looks ridiculous, no bicycle -- and of these reasons the greatest is the social image of the dirty old man and the asexual, undesirable older woman " (Comfort, 1974). Comfort went on to say that sexuality in later years is "a mental, social, and probably a physical, preservative of their status as persons, which our society already attacks in so many cruel ways." Table 19.1 shows the importance of sexuality to older people. This table clearly shows that the majority of the over 4,200 older people who responded to a mailed questionnaire enjoy sexual expression and they engage in it regularly. Fifty-eight percent of the questionnaires, however, were not returned so it is difficult to determine how representative Brecher's (1984) sample is.

Table 19.1*

PROPORTION OF MEN AND WOMEN WHO REMAIN SEXUALLY ACTIVE (WITH A PARTNER OR ALONE) AFTER AGE 50

	In their 50s	In their 60s	Age 70 and older
Women	93%	81%	65%
Men	98%	91%	79%

*Copyright 1984 by Consumers Union of United States, Inc. Mount Vernon, NY 10553. Reprinted by permission from CONSUMER REPORTS BOOKS, 1984.

It is important to keep in mind that most people, regardless of their age, do not wish to have sex pressed upon them, but as a society we "could stop turning it off." (Comfort, 1974). We need to acknowledge that those who wish to be sexually active should be given the opportunity to do so.

Changes in Sexuality in the Aging Female

Biologically, there is little sexual impairment in women as they age. If health remains good and if there is a desire to remain sexually active, women can continue to be sexually active until late in life.

Table 19.2*

FREQUENCY OF SEX (WITH A PARTNER OR ALONE) AMONG SEXUALLY ACTIVE MEN AND WOMEN AFTER AGE 50

	In their 50s	In their 60s	Age 70 and older
Women (Sex at least once a week)	73%	63%	50%
Men (Sex at least once a week)	90%	73%	58%

*Copyright 1984 by Consumers Union of United States, Inc., Mount Vernon, NY 10553. Reprinted by permission from CONSUMER REPORTS BOOKS, 1984.

One of the main barriers to a sexually active life among heterosexual women is the unavailability of suitable male partners. Women outlive men by 7 or 8 years and they also tend to marry men older than they, therefore most married women are eventually widowed. The average age of widowhood is 56 and by the age of 65, 52% are widowed; by age 75, 68% are widowed. At these same ages most men are married (National Institute on Aging, n.d.). In modern American society there is a double standard as it views older-younger lovers. It is still much more acceptable for men to court women much younger than themselves than it is for women to court men much their junior. Although this is changing somewhat, Ziegler & Seskin (1979) demonstrated that both the children and the parents of older women and younger men in relationships were quite negative toward these relationships. Ultimately, for either younger women/older men or younger men/older women relationships: "If we can get away from these narrow age-graded views--and away from stereotyping older people as wise but slow and the young as vigorous but impetuous--we may greatly enrich our own lives through intimate cross-age friendships " (Nass & Fisher, 1988).

Physiologically, older women are likely to experience the following changes, most of which are related to the ovaries producing less estrogen.   The vaginal tissue thins with age and the older woman takes longer to become aroused and to lubricate sufficiently for penetration--but these changes do not have to interfere with sexual pleasure.   If intercourse becomes painful then lubricating creams or estrogen replacement therapy (ERT) can help.   If lubricants are used they should be germ-free, like K-Y jelly so that they do not carry any infection.   If ERT is being considered, be sure to weigh the benefits against the possible side-effects.   Ask your physician about the pluses and minuses and consult consumer health organizations like the People's Medical Society and The Public Citizen Health Research Group to get their viewpoints.

Another important aspect of sexuality regardless of a person's age is self-concept.   Feeling physically attractive is important to everyone.   If beauty is seen as being represented only by the beauty contestants or the models in most advertising, then few people will be able to live up to these images.   If youth equals beauty then by definition, old age does not.   These are the stereotypes that people are faced with everyday.   We, as a society, need to expand our images of what beauty is.   We need to stop accepting being called young as being a compliment and accept that there is beauty in all ages.   As Zilbergeld (1978) commented, being apologetic about being old is not only bad for "good sex" but also bad for "good anything" (Nass & Fisher, 1988).   "Fortunately, the capacity to share empathic affection does not require virile muscles or perfect physical conditioning. It does not diminish with age" (Nass & Fisher, 1988).

Changes in Sexuality in Aging Men

Physiological changes that commonly occur in older men are the following: it takes longer to acheive an erection, the erection may be less firm, the force of ejaculation is diminished, there is less fluid ejaculated, the erection may be lost faster during or after sexual stimulation, and there is a longer refractory period between ejacuations (i.e., the time from one ejaculation to the next is increased).   Impotence (the inability to acheive an erection) is not a normal aspect of aging. Most frequently impotence results from disease processes, use of certain drugs including alcohol, fear of failure, mental or physical fatigue, or the belief that older people can't or shouldn't be sexually active.   As with women, good health and regular sexual activity promotes sexual functioning in later life among men.

Table 19.3*

ENYOYMENT OF SEX BY SEXUALLY ACTIVE MEN AND WOMEN
AFTER AGE 50

	In their 50s	In their 60s	Age 70 and older
Women (High enjoyment of sex)	71%	65%	61%
Men (High enjoyment of sex)	90%	86%	75%

*Copyright 1984 by Consumers Union of United States, Inc., Mount Vernon, NY 10553. Reprinted by permission from CONSUMER REPORTS BOOKS, 1984.

The ability to move from a focus on athletic intercourse does not come easily in our society with its competitive, performance-oriented models in every corner. But for the older person an anti-performance model for sexual activity may be more reliable and satisfying.

One such non-goal-oriented model for sex has been developed in the Far East: tantric sex. Here the emphasis is not on speeding up sex but rather on slowing things down in order to savor each moment fully. Lovers are encouraged to focus on their own touches and to imagine how it would feel to be receiving them. Orgasm is not emphasized. In fact, sensual arousal without orgasm is especially cherished. Since building up to orgasm is not the objective, sex that does not end in orgasm is not seen as failure (as it is in our society). Instead, it may be a most loving gesture--one that older friends can share with each other.

Seen from a tantric point of view, the quality of sex may actually improve with age. . . (Nass & Fisher, 1988).

Sexual Communications and Preconceived Notions

There are other ways to be sexually active besides sexual intercourse. Many people enjoy closeness, gentle caressing, touching, and massage. Other alternatives are self- or partner-stimulation either manually or with vibrators. Some people enjoy oral sexual stimulation. The key to enjoyment of sexual activity with another person is communication. One should tactfully let his/her partner know what makes one feel good and what causes discomfort (either physically or emotionally). One shouldn't assume that your partner knows how you feel. Communication should be on-going. It shouldn't be assumed that what is enjoyable one time will always be enjoyable -- moods change, aches and pains change, and situations change so it should not be assumed that there is only one best way to satisfy a partner or yourself. It should be kept in mind that all sexual encounters do not have to end with orgasm. It is the "joy of sex" that is important not the "job of sex" (i.e., doing what one thinks he/she is supposed to do rather that what one enjoys doing). The most important erogenous zone is the mind, and like other aspects of health, expectations will often be self-fulfilling. If a person believes that sex should not be enjoyed by older people, then he or she will probably not enjoy it. If a person believes that older people have as much right to their sexual expressions as any other adults, then he or she will be more likely to act on these beliefs. It is important to remember that stereotyping can come from within the group being stereotyped. Sexually active older adults may wrongly think that their peers can't or don't want to be sexually active.

As with other age groups, some people express their sexuality primarily or solely with people of the same sex. Some homosexual organizations for older adults like SAGE in New York City (see the resources at the end of this chapter) have been formed and they deal with both sexual and non-sexual aspects of the lives of older homosexuals. Above all, it is important to remember this about sexuality and older adults: "All older people are not alike. No stereotype of 'the aging' or 'the aged' can do justice to the richly variegated patterns of life as it is actually being lived by many in their later years" (Brecher, 1984).

Older Adults and Dating

An increasing number of divorced or widowed older people are faced with the question of whether or not they should begin dating. Bulcroft & O'Conner-Roden (1986) interviewed 45 older people who were actively dating. They found that ". . .not only do older couples' dates include the same activities as those of younger people, but they are often far more varied and creative." Dating " . . . is a critical, central part of elders' lives that provides something that cannot be supplied by family or friends" (Bulcroft & O'Conner-Roden, 1986). Said one interviewee in the Bulcroft & O'Connor-Roden study: "No matter how old they are, they are looking for this thing called love." There is no doubt about it, it does help to have a sexual partner if you wish to stay sexually active. Table 19.4 illustrates the differences in sexual activity between married and unmarried men and women.

Table 19.4*

PROPORTION OF OLDER MARRIED AND UNMARRIED WOMEN AND MEN
WHO ARE SEXUALLY ACTIVE

	In their 50s	In their 60s	Age 70 & older
Married women	95%	89%	81%
Unmarried women	88%	63%	50%
Married men	98%	93%	81%
Unmarried men	95%	85%	75%

*Copyright 1984 by Consumers Union of United States, Inc., Mount Vernon, NY 10223. Reprinted by permission from CONSUMER REPORTS BOOKS, 1984.

Adaptations in Sexuality

As mentioned in Chapter 1, a large percentage of older adults have one or more chronic disabilities. Because of this older adults are more likely to be using over-the-counter and prescription medications, therefore some adaptations to sexuality may be in order for many older adults. Listing all of these adaptations is beyond the scope of this book, but it is worthwhile mentioning that there is help available. Some helpful booklets are noted at the end of this chapter. For example, the Arthritis Foundation has published a pamphlet that addresses sexual activities for arthritics. It gives illustrations of a variety of sexual positions that are designed not to aggravate various types and sites of arthritis. Another booklet, The Sensuous Heart gives guidelines for sex after a heart attack.

Despite the so-called sexual revolution, sexuality is still a sensitive topic, even among health care professionals. It shouldn't be assumed that health care professionals will automatically address or be knowledgeable about sexuality concerns that older adults might have (particularly after undergoing surgery, after an illness, upon the diagnosis of a chronic disease, or upon being prescribed a new medication). It is up to the patient to bring up concerns if these concerns are not part of a patient education program. Older people need to recognize that doctors, nurses, physical therapists, occupational therapists, social workers, or patient educators may not be prepared to unabashedly discuss sexual concerns (most have not had specific training in these matters). If this is the case, then the patient needs to ask for a referral to someone who can adequately answer his or her questions.   An informed patient should always be alert to the possibility that a change in sexual functioning may be due to the treatment as well as the disease. It should never be assumed that sexuality should be eliminated because of an illness or a treatment.   Patients and their partners should not feel guilty about being concerned about sexuality even in the throes of a dangerous or debilitating disease.   People do not cease being sexual just because they or their partner is infirm.   Patients and their partners deserve to have all questions answered honestly and forthrightly without threat of embarrassment of health care professionals. By the same token, health care professionals cannot be expected to anticipate all the sexual functioning problems that may occur.   It is up to the patient and his or her partner to inform health care professionals about such concerns.

Kegel Exercises

One specific exercise for older adults is worth mentioning in this chapter because it can be helpful to all older adults whether they are healthy or infirm. Kegel exercises can help to prevent or control urinary incontinence (the leaking of urine), especially when lifting, coughing, sneezing, or laughing. Fear of incontinence during sexual activity could certainly be a deterrent to being sexually active.   Kegel exercises strengthen the pubococcygeus (pew-bo-cox-uh-gee-us), or PC muscle, which not only helps prevent urinary incontinence in both men and women, but the strengthening of the PC muscle has also been touted as an enhancement to sexual functioning. In women the PC muscle can tighten to produce more friction on the man's penis during intercourse or, according to some experts, a strengthened PC muscle increases sexual arousal in the woman as well.   In men a strong PC muscle may allow them to have better ejaculatory control and to have more intense orgasms.

To do Kegel exercises all you need to do is to contract the PC muscle as if you were interrupting a flow of urine.   If you aren't sure that you are doing the exercise properly, then you can begin by actually starting and stopping an actual flow of urine when urinating. Once you have a feel for the exercise then you can practice the exercise many times during the day.   Some experts recommend up to 200 contractions per day. The muscle can be squeezed quickly and released, gradually working up to one or two minutes and/or the muscle can be squeezed and held for up to ten seconds (beginning with three seconds and working up to ten seconds over a period of several weeks).   The held contractions should be continued for one to two minutes (beginning gradually and working up to the one or two minutes).   If you are not experiencing success with this exercise on your own, you may wish to try one of the commercial products on the market now (i.e., the Super Kegel) that help people to strengthen the PC and surrounding pelvic muscles.

Sex and Good Health

In general, people who exercise regularly, eat properly, don't smoke, don't drink to excess, and are wise in the use of any medications are more likely to look better, feel better, and have more positive attitudes about themselves and their sexuality. In addition to good health promoting good sex, the converse also seems to be true. Besides the pleasurable emotional, psychological, and physical sensations that accompany sexual activity, sex is also a good pain and stress reliever. Some arthritics report several hours of pain relief after sex and many people report profound relaxation and sound sleep following orgasms. "Not much is known yet about how sex relieves pain and stress, but it may have something to do with stimulation of endorphins, the morphinelike chemicals in the nervous system" (Nass & Fisher, 1988).

Summary

The study of sexual activity among older adults does not imply that all older adults must or should be sexually active, but for the majority who wish to be sexually active, they should not be categorically hampered or denied to be fulfilled. "Most people can and should expect to have sex long after they no longer wish to ride bicycles" (Comfort, 1974).

In general, the "use it or lose it" philosophy that is relevant to fitness and mental acuity is also applicable to sexuality. Men and women who are sexually active throughout their lives are less likely to have sexual problems in their later years.

References

Brecher, E.M. (1984). Love, sex and aging: A consumers union report, Boston: Little, Brown and Consumer Union.

Comfort. A. (1974). Journal of the American Geriatrics Society. 22 (10), 440-442.

Bulcroft, K., and O'Conner-Roden, M. (June, 1986). Never too late. Psychology Today.

Nass, G.D., & Fisher, M.P. (1988). Sexuality today. Boston: Jones and Bartlett.

National Institute on Aging. Answers about: The aging woman/the aging man. Washington, D.C.: U.S. Department of Health and Human Services.

White, S.C. (1984). The sensuous heart. (2nd ed.). Atlanta: Pritchett & Hull.

Zilbergeld, B. (1978). Male sexuality: A guide to sexual fulfillment. Boston: Little, Brown.

Additional Resources

American Heart Association (1983). <u>Sex</u> <u>and</u> <u>heart</u> <u>disease</u>. Dallas: American Heart Association. This is a 20 page pamphlet that discusses sexual activity in the presence of heart disease.

Arthritis Foundation. (1982). <u>Arthritis:</u> <u>Living</u> <u>and</u> <u>loving</u> <u>(information</u> <u>about</u> <u>sex)</u>. This 16 page pamphlet is available free of charge from your local Arthritis Foundation or from the national Arthritis Foundation office, 3400 Peachtree Road, N.E., Atlanta, GA 30326.

Doress, P.B. & Siegal, D.L. (1987). <u>Ourselves,</u> <u>growing</u> <u>older</u>. New York: Touchstone. Provides valuable information for aging women.

The Public Citizen Health Research Group was co-founded in 1971 by Ralph Nader and Sidney Wolfe "to fight for the public's health, and to give consumers more control over decisions that affect their health." They publish a monthly newsletter <u>Health</u> <u>Letter</u> for an annual subscription price of $18.00 per year. For more information write to: <u>Health</u> <u>Letter</u>, Circulation Department, 2000 P St., N.W., Washington, D.C. 20036.

The Super Kegel PC Fitness Program is available from DNA Research Group, Inc., P.O. Box 1066, Novato, CA 94948, (707)762-5321. This includes a special device used for Kegel exercises.

Senior Action in a Gay Environment (SAGE) is for gay men and women of all ages, caring about elders. For more information write: SAGE, 208 West 13th St., New York, NY 10011, (212) 741-2247.

The People's Medical Society (PMS) publishes the <u>Peoples'</u> <u>Medical</u> <u>Society</u> <u>Newsletter</u> bimonthly for an annual subscription rate of $15.00. They also publish books and pamphlets about consumer health issues.

Romance continues throughout the life cycle

Resources

Chapter 20
Resources

It is beyond the scope of this book to make a complete listing of resources in the areas of exercise, dance and gerontology. The following information is offered as a guide to resources which we have found to be helpful. They include resources for books, records, films, slides, videotapes, and audiotapes, as well as addresses of helpful organizations and associations. There are also resources and references listed at the end of each chapter

Books and Other Printed Materials

Addison, C. & Humphrey, E. (1979). _Fifty positive vigor exercises for senior citizens_. Reston, VA: AAHPERD Publications.

Adkins, O.B. (1983). _Get moving: Exercise for later life_. Cochranton, PA: Specialty Publishing Co.

Administration on Aging. (1968). _The fitness challenge in the later years: An exercise program for older adults_. Washington, DC: DHEW Publication No. (OHD) 75-20802.

Alexander, J., Berrow, D., Domitrovich, L., Donnelly, M., & McLean, C. (Eds.). (1986). _Women and aging: An anthology by women_. Corvallis, OR: Calyx Books.

American Association of Retired Persons. (1986). _Staying well: Healthy activities for healthy older persons_. Washington, DC: AARP.

American College of Sports Medicine. (1986). _Resource manual for guidelines for exercise testing and prescription_ (3rd ed.). Philadelphia: Lea & Febiger.

Bechdahl, J. (n.d.). _Dancing is a ball: A beginner's line dance manual_. Springfield, OH: Keep Movin' of the USA.

Beland, R.M. (1980). _Service-Learning: Programs for the aging_. (A guide to practicum and fieldwork experiences in health, fitness, Dance and Leisure Services). Reston, VA: The American Alliance for Health, Physical Education, Recreation and Dance.

Bassey, E.J. & Fentem, P.H. (1981). _Exercise: The facts_. Oxford, England: Oxford University Press.

Beigel, L. (1984). _Physical fitness and the older person: A guide to exercise for health care professionals_. Rockville, MD: Aspen Systems Corp.

Benison, B. (n.d.). The magic of movement. (Activities for those with limited movement). Oklahoma City: Melody House Publications.

Berland, T. (1986). Fitness for life. Glenview, IL: Scott, Foresman and Co.

Berryman-Miller, S. (1986). Benefits of dance and the process of aging and retirement for the older adult. Activities, Adaptations & Aging. Hawthorne Press.

Berryman-Miller, S. & Beal, R.K. (1988). Dance for the older adult. Reston, VA: American Alliance for Health, Physical Education, Recreation, and Dance.

Bernard, M. (Ed.). (1988). Positive approaches to ageing: Leisure and life-style in later life. Stoke-on-Trent, England: Beth Johnson Foundation Publications.

Bigelow, B. (1982). The heritage of the future. Washington, DC: The National Council on the Aging, Inc.

Caplow-Lindner, E., Harpaz, L. & Samberg, S. (1979). Therapeutic dance/movement: expressive activities for older adults. New York: Human Sciences Press.

Cayou, D.K. (1971). Modern jazz dance. Palo Alto, CA: Mayfield.

Clark, E. (1986). Growing old is not for sissies. Corte Madera, CA: Pomegranate Calendars & Books.

Clark, H.H. (Ed.) (1977, April). Exercise and aging. Physical Fitness Research Digest, Series 7 (2). Published by the President's Council on Physical Fitness and Sports, Washington, DC 20201.

Coombs, J. (1981). Aerobic dance for the older adult. Ottawa, Canada: Recreation Development Division.

Corbin, C.B., & Corbin, D.E. (1981).Homemade play equipment. Boston, MA: American Press.

Corbin, C.B., & Lindsey, R. (1988). Concepts of physical fitness with laboratories (6th ed.). Dubuque, IA: Wm. C. Brown.

Corbin, C.B., & Lindsey, R. (1984). The ultimate fitness book: Physical fitness forever. New York: Leisure Press.

Corbin, D.E. (1988). Jogging. Glenview, IL: Scott, Foresman & Co.

Corbin, D.E., Kagan, D., & Metal-Corbin, J. (1987). A content analysis of an intergenerational unit on aging in a sixth grade classroom. Educational Gerontology, 13, (5), 403-410.

Corbin, D.E., and Metal-Corbin, J. (1990). <u>Reach</u> <u>for</u> <u>it:</u> <u>A</u> <u>handbook</u> <u>of</u> <u>health,</u> <u>exercise</u> <u>and</u> <u>dance</u> <u>activities</u> <u>for</u> <u>older</u> <u>adults</u>. Dubuque, IA: Eddie Bowers Publishing Co.

Corbin, D.E., Metal-Corbin, J., & Barg, C. (1989). Teaching about aging in the elementary school: A one-year follow-up. <u>Educational Gerontology</u>, <u>15</u>, 103-109.

Corbin, D.E., Metal-Corbin, J., & Biddle, S. (1990). Educating children for lifetime health fitness: An intergenerational approach. <u>British</u> <u>Journal</u> <u>of</u> <u>Physical</u> <u>Education</u>.

Chrisman, D.E. (1980). <u>Body</u> <u>recall</u>. Berea, KY: Berea College.

deVries, H.A. (1974). <u>Vigor</u> <u>regained</u>. Englewood Cliffs, NJ: Prentice-Hall.

deVries, H.A., & Hales, D. (1974). <u>Fitness</u> <u>after</u> <u>50</u>. New York: Charles Scribner's Sons.

Dishman, R.K. (Ed.). (1988). <u>Exercise</u> <u>adherence:</u> <u>Its</u> <u>impact</u> <u>on</u> <u>public</u> <u>health</u>. Champaign, IL: Human Kinetics Books.

Doress, P.B. & Siegal, D.L. (Eds.). (1987). <u>Ourselves</u> <u>growing</u> <u>older:</u> <u>Women</u> <u>aging</u> <u>with</u> <u>knowledge</u> <u>and</u> <u>power</u>. New York: Touchstone.

Dychtwald, K. (Ed.). (1986). <u>Wellness</u> <u>and</u> <u>health</u> <u>promotion</u> <u>for</u> <u>the</u> <u>elderly</u>. Rockville, MD: Aspen Publication.

Ensign, C.P., McAdam, M. & Smith, E.L. (1988). <u>Healthline</u>. Madison, WI: Healthline, Inc.

Ferrini, A.F., & Ferrini, R.L. (1989). <u>Health</u> <u>in</u> <u>the</u> <u>later</u> <u>years</u>. Dubuque, IA: William C. Brown.

Fitt, S., & Riordan, A. (1980). <u>Dance</u> <u>for</u> <u>the</u> <u>handicapped:</u> <u>Focus</u> <u>on</u> <u>dance</u> <u>IX</u>. Reston, VA: American Alliance for Health, Physical Education, Recreation and Dance.

Flatten, K., Wilhite, B., & Reyes-Watson, E. (1988). <u>Exercise</u> <u>activities</u> <u>for</u> <u>the</u> <u>elderly</u>. New York: Springer.

Flatten, K., Wilhite, B., & Reyes-Watson, E. (1988). <u>Recreational</u> <u>activities</u> <u>for</u> <u>the</u> <u>elderly</u>. New York: Springer.

Fisher, P. (1988). <u>Creative</u> <u>movement</u> <u>for</u> <u>older</u> <u>adults:</u> <u>Exercises</u> <u>for</u> <u>the</u> <u>fit</u> <u>and</u> <u>frail</u>. New York: Human Sciences.

Ford, J., & Sinclair, R. (1987). <u>Sixty</u> <u>years</u> <u>on:</u> <u>Women</u> <u>talk</u> <u>about</u> <u>old</u> <u>age</u>. London: The Women's Press.

Foster, P.M. (Ed.). (1983) <u>Activities</u> <u>and</u> <u>the</u> <u>"well</u> <u>elderly"</u>. New York: Haworth Press.

Frankel, L.J., & Richard, B.B. (1977). Be alive as long as you live. Charleston, WV: Preventicare Publications.

Garnet, E.D. (1982). Chair exercise manual: An audio-assisted program of body dynamics. Princeton, NJ: Princeton Book Co.

Garnet, E.D. (1982). Movement is life: A holistic approach to exercise for older adults. Princeton, NJ: Princeton Book Co.

Golub, S., & Freedman, R.J. (Eds.). (1985).Health needs of women as they age. New York: The Haworth Press.

Gowitzke, B. (1981). Folk dance for the older adult. Canada: Recreation Development Division.

Harris, J.A., Pittman, A. & Waller, M. (1988). Dance awhile (6th ed). New York: Macmillan.

Hecox, B. (1983). Movement activities for older adults. Journal of Physical Education, Recreation and Dance. 54, (5), 47-48.

Hill, K. (1976). Dance for physically disabled persons. Reston, VA: American Alliance for Health, Physical Education, Recreation and Dance.

Hurley, O. (1988). Safe therapeutic exercise for the frail elderly: An introduction. Albany, NY: Center for the Study of Aging.

Jable, T. (Ed.). (1989). Aging and health, exercise, recreation and dance: 1978-1988. William Paterson College. Compiled by the Research Committee of the Council on Aging and Adult Development of AAHPERD. Available from: Department of Movement Science and Leisure Studies, The William Paterson College of New Jersey, Wayne, NJ 07470.

Jamieson, R.H. (1982). Exercises for the elderly. Verplanck, NY: Emerson Books, Inc.

Joyce, M. (1973). First steps in teaching creative dance. Palo Alto, CA: National Press.

Kaplan, M. (1983). Leisure, recreation, culture and aging: An annotated bibliography. Washington, DC: The National Council on the Aging, Inc.

Kart, C.S., Metress, E.K., & Metress, S.P. (1988). Aging, health and society. Boston: Jones and Bartlett.

Kennedy, D.W., Austin, D.R., & Smith, R.W. (1987). Special recreation: Opportunities for persons with disabilities. Philadelphia: Saunders College Publishing.

Koss, R. (n.d.). <u>Aging</u> <u>and</u> <u>health--changing</u> <u>life-styles</u>. Available from: Ramapo College of New Jersey, 505 Ramapo Valley Road, Mahwah, NJ 07430.

Koss, R. (1986). Moving into the third age: AAHPERD serves a new clientele. <u>Journal</u> <u>of</u> <u>Physical</u> <u>Education,</u> <u>Recreation</u> <u>and</u> <u>Dance</u>, <u>57</u>, (1), 30-31.

Kuntzleman, C. & Kuntzleman, B. (1978). <u>Fitness</u> <u>is</u> <u>ageless</u>. Spring Arbor, MI: Arbor Press.

Lang, D. & Stinson, W. (n.d.). <u>Project</u> <u>towers</u> <u>resource</u> <u>guide:</u> <u>A</u> <u>wellness</u> <u>program</u> <u>for</u> <u>the</u> <u>elderly</u>. Emporia, KS: Healthcomm.

Lerman, L. (1984). <u>Teaching</u> <u>dance</u> <u>to</u> <u>senior</u> <u>adults</u>. Chicago: Charles C. Thomas.

Leslie, D. (Ed.). (1989). <u>Mature</u> <u>stuff:</u> <u>Physical</u> <u>activity</u> <u>for</u> <u>the</u> <u>older</u> <u>adult</u>. Reston, VA: AAHPERD Publications.

Levete, G. (1982). <u>No</u> <u>handicap</u> <u>to</u> <u>dance:</u> <u>Creative</u> <u>improvisation</u> <u>for</u> <u>people</u> <u>with</u> <u>or</u> <u>without</u> <u>disabilities</u>. London: Souvenir Press, Ltd.

Leviton, D., & Santoro, L.C. (Eds.) (1980). <u>Health,</u> <u>physical</u> <u>education,</u> <u>recreation,</u> <u>and</u> <u>dance</u> <u>for</u> <u>the</u> <u>older</u> <u>adult:</u> <u>A</u> <u>modular</u> <u>approach</u>. Reston, VA: American Alliance for Health, Physical Education, Recreation, and Dance.

Lindner, E.C. (1982). Dance as a therapeutic intervention for the elderly. <u>Educational</u> <u>Gerontology</u>, <u>8</u>, 167-174.

Lindner, E.C., & Harpaz, L. (1983). Shared movement programs: Children and older adults. <u>Journal</u> <u>of</u> <u>Physical</u> <u>Education,</u> <u>Recreation</u> <u>and</u> <u>Dance</u>, <u>54</u>, (5), 44-45.

Lockhart, A., & Pease, E. (1977). <u>Modern</u> <u>dance,</u> <u>building</u> <u>and</u> <u>teaching</u> <u>lessons</u>. (5th ed). Dubuque, IA: William C. Brown.

Long, J. & Wimbush, E. (1985). <u>Continuity</u> <u>and</u> <u>change:</u> <u>Leisure</u> <u>around</u> <u>retirement</u>. London, England: The Sports Council and Economic and Social Research Council.

Mason, K.C. (1974). <u>Dance</u> <u>therapy:</u> <u>Focus</u> <u>on</u> <u>dance</u> <u>VII</u>. Reston, VA: American Alliance for Health, Physical Education, Recreation and Dance.

McPherson, B.D. (Ed.). (1984). <u>Sport</u> <u>and</u> <u>aging:</u> <u>The</u> <u>1984</u> <u>Olympic</u> <u>Scientific</u> <u>Congress</u> <u>proceedings</u> (Vol.5). Champaign, IL: Human Kinetics.

Metal-Corbin, J. (1983). Shared movement programs: College students and older adults. <u>Journal</u> <u>of</u> <u>Physical</u> <u>Education,</u> <u>Recreation</u> <u>and</u> <u>Dance</u>, <u>54</u>, (5), 46, 50.

Metal-Corbin, J., & Foltz, R. (1985). All my grandmothers could sing: An interdisciplinary and intergenerational choreographic work. Journal of Physical Education, Recreation and Dance, 55, (9), 52-55.

Mid-America Arts Alliance. (1984). Through the looking glass: Drawings by Elizabeth Layton. Kansas City: Mid-American Arts Alliance.

Missinne, L., & Fischer, E. (1981). All you could forget about older people. R & E Publishers, P.O. Box 2008, Saratoga, CA 95070.

Morgan, K. (1987). Sleep and Ageing. London: Croom Helm.

National Council on the Aging, Inc. (1982). Service learning in aging: Implications for health, physical education, recreation and dance. Washington, DC: National Concil on the Aging, Inc.

Ostrow, A. (1984). Physical activity and the older adult: Psychological perspectives. Pennington, NJ: Princeton Books.

Painter, C. (1985). Gifts of age. San Francisco: Chronicle Books.

Parker, B. (1983). Sit down and shape up. Champaign, IL: Leisure Press/Human Kinetics.

Penner, D. (1989). Eldercise. Waldorf, MD: AAHPERD Publications.

Piscopo, J. (1985). Fitness and aging. New York: Macmillan.

President's Council on Physical Fitness. (1984). Walking for exercise and pleasure. Washington, D.C.: U.S. Government Printing Office, Supt. of Documents.

Price, W., & Lyon, L. (1987). A national directory of physical fitness programs for older adults. (2nd ed.). Saranac Lake, NY: North Country Community College Press.

Price, W., & Lyon, L. (1983). Fitness programs for the aged: A study of college and university involvement. Journal of Physical Education, Recreation and Dance, 54, (5), 43-51.

Pruett, D.M. (1983). Dance for older adults. Journal of Physical Education, Recreation and Dance, 54, (5), 43-51.

Raven, P.B., & Wilson, J.R. (1988, June). Exercise for the elderly. Sports Medicine Digest, 10, 6.

Rikkers, R. (1986). Seniors on the move. Champaign, IL: Leisure Press/Human Kinetics.

Schade, C., & Johnson, L. (1986). Prime time aerobics. San Diego: 3089 C. Clairemont Dr., #130, San Diego, CA 92117.

Schultz, S. (1980). <u>Let's get moving: A fitness program developed for those over sixty</u>. Mayville, ND: Mayville State College.

Shea, M.M. (1986). Senior aerobics: Improving cardiovascular fitness. <u>Journal of Physical Education, Recreation and Dance</u>, <u>57</u>, (1), 48-49.

Sherbon, E. (1982). <u>On the count of one: modern dance methods</u>. (3rd ed.). Palo Alto, CA: Mayfield.

Shephard, R.J. (1987). <u>Physical activity and aging</u>, (2nd ed.). Rockville, MD: Aspen Publishers, Inc.

Smith, E.L. (Ed.). (1985, April). Exercise and aging. <u>Topics in Geriatric Rehabilitation</u>. (Whole issue), <u>1</u>, 1.

Sobul, A.L. (n.d.). <u>Modified exercises or senior adults</u>. Shaker Heights, OH: MESAG, 3555 Tolland Rd. 44120.

Stempfly, P. (n.d.). <u>Keep movin'</u>. Springfield, OH: Wonderhouse Press.

Strenger, L.A. & Smith, C.M. (1985, February). <u>Healthy moves for older adults</u>. Health, Physical Education, Recreation and Dance Monograph No. One (Report No., ISBN-0-89333-034-5). Washington, DC: ERIC Clearinghouse on Teacher Education.

Teaff, J.D. (1985). <u>Leisure services with the elderly</u>. St. Louis: Times Mirror/Mosby College Publishing.

Teague, M.L. (1987). <u>Health promotion: Achieving high-level wellness in the later years</u>. Indianapolis: Benchmark.

Thomson, C., & Warren, B. (Eds.). (1981). <u>The thunder tree</u>. Lancaster, England: LUDUS Dance Co.

Tinsley, H.E.A. (1982). <u>The psychological benefits of leisure activities for the elderly</u>. Research report. Washington, DC: NRTA-AARP Andrus Foundation.

Travelers Insurance Companies. (n.d.). <u>Pep up your life: A fitness book for seniors</u>. Hartford, CT: The Travelers Insurance Companies, One Tower Square, 06115.

Ventura-Merkel, C. (1983). <u>Cultural programs for and by older adults: A catalogue of program profiles</u>. Washington, DC: The National Council on the Aging, Inc.

<u>Walk to better health: A program of Swedish walking</u>. (n.d.). Baltimore: Maryland Commission on Physical Fitness.

<u>Walking as an exercise</u>. (1984). Deer Park, NY: The Langer Foundation for Biomechanics and Sports Medicine Research, Inc.

Wantz, M.S., & Gay, J.E. (1981). <u>The aging process: A health perspective</u>. Cambridge, MA: Winthrop Publishers, Inc.

Warren, B., & Nadeau, R. (n.d.). <u>Using the creative arts in therapy: The power of the arts experience to expand human horizons</u>. Cambridge, MA: Brookline Books.

Williams, J.L., & Downs, J. (1984). <u>Educational activity programs for older adults</u>. New York: Haworth Press.

Records and Cassette Tapes

Records and cassette tapes suitable for exercise and dance are available from the following sources. Records and tapes made by major manufacturers are available through local record stores. For additional sources, visit the record and tape department of your school or public library.

Companies

Dance Record Distributor (formerly Folkraft Records)
P.O. Box 404
Florham, NJ 07932
(201) 377-1885

Educational Activities, Inc.
P.O. Box 392
Freeport, NY 11520

Hoctor Records
115 Manhattan Street
Waldwick, NJ 07463

Kimbo Dance Records (also parachute source)
10 N. 3rd Ave.
Long Branch, NJ 07740
1-800-631-2187

Specific Selections

Garnet, E.D. (1982). <u>Chair exercise manual: An audio assisted program</u>. Princton Book Co., Princeton, NJ.

Gibbs, N. <u>Wheels, reels, and squares</u>. (Record Album). American Health Care Association, 1200 15th Street, N.W., Washington, DC: 20005.

Lindner, E.C., & Harpaz, L. (1987). <u>Come dance again on your feet or in your seat</u>. (Record, cassette, manual). P.O. Box 993, Woodside, NY 11377.

Lindner, E.C., & Harpaz, L. <u>Special dancing: On your feet or in your seat</u>. (Record, cassette, manual). P.O. Box 993, Woodside, NY 11377.

MacCallum, M. <u>Choreographed</u> <u>aerobic</u> <u>fitness</u> <u>for</u> <u>active</u> <u>older</u> <u>Canadians</u>. (Cassette and instructional manual). 905 Standard Life Center, 10405 Jasper Ave., Edmonton, Alberta, Canada T5J 3N4.

Reed, J. <u>Wheelchair</u> <u>workout</u>. 12275 Greenleaf Ave., Potomac, MD 20854.

Switkes, B. <u>Armchair</u> <u>fitness</u>. CMI, 2420 K Street, N.W., Washington, DC 20037.

<u>Sittercise</u> and <u>Seatworks</u>. Kimbo Educational, P.O. Box 477E, Long Branch, NJ 07740.

Sorine, S. <u>For</u> <u>the</u> <u>young</u> <u>at</u> <u>heart:</u> <u>Fitness</u> <u>for</u> <u>seniors</u>. Kimbo Educational, P.O. Box 477E, Long Branch, NJ 07740.

<u>Keys</u> <u>to</u> <u>life</u> and <u>Light'n</u> <u>lively</u>. Melody House Publishing Company, 819 N.W. 92nd Street, Oklahoma City, OK 73114.

For stress management tapes, see Chapter 16.

Films and Videotapes

<u>A</u> <u>coming</u> <u>of</u> <u>age</u>. (Film). (1976). SAGE Project. University of Minnesota, AV Library Service 1313 Fifth St., S.E., Suite 108, Minneapolis, MN 55414.

<u>Dance</u> <u>movement</u> <u>as</u> <u>therapy</u> <u>for</u> <u>older</u> <u>adults</u>. (Film). American Dance Therapy Association, 2000 Century Plaza, Suite 108, Columbia, MD 21044.

<u>Don't</u> <u>take</u> <u>it</u> <u>easy</u>. TV ONTARIO. University of Minnesota, AV Library Service, 1313 Fifth St., S.E., Suite 108, Minneapolis, MN 55414.

<u>The</u> <u>Good</u> <u>Life</u> (Film). The Travelers Film Library, One Tower Square, Hartford, CT 06115.

Griffith, B.R., & Martin, P. <u>Sodanceabit</u>, (Videotape, Manual). 1401 Anaheim Place, Long Beach, CA 90804.

<u>Health,</u> <u>fitness</u> <u>and</u> <u>leisure</u> <u>for</u> <u>a</u> <u>quality</u> <u>life</u>. (Film). American Alliance for Health, Physical Education, Recreation and Dance, 1900 Association Dr., Reston, VA 22091.

Leviton, D. (Producer), and Callahan, G. (Director). <u>Smiles:</u> <u>The</u> <u>Adults</u> <u>Health</u> <u>and</u> <u>Development</u> <u>Program</u> (Film). Adults Health and Development Program, PEHR Building, University of Maryland, College Park, MD 20740.

Leviton, D. <u>The</u> <u>Adults</u> <u>Health</u> <u>and</u> <u>Development</u> <u>Program:</u> <u>More</u> <u>than</u> <u>just</u> <u>fitness</u> (Videotape). Adult Health and Development Program, PEHR Building, University of Maryland, College Park, MD 20740.

Martin, P. & Grifith Railey, B. Social dance aerobics. (Videotapes). 429 Jaycee Drive, San Luis Obispo, CA 93401.

*Metal-Corbin, J. (Project Director), Bottum, D. (Director and Producer, & Corbin, D.E. (Writer/Narrator). (1985). Age doesn't matter: Weaving dance and aging into a fifth grade curriculum. (Videotape). University Television, University of Nebraska at Omaha, Omaha, NE 68182.

*Metal-Corbin, J. (Director/ Choreographer), Langdon, J. (Producer and Director), & Greenblatt, D. (Composer). (1986). Out of the shadow, into the light. (Videotape). A concert dance for older women. University Television, University of Nebraska at Omaha, Omaha, NE 68182.

*Metal-Corbin, J. (Project Director), & Scollon, W. (Director and Producer). (1983). Old friends: An intergenerational approach to dance. (Videotape). University Television, University of Nebraska at Omaha, Omaha, NE 68182.

*Metal-Corbin, J. (Director/Choreographer), Scollon, W. (Director and Producer), & Foltz, R. (Composer). (1985). All my grandmothers could sing. (Videotape). A concert dance for older women. University Television, University of Nebraska at Omaha, Omaha, NE 68182.

*Metal-Corbin, J. (Director/Choreographer & Langdon, J. (Producer and Director). (1988). A good age: A collection of dances for women over fifty-five. (Videotape). University Television, University of Nebraska at Omaha, Omaha, NE 68182.

Riordan, A. A very special dance. (Videotape or film). AAHPERD Publications, 1900 Association Dr., Reston, VA 22091.

ROM dance. (Videotape, manual). Central Chapter of the Arthritis Foundation, 2501 North Star Road, Columbus, OH 43221.

Slow golden aerobics. (1987). (Videotape). Public Relations & Marketing, HCA L.W. Blake Hospital, Bradenton, FL 33529, (813) 792-3295.

Simmons, R. The silver foxes (Videotapes, Vol. 1 & 2). Lorimar Home Video. Available in video stores throughout the country.

Young, T. Young at heart fitness for life. (Videotape). Young at Heart Fitness for Life, 107 North Main, Lansing, KS 66048 (913) 727-2263.

*An order form for these videotapes is located at the end of this chapter.

Other Resources for films and videotapes

Arnold, D. Media Exchange Committee Chair, the Council on Aging and Adult Development, American Alliance for Health, Physical Education, Recreation, and Dance, 1233 Pitman Ave., Palo Alto, CA 94301. Maintains a listing of media related to aging and health, physical education, recreation and dance.
Van Clief, B. Institute of Creative Research, Lewis Clark State College, Lewiston, ID 83501. Maintains a collection of videotapes pertaining to health, physical education, recreation, and dance.

Yahnke, R. (1987). <u>The great circle of life: A guide to films on aging</u>. The General College, 106 Nicholson Hall, 216 Pillsburg Dr., S.E., Minneapolis, MN 55455.

Exercise and Dance Prop Sources

Recreational Parachute:
(12 foot multi-colored, 7 handles)
Medical & Activities Sales
P.O. Box 4068
Omaha, NE 68104
1-800-541-9152

Chiffon Scarves:
Gopher Athletics
P.O. Box O
Owatonna, MN 55060
1-800-535-0446

Hoops:
Things from Bell
230 Mechanic St.
Princeton, WI 54968
1-800-543-1458

A Group that "Nose" their Exercises

Associations and Organizations Pertaining to Aging

Administration on Aging
Dept. of Health and Human Services
Washington, D.C. 20201

Advocates Senior Alert Process
1334 G St. NW
Washington, D.C. 20005
(202) 737-6340

American Academy of Geriatric Dentistry
2 N. Riverside Plaza
Chicago, IL 60603

American Alliance for Health, Physical Education,
   Recreation & Dance
Council on Aging and Adult Development
1900 Association Drive
Reston, VA 22091

American Association for Geriatric Psychiatry
230 N. Michigan Avenue, Suite 2400
Chicago, IL 60601

Practicing the "Hand Jive"

American Association of Homes for the Aging
1050 17th St., N.W., Suite 770
Washington, D.C. 20036

American Association of Retired Persons
              and
National Retired Teachers Association
1909 K Street, N.W.
Washington, D.C. 20006
(202) 872-4700

American College of Nursing Home Administrators
4650 East-West Highway
Washington, D.C. 20014

American Geriatrics Society
10 Columbus Circle
New York, NY 10019

American Nurses Association, Inc.
Council of Nursing Home Nurses
Division on Gerontological Nursing Practice
2420 Pershing Road
Kansas City, MO 64108

American Nursing Home Association
1200 15th St., N.W.
Washington, D.C. 20005

American Psychiatric Association
Council on Aging
1700 18th St., N.W.
Washington, D.C. 20009

American Psychological Association
Division of Adult Development and Aging
1200 17th St., N.W.
Washington, D.C. 20036

American Public Health Association
Section on Gerontological Health
1015 18th St., N.W.
Washington, D.C. 20036

Asian and Pacific Coalition on Aging
1851 S.W. Moreland Ave.
Los Angeles, CA 90006

Asociacion Nacional por Personas Mayores
(National Association for Spanish Speaking Elderly)
1730 W. Olympic Blvd., Suite 401
Los Angeles, CA 90015

Association for Gerontology in Higher Education
1835 K St., N.W.
Washington, D.C. 20036

Association for Humanistic Gerontology
1711 Solano Avenue
Berkeley, CA 94707

Boston Women's Health Book Collective
47 Nichols Avenue
Watertown, MA 02172
(617) 924-0271

Canadian Association on Gerontology/Association Canadienne de
      Gerontologie
722 16th Avenue, N.E.
Calgary, Alberta T2E 6V7

Elderhostel
100 Boylston Street
Suite 200
Boston, MA 02116

Gerontological Society of America
1835 K St., N.W., Suite 305
Washington, D.C. 20006

Grandparents'-Children's Rights, Inc.
5728 Bayonne Ave.
Haslett, Mi 48840
(517) 339-8663

Gray Panthers
311 S. Juniper St., Suite 601
Philadelphia, PA 19107
(215) 545-6555

International Center for Social Gerontology
425 13th St., N.W., Suite 840
Washington, D.C. 20004

International Federation on Aging
1909 K Street, N.W.
Washington, D.C. 20006

International Senior Citizens Association. Inc.
11753 Wilshire Blvd.
Los Angeles, CA 90025

Melpomene Institute for Women's Health Research
2125 Hennepin Ave.
Minneapolis, MN 55413
(612) 378-0545

National Association for Human Development
1750 Pennsylvania Ave., N.W.
Washington, D.C. 20066

National Association for Lesbian and Gay Gerontology
1835 Market St.
San Francisco, CA 94103
(415) 626-7000

National Association for Widowed People
P.O. Box 3564
Springfield, IL 62708

National Association of Area Agencies on Aging
1828 L Street, N.W., Suite 404
Washington, D.C. 20036

National Association of Mature People
918 16th St., N.W.
Washington, D.C. 20006

National Association of Retired Federal Employees
1533 New Hampshire Ave., N.W.
Washington, D.C. 20036

National Association of State Units on Aging
1828 L St., N.W., Suite 500
Washington, D.C. 20036

National Caucus and Center on the Black Aged
1424 K St., N.W.
Washington, D.C. 20005
(202) 637-8400

National Citizens' Coalition for Nursing Home Reform
1424 16th St., N.W., Suite 204
Washington, D.C. 20036

National Committee on Careers for Older Americans
1414 22nd St., N.W., Room 602
Washington, D.C. 20037

National Council on the Aging, Inc.
600 Maryland Ave., S.W.
West Wing 100
Washington, D.C. 20024
(202) 466-7834

National Council of Senior Citizens
925 15th St.
Washington, D.C. 20005
(202) 347-8800

National Geriatric Society
212 W. Wisconsin Avenue
Milwaukee, WI 53203

National Indian Council on Aging, Inc.
P.O. Box 2088
Albuquerque, NM 87103

National Institute of Senior Centers
600 Maryland Ave., S.W., West Wing 100
Washington, D.C. 20024

National Interfaith Coalition on Aging
P.O. Box 1924
298 S. Hull St.
Athens, GA 30603
(404) 353-1331

National Pacific/Asian Resource Center on Aging
811 First Ave., Suite 210
Seattle, WA 98104
(206) 622-5124

National Senior Citizens' Law Center
1302 18th St., N.W., Suite 701
Washington, D.C. 20036
(202) 887-5280

National Voluntary Organization for Independent Living for the
      Aging (NVOILA)
600 Maryland Ave., S.W., West Wing 100
Washington, D.C. 20024

Older Women's League (OWL)
730 11th St., N.W., Suite 750
Washington, D.C. 20005
(202) 783-6686

Outdoor Vacations for Women Over 40
P.O. Box 200
Groton, MA 01450
(617) 448-3331

Retired Officers Association
1625 I Street, N.W.
Washington, D.C. 20006

Senior Action in a Gay Environment (SAGE)
208 W. 13th St.
New York, NY 10011
(212) 741-2247

Southern Gerontological Society
Gerontology Center
Georgia State University
Atlanta, GA 30303

The Supportive Older Women's Network (SOWN)
2805 N. 47th St.
Philadelphia, PA 19131
(215) 477-6000

Theos Foundation (Helps widowed people through their grieving)
Penn Hills Mall, Suite 410
Pittsburgh, PA 15235
(412) 243-4299

Urban Elderly Coalition
1828 L St., N.W.
Washington, D.C. 20036

Vacation and Senior Centers Association
275 Seventh Ave.
New York, NY 10001
(212) 645-6590

Western Gerontological Society
785 Market St., Room 1114
San Francisco, CA 94114

Women's Association for Research in Menopause (WARM)
128 E. 56th St.
New York, NY 10022

Women's Midlife Resource Center
1825 Haight St.
San Francisco, CA 94117
(415) 221-7417

The Villers Foundation (Funds projects that empower older people)
1334 G St., N.W.
Washington, D.C. 20005
(202) 628-3030

Intergenerational Organizations

Center for Intergenerational Learning
Temple University Institute on Aging
206 University Services Building
Philadelphia, PA 19122
(215) 787-6970
Director: Nancy Z. Henkin

Generations Together
811 William Pitt Union
University of Pittsburgh
Pittsburgh, PA 15260
(412) 624-5470
Director: Sally Newman

Understanding Aging, Inc.
Center for Understanding Aging
Framingham State College
Framingham, MA 01701
Director: Fran Pratt

Community Education Center on Aging
2723 Foxcroft Road, Suite 211
Little Rock, AR 72207

Wisconsin Positive Youth Development Initiative, Inc.
30 W. Mifflin Street, Suite 310
Madison, WI 53703

New Age, Inc.
1212 Roosevelt
Ann Arbor, MI 48104

Intergenerational Clearinghouse
Retired Senior Volunteer Program of Dane County, Inc.
540 W. Olin Avenue
Madison, WI 53715

Health-Related Organizations

American Cancer Society
5099 Clifton Road
Atlanta, GA 30329

Alzheimer's Association
700 E. Lake Street
Chicago, IL 60601-5997
1-800-621-0379

American College of Sports Medicine
1440 Monroe St.
Madison, WI 53706

American Dance Therapy Association
Suite 230
2000 Century Plaza
Columbia, MD 21044

American Dental Association
Department of Public Information and Education
211 E. Chicago Ave.
Chicago, IL 60611
(312) 440-2500

American Diabetes Association (ADA)
National Service Center
1660 Duke St.
Alexandria, VA 22314
(800) 232-3472

American Digestive Disease Society
7720 Wisconsin Ave.
Bethesda, MD 20814
(301) 652-9293

American Foundation for the Blind
15 W. 16th St.
New York, NY 10011
(212) 620-217

American Heart Association
National Center
7320 Greenville Ave.
Dallas, TX 75231
(214) 373-6300

American Institute for Cancer Research
500 N. Washington St.
Falls Church, VA 22046
(703) 237-0159

American Massage & Therapy Association
P.O. Box 1270 - 310 Cherokee Street
Kingsport, TN 37662

The Arthritis Foundation
1314 Spring St., N.W.
Atlanta, GA 30309
(404) 872-7110

Arthritis Information Clearinghouse
P.O. Box 9782
Arlington, VA 22209
(703) 588-8250

Cancer Information Service (CIS)
(800) 4-CANCER

Continence Restored, Inc.
785 Park Ave.
New York, NY 10021

Diabetes Center, Inc.
P.O. Box 739
Wayzata, MN 55391
(800) 848-2793

Help for Incontinent People (HIP)
P.O. Box 544
502 Park Drive
Union, SC 29379
(803) 585-8789

Hysterectomy Educational Resources and Services (HERS)
422 Bryn Mawr Ave.
Bala Cynwyd, PA 19004
(215) 667-7757

International Dental Health Foundation, Inc.
11800 Sunrise Valley Drive
Reston, VA 22091

Make Today Count (Support for people with cancer)
P.O. Box 222
Osage Beach, MO 65065
(303) 348-1619

National Digestive Diseases Information Clearinghouse
1255 23 St. N.W., Suite 275
Washington, D.C. 20037
(202) 296-1138

National Cancer Survivors Network
P.O. Box 4543
Albuquerque, NM 87196
(505) 268-7388

National Self-Help Clearinghouse
33 W. 42nd St.
New York, NY 10036
(212) 840-1259

People's Medical Society
14 E. Minor St.
Emmaus, PA 18049
(215) 967-2136

Public Citizens Health Research Group
2000 P St., N.W.
Washington, D.C. 20036

United Ostomy Association, Inc.
2001 W. Beverly Blvd.
Los Angeles, CA 90057
(213) 413-5510

Videotape Order Form

University of
Nebraska
at Omaha

University Television
KYNE-TV Channel 26
The Omaha Production Center
for the Nebraska ETV Network
Omaha, NE 68182-0022
(402) 554-2516

OLD FRIENDS: AN INTERGENERATIONAL APPROACH TO DANCE

AGE DOESN'T MATTER: WEAVING DANCE AND AGING INTO A 5TH GRADE CURRICULUM

ALL MY GRANDMOTHERS COULD SING

OUT OF THE SHADOW, INTO THE LIGHT

A GOOD AGE: A COLLECTION OF DANCES BY WOMEN OVER FIFTY FIVE

These programs are designed for the professional, paraprofessional or student involved in teaching or planning activity programs for the older adult. Each program takes a unique look at the older adult through the medium of dance.

OLD FRIENDS introduces you to a variety of dance and expressive movement activities including dancing in chairs, circle and group dance, and improvisational studies. It is an ideal tape for leaders in dance, physical education, recreation and gerontology.

AGE DOESN'T MATTER documents a dance residency for the Nebraska Arts Council (Artists-in-Education) that provided fifth grade students with an opportunity to learn about the aging process through an interdisciplinary approach using dance, health education, language arts, social studies and art. Older adults ranging from 50 to 100 years of age visited the classroom and students went to residences for older people.

ALL MY GRANDMOTHERS COULD SING looks back at the life of an older woman through dance and music. Poetry is from the book *All My Grandmothers Could Sing;* music composed by Roger Foltz and the program choreographed by Josie Metal-Corbin.

OUT OF THE SHADOW, INTO THE LIGHT is a multi-media presentation integrating dance, art, music and issues on aging. The five dances depict universal messages about growing older, about women striving to achieve their identities, and about married life. The dances are based on the drawings of septuagenarian artist Elizabeth Layton and are performed by dancers ranging from 20 to 84 years of age.

A GOOD AGE integrates dance, interviews, music, poetry, and unusual dance spaces in a television program that provides a unique insight into the lives of older women. The women interviewed range in age from 55 to 96 and they talk candidly about such topics as men, friendship, love and their philosophy of life. The interviews precede dances with the same themes.

To order any or all of the programs (VHS tape only), please complete the form below and return it with check or money order to:
University Television, Engineering Building Room 200, University of Nebraska at Omaha, 60th & Dodge Streets, Omaha, Nebraska, 68182. (Orders must be accompanied by check or money order made out to University Television.)

You may also order a preview sampler showing a 5 minute segment of each program (on VHS tape). The only charge for the preview sampler is return postage.

Old Friends	Age Doesn't Matter	All My Grandmothers	Out of the Shadow	A Good Age
___Purchase $50 ___Preview Sampler	___Purchase $50 ___Preview Sampler	___Purchase $50 ___Preview Sampler	___Purchase $50 ___Preview Sampler	___Purchase $50 ___Preview Sampler

Ship to:

_____

_____

_____

_____

University of Nebraska at Omaha   University of Nebraska - Lincoln   University of Nebraska Medical Center

Subject Index